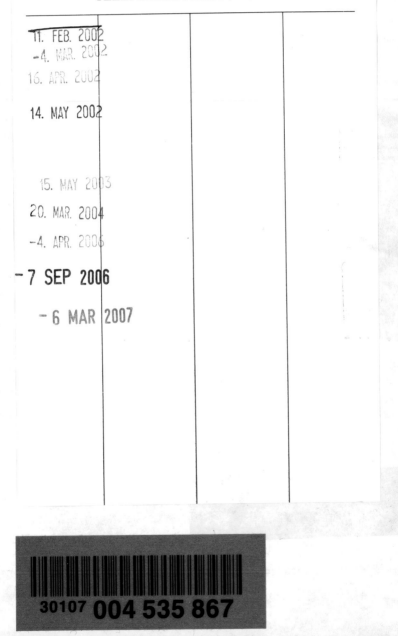

Privacy and Press Freedom

RAYMOND WACKS

Professor of Law
The University of Hong Kong

BLACKSTONE
PRESS LIMITED

First published in Great Britain 1995 by Blackstone Press Limited, 9–15 Aldine Street, London W12 8AW. Telephone 0181-740 1173

ISBN: 1 85431 454 8

British Library Cataloguing in Publication Data
A CIP catalogue record for this book is available from the British Library.

Typeset by Montage Studios Limited, Tonbridge, Kent
Printed by Bell and Bain Limited, Glasgow

Contents

Contents

6 Remedies

Trespass and nuisance — Breach of confidence — Other remedies

7 The Future

Index

Preface

Impossibly, 25 years have passed since my interest in the subject of 'privacy' was first kindled. And still the quotation marks. Still the uneasy feeling that this perplexing concept is no nearer being understood — especially by me. But, most importantly, still no legal protection against the gratuitous exposure of private lives by the press. And hence this attempt to reappraise the state of the law. Legislation which once seemed imminent, now appears remote. It therefore seems timely to look again at this difficult question.

The allure of 'privacy' remains undimmed. What fascinated me in 1971 continues its sway. Indeed, the case for the legal recognition of our right to control intimate information about us is, if anything, more compelling. Yet, both in England where the law still bars entry, and (ironically) in the United States where it first gained admission, the 'right to privacy' is embattled.

The English courts, with their conventional distaste for nebulous rights and a healthy distrust of 'theory', generally persist in their hostility toward 'privacy', and habitually look to Westminster for action. None materialises. The common law stumbles haltingly to fashion remedies for deserving plaintiffs whose 'privacy' has been infringed by an increasingly sensationalist press. In the United States, the right's domicile of origin, while 'privacy' flourishes as a synonym for freedom, the interests of victims of unwanted publicity are routinely vanquished by the irresistible power of the claims of free speech.

My devotion to the right of 'privacy' was, as some readers will know, tempered by scepticism surrounding its apparently relentless advance toward dominion over almost every species of human behaviour transacted 'in private'. I first expressed these anxieties in an article in *The Law Quarterly Review* and in my monograph, *The Protection of Privacy*, both in 1980. My exhortation to restrict 'privacy' to the right to control 'personal information', developed in my 1989 book *Personal Information: Privacy and the Law*, has gone almost entirely unheeded, although I understand that it may have influenced the deliberations of the Australian Law Reform Commission and the Calcutt Committee. Academic lawyers cherish such small pleasures.

That I refrain in these pages from again pursuing this argument at any length does not constitute a white flag. I still think Warren and Brandeis got it right, and that by locating as the core of the problem the protection of 'personal information', a number of difficulties might at least be made more manageable. Where appropriate (or convenient) I draw directly on these ideas, although I advance several new ones, some alarmingly at odds with those expressed in these and other earlier works. This is, after all, my first attempt to consider in greater detail the specific question promised by the title of this book. And the law, like me, has, I hope, matured.

It is important to emphasise that my purpose here is a modest one. Doubly so. First, the primary objective is to analyse the extent to which the law of England affords protection against unwanted press publicity. The scope is largely confined, in other words, to the perennial problem of whether legal remedies are available in circumstances in which private aspects of an individual's life are gratuitously published by the press. Secondly, although the principle of free speech inevitably figures largely in this debate, I have, in view of recent public disquiet, tried to stray as little as possible from the particular problem of the infringement of 'privacy' by the media, especially by newspapers.

My principal debt of gratitude is to Jamie Smith. When the University of Hong Kong kindly awarded me funds to secure the benefit of a research assistant, I had no idea what I could ask him to do, whether he would do what I asked him, or even whether it was possible to work alongside another labourer, for I have always toiled single-handedly. My apprehension was wholly unwarranted. I could not have hoped for a brighter, more congenial or conscientious partner.

Warm thanks are due, again, to Alistair MacQueen and Heather Saward of Blackstone Press for their patient and friendly encouragement, and to the anonymous editor for his or her meticulous checking of the many hundred references that this study has spawned.

I have endeavoured to state the law in the light of materials available to me on 3 June 1995.

Raymond Wacks
HongKong
11 June 1995

Table of Cases

Table of Cases

Table of Cases

Table of Cases

Table of Statutes

Table of Statutes

1

Introduction

Privacy postponed

The pattern is familiar. Private lives are made public spectacle by the tabloids. A general sense of unease ensues. Politicians appear to fret. Judges lament the incapacity of the common law to help. Committees are established. 'Privacy' legislation is proposed. Alarms are sounded by the quality press about the onslaught against freedom of speech. Inertia settles on politicians, reluctant to offend newspaper editors. The debate subsides until the next series of sensationalist disclosures.

If there is a trace of cynicism in this synopsis, it may be a consequence of a quarter of a century's scrutiny of the pitch and toss of this remarkable contest between Parliament and the press.[1]

Nor should anyone be surprised that in pursuit of profit or fun, the tabloids, happily untrammelled by legal or moral norms to the contrary, pander to our prurience and voyeurism. It would be odd if it were otherwise. Intimate facts about celebrities are evidently of considerable interest to many consumers, not only of newspapers, but of television, books, and, most recently, of the Internet. Thus, to take only the most conspicuous example, the vicissitudes of the private life of the Princess of Wales have long been regarded as fair game by the media. And in

---

[1] See, perhaps, R Wacks, *The Protection of Privacy* (London: Sweet & Maxwell, 1980), hereafter referred to as '*Protection of Privacy*'; Wacks, 'The Poverty of "Privacy"' (1980) 96 LQR 73; Wacks, 'Privacy and the Practitioner' [1983] PL 260; Wacks, *Personal Information: Privacy and the Law* (Oxford: Clarendon Press, 1989, reprinted with new preface and corrections, 1993), hereafter referred to as '*Personal Information*'; Wacks, 'The Right to Privacy' in Wacks (ed), *Human Rights in Hong Kong* (Hong Kong: Oxford University Press, 1992) and Wacks (ed), *Privacy*, vol 1, 'The Concept of Privacy', vol 2, 'Privacy and the Law' (International Library of Essays in Law and Legal Theory) (London: Dartmouth, 1993; New York: New York University Press, 1993), hereafter referred to as '*Privacy I*' or '*Privacy II*'.

their desire to satisfy the apparently insatiable appetite for facts and photographs, the press has not shrunk from surreptitious surveillance, intercepting telephone conversations, and publishing the fruits of hidden cameras.

In 1990 the Princess joined the LA Fitness Centre in Isleworth, Middlesex, under a pseudonym in order, presumably, to avoid publicity. The owner of the gym, Mr Bryce Taylor, had other ideas. He invested £2,524 in a Leica M6 camera, renowned for its inaudible shutter and winding-on mechanism, and placed it above the false ceiling so that, hidden from view, it looked down on to a particular exercise machine. He then ran 80 feet of pneumatic cable from the camera to his office from where he could depress the shutter by virtue of a pulse of air sent down the cable by a rubber bulb.

It has been suggested that, from the outset, Taylor was in collusion with at least one tabloid, the *Mirror* (which the newspaper strongly denies),[2] but, aided or acting alone, what seems clear is that during the months of April and May 1993, approximately 50 'pin-sharp' photographs of the Princess performing her exercises were taken. They were sold to the *Mirror*, allegedly for £125,000. The *Sunday Mirror* published some of them on 7 November 1993, lamenting on its front page that the pictures posed a serious security risk to Diana. Further photographs were published in the *Mirror* the following day.

Within a week the Princess obtained an injunction to prevent further publication of the photographs and issued a writ claiming breaches of confidence, contract and fiduciary duty. The *Mirror* apologised to the Princess and withheld Taylor's promised £125,000 pending the outcome of the litigation. The court was ultimately denied an opportunity to rule on the matter, for it was settled, reportedly for a sum of almost £1 million, with £500,000 for Bryce, £200,000 to allow him to pay tax on this sum, and another £25,000 to enable him to settle the cost of his legal aid. The Princess received £25,000 for a charity of her choice. It has been alleged that 'the biggest contributor to the syndicate's cost was the *Mirror* itself, backed by a consortium of other newspapers who, as the case grew nearer, feared a Diana victory in the courts and a sudden new judge-made law of privacy which would stand forever'.[3] If this extraordinary suggestion is true, it may be because the *Mirror's* legal

---

[2]See, 'How the Snoop Won the Photo Finish', *Sunday Times*, 12 February 1995; and, 'The Princess Wins Her Prints', *The Independent*, 9 February 1995.
[3]*Private Eye*, 24 February 1995, 7. The authority of this source may be regarded as suspect, but if this remarkable allegation were untrue, it would surely have been denied by the press. It has not.

advisers formed the view that the circumstances of this case fell within existing breach of confidence principles. The court was therefore denied an opportunity to consider the kinds of arguments advanced in Chapter 3. The fact that the *Mirror* blinked may be of more than passing significance.

In any event, the newspaper would almost certainly have argued that the Princess was not averse to publicity and had even colluded with the press in the past, permitting herself to be photographed in swimwear and disclosing her private feelings to journalists. This argument, a central element in the American tort of 'privacy', is not unknown to our own law of confidence (see Chapter 3) but its fate in this case would, at the very least, have provided an important clarification of the position.

Privacy Bills

In its recognition of the general failure of the common law to mirror American developments the United Kingdom legislature has, on several occasions, sought (without success) to create a statutory 'right of privacy'. The most comprehensive Bill, introduced in 1969,[4] was the result of an investigation by a Committee of JUSTICE into the inadequacies of the common law. Eschewing mere tinkering with the law of, for instance, trespass and nuisance, to provide remedies for invasions of 'privacy', and the enactment of piecemeal legislation, it recommended instead a bill to create 'a general right of privacy applicable in all situations'.[5] During the second reading debate, the Home Secretary, Mr James Callaghan MP, argued (with some justification) that the kinds of activity that were genuinely objectionable required clearer definition. He also expressed concern that the Bill vested too much discretion in the courts and that it might generate

[4]A Right of Privacy Bill was introduced in the House of Lords by Lord Mancroft on 14 February 1961. It was restricted to the 'public disclosure' element of 'privacy'. Though it attracted the support of Lord Denning in the House of Lords and passed its second reading by 74 votes to 71, the Bill was withdrawn during the committee stage for lack of government support. A second Right of Privacy Bill was introduced by Mr Alexander Lyon MP under the 10-minute rule on 8 February 1967. It applied to 'intrusion' as well as 'public disclosure', but proceeded no further than its first reading. A further attempt to introduce a Right of Privacy Bill was made by Mr Brian Walden MP on 26 November 1969. The Bill was similar, in all material respects, to that proposed by JUSTICE (the British Section of the International Commission of Jurists) in its report, *Privacy and the Law* (1970). Mr William Cash MP proposed a 'privacy' Bill in 1987, Mr John Browne MP in 1987, and Lord Stoddart in 1989. In the same year Mr Tony Worthington MP introduced a Right of Reply Bill.
[5]JUSTICE, *Privacy and the Law*, para 128.

'unwarranted litigation'.[6] The matter, he persuaded the House, warranted a full investigation. The proposer, Mr Brian Walden MP, withdrew his Bill. (With few modifications it emerged again almost 20 years later as a private member's Bill proposed by Mr William Cash MP. Though it attracted considerable support, it eventually lapsed.)

Following the withdrawal of the Walden Bill, a Committee on Privacy was appointed on 13 May 1970 under the chairmanship of Kenneth Younger with the following terms of reference:

> To consider whether legislation is needed to give further protection to the individual citizen and to commercial and industrial interests against intrusions into privacy by private persons and organisations, or by companies, and to make recommendations.

The committee rejected, by a majority, the creation of a general right of privacy, preferring instead a 'piecemeal approach'.[7] It took the view that 'privacy' was 'a basic need, essential to the development and maintenance both of a free society and of a mature and stable individual personality'.[8] But the 'best way to ensure regard for privacy is to provide specific and effective sanctions against clearly defined activities which unreasonably frustrate the individual in his search of privacy'.[9]

The committee concluded that a general right would create uncertainty, although there is less substance in its claim that such a right would burden the court with 'controversial questions of a social and political character',[10] for this is to accept the doubtful view that the courts do not concern themselves with such issues anyway. It recommended:

(a) The creation of a new crime and a new tort of unlawful surveillance.

(b) The creation of a new tort of disclosure or other use of information unlawfully acquired.

(c) Reference to the Law Commissions of the law relating to breach of confidence with a view to its clarification and statement in legislative form.

The proposals of the Law Commission and the Scottish Law Commission are examined in Chapter 3.

---

[6]794 *Hansard*, HC, col 943 (23 Jan 1970).
[7]Committee on Privacy, *Report of the Committee on Privacy*, Cmnd 5012, 1972, para 659.
[8]*Ibid*, para 113.
[9]*Ibid*, para 663.
[10]*Ibid*, para 653.

Other attempts to introduce legislation have followed.[11] But the tempest truly began to blow in 1990 after severe gales in large parts of Britain resulted in the well-known television actor, Gorden Kaye's, being seriously injured when a piece of timber smashed his car windscreen causing a splinter to enter his brain. As he lay in a coma attached to a life-support machine, two journalists of the tabloid *Sunday Sport*, ignoring a notice prohibiting entry, gained access to his room, photographed and attempted to 'interview' him. Following an unsuccessful attempt to enjoin publication, the newspaper printed the photograph on its front page, unashamedly admitting how it had been obtained.

The High Court awarded Kaye an interlocutory injunction prohibiting publication, but this was partially discharged by the Court of Appeal which held that (since there had been no trespass to the person, libel or passing off)[12] the only cause of action available to him was malicious falsehood. The court admitted that English law recognised no 'right of privacy' and (not for the first time) urged legislative action. This decision is further examined in Chapters 2, 3, and 4.

By coincidence, a committee chaired by Mr David Calcutt QC was already in the process of putting the finishing touches to its report when the *Kaye* case broke. It had been formed to consider (not for the first time) the conduct of the press in publishing intimate facts about the lives of the royal family and certain politicians. Its report of June 1990[13] recommended (not for the first time) that the press be given a 'last chance' to regulate itself; a new Press Complaints Commission (PCC) would replace the largely discredited Press Council. It decided that a statutory civil right of 'infringement of privacy' was inappropriate because reform should only fill in existing gaps in protection. Doorstepping, bugging, and use of long-range cameras should be unlawful. Reporting restrictions in respect of children and victims of sex offences should be enhanced. If these proposals proved ineffectual, a statutory press tribunal, presided over by a judge, should be established.

Newspaper readers were, in the meantime, treated, courtesy of the *Sunday Times*, to the serialisation in June 1992 of Andrew Morton's book on the Princess of Wales, after the PCC received assurances from the Queen's Private Secretary that neither the Princess nor her friends had

---

[11]For a lively account of various inquiries into the British press since 1947 as well as some keen insights by an experienced journalist, see R Snoddy, *The Good, the Bad and the Unacceptable: The Hard News about the British Press* (London: Faber, 1992).

[12]*Kaye v Robertson* [1991] FSR 62.

[13]Committee on Privacy and Related Matters, *Report of the Committee on Privacy and Related Matters*, Cm 1102, 1990.

cooperated with the author. The Chairman of the PCC, Lord McGregor of Durris, subsequently learned that this was not the case. The Duchess of York was photographed with her 'financial adviser', John Bryan in France by a freelance journalist using a zoom lens. Mr Bryan failed to obtain an injunction in France because there was no proof that the pictures existed, and in London on the ground that English law did not protect 'privacy'. However, he successfully obtained damages later in respect of invasion of private life in the French courts. The 'Dianagate' tapes (revealing the content of intimate telephone conversations conducted by the Princess of Wales) were published by the press. And so on. And on . . .

The disclosures were not confined to royalty. Several politicians' private, mostly sex, lives were the subject of newspaper articles, including Clare Short (whose complaint was the first to be heard by the new PCC in 1991), Paddy Ashdown, Virginia Bottomley, and David Mellor.

The recommendations of the Calcutt Committee's report are discussed in the appropriate places in the Chapters that follow. Suffice it to say here that it was only after that report that the press took steps to 'clean up its act'. A Code of Practice was adopted by the Newspaper Publishers Association and the Newspaper Society formulating ethical standards for journalists and editors. The new PCC, whose job is to adjudicate complaints of breaches of the code, has the power to censure journalists and newspapers, and to require publication of its adjudications, but not to enforce a right of reply, award compensation or impose fines. While the old Press Council would not hear a complaint unless the complainant waived his[14] right to sue, this preposterous requirement has been abandoned by the new PCC.

The membership of the PCC is dominated by representatives of the press. This is not a criticism; the body's legitimacy is always likely to be in inverse proportion to the number of outside members. It may also draw on the readers' complaints ombudsmen appointed by individual newspapers, who monitor the performance of both the press and the PCC itself.

In his 1993 report on the effectiveness or otherwise of the new dispensation, Sir David Calcutt was unimpressed. He recalled that the proposals in his earlier report were primarily directed towards the protection of 'privacy' for private individuals. But most of the

---

[14]In the unfortunate contest between non-sexist pronouns and non-cumbersome expression, the latter has, in this book, generally prevailed.

disclosures since 1990 concerned politicians and royalty: 'public figures'. Nevertheless:

> ... persons discharging public functions must be prepared to expect
> the level of [protection of their privacy] to be reduced to the extent,
> but only to the extent, that it is necessary for the public to be informed
> about matters directly affecting the discharge of their public func-
> tions.[15]

He proposed defrosting the measures suggested in the earlier report
which had been kept on ice. Self-regulation, he concluded, had failed.
A legal framework was required. Its main feature was a statutory
tribunal, the Press Complaints Tribunal (PCT) with jurisdiction over all
newspapers, magazines and journals. It would enforce a code of
practice and have the power to award damages and impose fines. It
could also require publishers to apologise in a form specified by the
tribunal.

The Tribunal would be chaired by a judge appointed by the Lord
Chancellor. There would be a right of appeal to the Supreme Court of
Judicature. The complainant would obtain legally enforceable redress
before the PCT and could not, therefore, also sue in the ordinary courts.
The Tribunal would be publicly funded (though the funds would be
recouped from the press industry by levy).

He recommended the creation of a crime and tort of unlawful entry
into private property, or placing a surveillance device there, or taking a
photograph or recording the voice of anyone, with the intention of
obtaining personal information with a view to its publication.[16] It would
be a defence if the act were done to prevent, detect or expose a crime or
other seriously antisocial conduct, to protect public health or safety, to
prevent the public being misled by a public statement or action, or for
the purpose of informing the public about matters directly affecting the
discharge of any public function of the individual concerned, or done
under lawful authority. Sir David also recommended that the government 'should now give further consideration to the introduction of a
new tort of infringement of privacy'.[17]

In March 1993 the National Heritage Select Committee rejected the
establishment of a statutory tribunal, preferring instead the creation of

---

[15]Sir David Calcutt QC, *Review of Press Self-Regulation*, Cm 2135, 1993, para 4.38.
[16]This last requirement is curious, for not only would it raise difficult problems of proof,
but, more importantly, it ought to be irrelevant. See Chapter 5.
[17]Calcutt (note 15 above), para 7.42.

yet another self-regulatory organ, the Press Commission, to enforce a new Press Code.[18] Where factual errors or breaches of the Code have occurred, the Commission should be able to order the publication of its adjudications and of a correction and appropriate apology. It should also have the power to award compensation, or impose fines where it judges that a breach of the Code is such as to have brought journalism into disrepute.

Appointments to the Press Commission should be entrusted to the appropriate representative bodies of the industry. Compliance with the Code of Practice should be a term of every journalist's contract of employment and every freelancer should be told that his or her work will not be accepted unless the material has been obtained in compliance with the Code.

Journalists should be required to provide proof of identity and a copy of the Code to those they seek to interview and photograph. Consideration should also be given to printing copies of the Code in other languages that are used by significant groups in Britain.

The committee urged the introduction of a new statutory tort of infringement of privacy.[19] Its proposed Protection of Privacy Bill would create several new criminal offences: placing a surveillance device on private property without the consent of the lawful occupant, with intent to obtain personal information; using a surveillance device (whether on private property or elsewhere) in relation to an individual who is on private property, without the consent of the individual to such use, with intent to obtain personal information about that individual; taking a photograph, or recording the voice, of an individual who is on private property, without his or her consent to the taking or recording, with intent that the individual shall be identifiable; publishing of a recording or an intimate photograph of an individual taken without consent; entering private property without the consent of the lawful occupant with intent to obtain personal information; the buying, selling or retention of any recording without the permission of the person on the tape, or of any material obtained through eavesdropping or use of long-range cameras where any of the parties was aware that the material was procured through illegal means or suspected it to be so

---

[18]National Heritage Select Committee, *Fourth Report, Privacy and Media Intrusion*, 294–I, 1993.

[19]As did the Lord Chancellor's Department which, in July 1993, published a consultation paper, *Infringement of Privacy* (Lord Chancellor's Department and Scottish Office, 1993). Like the report by the National Heritage Select Committee, the consultation paper 'concentrates on the question whether there should be a general civil wrong of infringement of privacy; it is not concerned only with the press' (*ibid*, para 2.8).

obtained; and publication of any recording or material so obtained even where no financial transaction was involved; and deliberate interception of calls made on mobile telephones.

It would be a defence that the act had been done in the public interest for the purpose of preventing, detecting or exposing the commission of any crime; or for the purpose of preventing the public from being harmfully misled by some public statement or action of the individual concerned; or for the purpose of informing the public about matters directly affecting the discharge of any public functions of the individual concerned; or for the protection of health and safety; or under any lawful authority.

The committee proposed that the following acts be tortious: obtaining and/or publishing harmful or embarrassing personal material or photographs; or obtaining and/or publishing private information (e.g., medical records) or photographs without the permission of the person concerned or, where that person is not in a position to give permission, by his or her next of kin; or publishing inaccurate or misleading personal information; or violating the peace of another by intruding upon, or persistently communicating with him or her.

It also recommended that further consideration be given to the introduction of legislation on breach of confidence and suggested that the government examine s. 7 of the Conspiracy and Protection of Property Act 1875 with a view to incorporating into the Protection of Privacy Bill comparable besetting and harassment provisions in the context of unreasonable invasion of privacy and changing its terms to reflect altered circumstances since that date. Such changes could possibly include the need to curtail sexual harassment, noise pollution, etc. Among specific journalistic practices it recommended that the press should not identify relatives of an accused person when identification is likely to put at risk their physical or mental health or security.

A statutory Press Ombudsman was proposed, with powers to supervise the wording, position and format of corrections, apologies and retractions; to publish with an adjudication whenever he thinks it appropriate, the names of those responsible for a serious breach of the Code, to order the payment of compensation, and to impose fines. Where a newspaper refuses to pay a fine or compensation which has been ordered by the Ombudsman, he should be able to seek a court order requiring it to be paid. Similarly, where a newspaper dissents from the Ombudsman's decision, it should be entitled to ask the court to discharge the order.

These proposals have generated considerable debate, not to say anxiety, especially among the press.[20] But the prospect of English law reinventing such a 'privacy' tort, revealed to exist in our law by two Americans, remains doubtful. It is to that remarkable discovery in 1890 that I now turn.

The American law

The common law

Warren and Brandeis's famous finding, that the common law implicitly recognised the 'right to privacy',[21] 'enjoys the unique distinction of having initiated and theoretically outlined a new field of jurisprudence'.[22] Drawing upon English cases of, in particular, breach of confidence, property, copyright, and defamation, they argued that these cases were merely instances and applications of a general 'right to privacy'. The common law, they claimed, albeit under different names and forms, protected an individual whose 'privacy' was invaded by the likes of snooping journalists. In so doing, the law acknowledged the importance of the spiritual and intellectual needs of man. In their celebrated rhetoric:

> The intensity and complexity of life, attendant upon advancing civilization, have rendered necessary some retreat from the world, and man, under the refining influence of culture, has become more sensitive to publicity, so that solitude and privacy have become more essential to the individual; but modern enterprise and invention have, through invasions upon his privacy, subjected him to mental pain and distress, far greater than could be inflicted by mere bodily injury.[23]

---

[20]See generally, Snoddy (note 11 above).

[21]S D Warren and L D Brandeis, 'The Right to Privacy' (1890) 4 Harv L Rev 193. (This seminal essay is reprinted in Wacks, *Privacy II* (note 1 above), 3). Several other important contributions to the literature may be found in *Privacy I* and *II* (note 1 above). William Prosser describes Warren and Brandeis's article as 'the outstanding example of the influence of legal periodicals upon the American law' (W Prosser, 'Privacy' (1960) 48 Calif L Rev 383; Wacks, *Privacy II* (note 1 above), 47). See too W F Pratt, 'The Warren and Brandeis Argument for a Right to Privacy' [1975] PL 161; H Kalven, 'Privacy in Tort Law: Were Warren and Brandeis Wrong?' (1966) 31 Law & Contemp Probs 326 (Wacks, *Privacy II* (note 1 above), 31); R Gavison, 'Too Early for a Requiem: Warren and Brandeis Were Right on Privacy vs Free Speech' (1992) 43 SC L Rev 437.

[22]W Larremore, 'The Law of Privacy' (1912) 12 Colum L Rev 693.

[23]Warren and Brandeis (note 21 above), 196.

The common law, they contended, had developed from the protection of the physical person and corporeal property to the protection of the individual's 'Thoughts, emotions and sensations'.[24] But, as a result of threats to 'privacy' from recent inventions and business methods and from the press, the common law needed to go further. An individual's right to determine the extent to which his thoughts, emotions, and sensations were communicated to others was already legally protected, but only in respect of authors of literary and artistic compositions and letters who could forbid their unauthorised publication. And though English cases recognising this right were based on protection of property, in reality they were an acknowledgement of 'privacy', of 'inviolate personality'.[25]

In 1902, the New York Court of Appeals was given an opportunity to consider the Warren and Brandeis thesis. The plaintiff complained that her picture had been used without her consent to advertise flour.[26] The majority rejected the 'privacy' argument, it had 'not as yet an abiding place in our jurisprudence, and . . . cannot now be incorporated without doing violence to settled principles of law'.[27] Three years later in a case involving similar facts the Supreme Court of Georgia explicitly adopted the Warren and Brandeis thesis.[28]

The new cause of action spawned a huge body of case law and academic comment. Almost every American State has incorporated the 'right to privacy' into its law. Yet, despite the authors' almost exclusive reliance on English decisions,[29] no similar development has occurred in England.

The American common law, following Prosser, recognises not one tort, 'but a complex of four'.[30] The four relatively discrete torts are described by Prosser as:

(a) Intrusion upon the plaintiff's seclusion or solitude, or into his private affairs.

(b) Public disclosure of embarrassing private facts about the plaintiff.

(c) Publicity which places the plaintiff in a false light in the public eye.

---

[24] *Ibid*, 195.
[25] *Ibid*, 205.
[26] *Roberson* v *Rochester Folding Box Co.* 171 NY 538, 64 NE 442 (1902).
[27] 64 NE 442, 450.
[28] *Pavesich* v *New England Life Insurance Co.* 122 Ga 190, 50 SE 68 (1905).
[29] Especially *Prince Albert* v *Strange* (1849) 2 De G & Sm 652, 64 ER 293; (on appeal) (1849) 1 Mac & G 25, 41 ER 1171.
[30] Prosser (note 21 above), 383. Adopted by the American Restatement (Second) of the Law of Torts, § 652A.

(d) Appropriation, for the defendant's advantage, of the plaintiff's name or likeness.

This formulation (though it has been criticised)[31] has exercised a considerable influence on the American courts. Indeed, in their willingness to accept it, not only have they resisted the application of the law of 'privacy' to other fact situations, but, more importantly, the courts have failed to question its theoretical coherence. In particular, the inclusion of the 'false light' and 'expropriation' categories is, at best, a questionable application of 'privacy' to circumstances that have only the most tenuous relationship to the concept as conceived by Warren and Brandeis. The elements of each of the torts may be briefly described as follows.

Intrusion upon the plaintiff's seclusion or solitude or into his private affairs
The wrongful act consists in the intentional interference with the plaintiff's solitude or seclusion. It includes the physical intrusion into the plaintiff's premises and eavesdropping (including electronic and photographic surveillance, 'bugging', and telephone-tapping). Three requirements must be satisfied:[32]

(a) There must be an actual prying (disturbing noises or bad manners will not suffice).
(b) The intrusion must offend a reasonable man.
(c) It must be an intrusion into something private.

---

[31]It has been argued, in particular, that Prosser's division undermines the essential unity of the law's protection of 'privacy' based on the right to, in Warren and Brandeis's phrase, an 'inviolate personality' (Warren and Brandeis (note 21 above), 205). Professor Bloustein attacks Prosser's atomisation on the ground that at the heart of the law's protection of 'privacy' is the recognition of 'human dignity': an invasion of 'privacy' is 'demeaning to individuality … an affront to personal dignity' (E Bloustein, 'Privacy as an Aspect of Human Dignity: An Answer to Dean Prosser' (1964) 39 NYU L Rev 962, 973; Wacks, *Privacy II* (note 1 above), 100). A similar argument is made by S Benn, 'Privacy, Freedom and Respect for Persons' (1971) 13 Nomos 1 (Wacks, *Privacy I* (note 1 above), 281). Cf H Gross, 'The Concept of Privacy' (1967) 42 NYU L Rev 34 (Wacks, *Privacy I* (note 1 above), 77). The debate seems misplaced for Prosser's account is (despite the normative interpretation it often receives) largely descriptive of the existing law. Bloustein, on the other hand, is identifying (rightly or wrongly) at a higher level of abstraction, a broader explanation for the law's protection of 'privacy'. Issue is never seriously joined.
[32]W Prosser and W P Keeton, *The Law of Torts*, 5th ed (St Paul, Minn: West Publishing Co., 1984), 855; Restatement (Second) of the Law of Torts, § 652B.

Public disclosure of embarrassing private facts about the plaintiff
This is the principal concern of this book. Three elements of the tort are indicated by Prosser and Keeton:[33]

(a) There must be publicity (disclosure to a small group of people would not suffice).
(b) The facts disclosed must be private facts (publicity given to matters of public record is not tortious).
(c) The facts disclosed must be offensive to a reasonable man of ordinary sensibilities.

Publicity which places the plaintiff in a false light in the public eye
According to Prosser and Keeton,[34] this tort normally arises in circumstances in which some opinion or utterance (such as spurious books or views) is publicly attributed to the plaintiff or where his picture is used to illustrate a book or article with which he has no reasonable connection. The overlap with the tort of defamation is at once apparent, and, though the false light 'need not necessarily be a defamatory one', an action for defamation will invariably lie in such cases. The publicity must be 'highly offensive to the ordinary reasonable man'.[35]

Appropriation, for the defendant's advantage, of the plaintiff's name or likeness
Under the common law tort the advantage derived by the defendant need not be a financial one.[36] It has, for instance, been held to arise where the plaintiff was named as father in a birth certificate. The statutory tort (which exists in several States) normally requires the unauthorised use of the plaintiff's identity for commercial (usually advertising) purposes; the New York statute, upon which most of the current legislation is modelled, confines itself to advertising for 'purposes of trade'.[37] The recognition of this tort establishes what is now called a 'right of publicity' under which an individual is able to decide how he wishes to exploit his name or image commercially. The protection of this

---

[33]*Ibid*, 856–7; Restatement (Second) of the Law of Torts, § 652D.
[34]*Ibid*, 863–4; Restatement (Second) of the Law of Torts, § 652E.
[35]Restatement (Second) of the Law of Torts, § 652E, comment b.
[36]Prosser and Keeton (note 32 above), 853; Restatement (Second) of the Law of Torts, § 652C, comment b.
[37]New York Civil Rights Law 1921, titles 50–1.

essentially proprietary interest has little connection even with the protection of a general 'right to privacy'.

It is only the torts of 'intrusion' and 'public disclosure' that 'require the invasion of something secret, secluded or private pertaining to the plaintiff'.[38] The torts of 'appropriation' and 'false light' are thus not properly conceived as aspects of 'privacy'. 'False light' is closer to defamation than 'privacy', and 'appropriation' is essentially a proprietary wrong.

Constitutional law

Until the US Supreme Court's controversial decision in *Griswold* v *Connecticut*[39] declaring unconstitutional a Connecticut statute which prohibited the use of contraceptives on the ground that it violated the right of marital privacy — a right 'older than the Bill of Rights'[40] — the constitutional protection of 'privacy' did not significantly extend beyond the torts recognised by the common law. Though the US Constitution itself is silent in respect of the 'right of privacy', through several of the Amendments (particularly the First, Third, Fourth, Fifth and Ninth) the Supreme Court has recognised, *inter alia*, the right of 'associational privacy',[41] 'political privacy'[42] and 'privacy of counsel'.[43]

In attempting to come to terms with its earlier rulings in *Olmstead* v *United States*[44] and *Goldman* v *United States*,[45] that electronic surveillance was *not* a search and seizure within the meaning of the Fourth Amendment and therefore *not* constitutionally regulated, the Supreme Court has sought to set the limits of protection against eavesdropping and unlawful searches. The incremental development of Supreme Court 'privacy' doctrine has continued (notably in *Roe* v *Wade*[46] and *Planned Parenthood of Southeastern Pennsylvania* v *Casey*),[47] invalidating abortion statutes on the ground that they invade a constitutional right of privacy, but has provoked critical responses which suggest the possibility that the doctrine might one day be checked.

---

[38]Prosser (note 21 above), 407.
[39]381 US 479 (1965).
[40]*Ibid*, 486.
[41]*NAACP* v *Alabama* 357 US 449 (1958).
[42]*Sweezy* v *New Hampshire* 354 US 234 (1957).
[43]*Massiah* v *United States* 377 US 201 (1964).
[44]277 US 438 (1928).
[45]316 US 129 (1942).
[46]410 US 113 (1973).
[47]112 S Ct 2791 (1992)

An opportunity arose in *Bowers* v *Hardwick*.[48] By five to four, the Court held that the privacy protection of the due process clause does not extend to homosexual acts between consenting adults in private. However, the majority judgment rested, not on the basis of the unsatisfactory enlargement of the constitutional concept of privacy, but on the narrower ground that: 'No connection between family, marriage, or procreation on the one hand and homosexual activity on the other has been demonstrated'.[49]

In the light of decisions such as *Griswold*, *Roe*, *Hardwick* and *Casey*, it is perhaps not surprising that 'privacy' discourse has expanded well beyond Warren and Brandeis's limited concern to establish a legal means of containing unwanted publicity. Though aspects of their original formulation of 'inviolate personality' have had a powerful influence on the concept of 'personhood'[50] as an essential philosophical basis of 'privacy', even this idea has been deployed in an expansive attempt to locate the right to privacy within a theory of democracy.

Thus two recent discussions proceed from explicitly political perspectives of State power. After rejecting both Michelman's republican account[51] and Rubenfeld's anti-totalitarian, Foucauldian analysis of 'privacy',[52] Schnably[53] argues that,

> ... privacy theory needs to make a decisive break from the idea of cordoning individuals from State power. That ideal is a chimera. Rather ... a theory of privacy needs to ask how the power of the State *should* be deployed both to foster individual responsibility and freedom in decision-making and to make the politics that directs the deployment of State power more democratic.[54]

---

[48]478 US 186 (1986).

[49]*Ibid*, 191.

[50]See J Reiman, 'Privacy, Intimacy, and Personhood' (1976) 6 Philosophy and Public Affairs 26; D A J Richards, 'Sexual Autonomy and the Constitutional Right to Privacy: A Case Study in Human Rights and the Unwritten Constitution' (1979) 30 Hastings LJ 965; J B Craven, 'Personhood: The Right to Be Let Alone' (1976) Duke LJ 699; S J Schnably, 'Beyond *Griswold*: Foucauldian and Republican Approaches to Privacy' (1991) 23 Conn L Rev 861; and J Rubenfeld, 'The Right of Privacy' (1989) 102 Harv L Rev 737, 739 (Wacks, *Privacy II* (note 1 above), 303).

[51]F Michelman, 'Law's Republic' (1988) 97 Yale LJ 1493 (Wacks, *Privacy II* (note 1 above), 255).

[52]Rubenfeld (note 50 above).

[53]Schnably (note 50 above).

[54]*Ibid*, 875.

Properly understood, the right to privacy addresses the problem of unequal power and the way it distorts individuals' attempts to come to grips with moral issues.[55]

A similar political strategy informs Thomas's analysis of *Bowers* v *Hardwick*.[56] He too rejects the approaches of Michelman and Rubenfeld, postulating instead an 'individual right of corporal integrity' from which he derives 'a right to be free from homophobic violence'.[57] Contending that 'the argument from privacy is predominantly an axiological case against the legal regulation of private, consensual sexual conduct', Thomas claims,[58]

> The corporal paradigm ... differs from the privacy framework in that its case against homosexual sodomy laws relies first and primarily on concepts about power and the State taken from political theory.... sodomy statutes necessarily presuppose a political conception regarding the relationship between the arm of the State and the body of the individual.... the corporal model permits us to apprehend the unique way in which homosexual sodomy law has historically promoted and reflected illegitimate power relationships among the citizens who make up the body politic.

Since its seminal decision in *Griswold*, the expression by the Supreme Court of unenumerated rights,[59] including 'privacy', has inevitably led not only to its colonisation of liberties, but has resulted in confusion between the political and social foundations of 'privacy', on the one hand, and its explication as an individual right, on the other.

It is difficult not to support the libertarian and feminist assault on the State's intrusion into private and even public lives, but the concept of 'privacy' is ill-suited to this task. Arguments about the nature and limits of State power are fundamental to any serious consideration of constitutional freedom, but they are far from conclusive; nor may they be substituted for the difficult and careful analysis that is required when attempting to delineate the precise nature of the right that it is sought to protect. This incarnation of so-called 'decisional privacy' is best resisted. It is a far cry from Warren and Brandeis's original formulation

---

[55]*Ibid*, 933.
[56]K Thomas, 'Beyond the Privacy Principle' (1992) 92 Colum L Rev 1431.
[57]*Ibid*, 1512.
[58]*Ibid, loc cit* 1513.
[59]*Ibid*.

of a cause of action to protect the individual against injurious disclosures of private facts.

The international dimension

A similarly generous 'right to privacy' is an acknowledged human right, and is recognised in most international instruments stating human rights.[60] So, for example, Article 12 of the United Nations Declaration of Human Rights and Article 17 of the International Covenant on Civil and Political Rights (ICCPR) both provide,[61]

(1)   No one shall be subjected to arbitrary or unlawful interference with his privacy, family, home or correspondence, nor to unlawful attacks on his honour and reputation.
(2)   Everyone has the right to the protection of the law against such interference or attacks.

Article 8 of the European Convention on Human Rights (ECHR) declares:

(1)   Everyone has the right to respect for his private and family life, his home and his correspondence.
(2)   There shall be no interference by a public authority with the exercise of this right except such as is in accordance with the law and is necessary in a democratic society in the interests of national security, public safety or the economic well-being of the country, for the prevention of disorder or crime, for the protection of health or morals, or for the protection of the rights and freedoms of others.

These rights are of fundamental importance to a free society, but their relevance to 'privacy', as here understood, and especially to free speech,

---

[60]Similar provisions exist in the American Declaration of the Rights and Duties of Man (Articles V, XI and IX) and the American Convention on Human Rights (Article 11(2)). The bills of rights of several domestic jurisdictions have adopted these or similar provisions. Perhaps the most recent example is the new South African constitution which provides in s. 13: 'Every person shall have the right to his or her personal privacy, which shall include the right not to be subject to searches of his or her person, home or property, the seizure of private possessions or the violation of private communications'.
[61]In the UN Declaration the article is not divided into paragraphs.

is limited.[62] More important in the present context is the extent to which, and manner in which, freedom of speech, also an internationally recognised right, is reconciled with 'privacy'.

Article 19 of the United Nations Universal Declaration provides:

> Everyone has the right to freedom of opinion and expression; this right includes freedom to hold opinions without interference and to seek, receive and impart information and ideas through any media and regardless of frontiers.

Article 19 of the ICCPR declares:

> (1) Everyone shall have the right to hold opinions without interference.
>
> (2) Everyone shall have the right to freedom of expression; this right shall include freedom to seek, receive and impart information and ideas of all kinds, regardless of frontiers, either orally, in writing or in print, in the form of art, or through any other media of his choice.
>
> (3) The exercise of the rights provided for in paragraph (2) of this article carries with it special duties and responsibilities. It may therefore be subject to certain restrictions, but these shall only be such as are provided by law and are necessary —
>
> (a) For respect of the rights or reputations of others;
>
> (b) For the protection of national security or of public order (*ordre public*), or of public health or morals.

A similar formulation is adopted by Article 10 of the ECHR, but to the exceptions stipulated in paragraph (2) are added, *inter alia*, restrictions 'for preventing the disclosure of information received in confidence'. Thus, along with the law to protect the reputation 'or rights of others', the equitable remedy for breach of confidence may constitute a legitimate limitation of the general right.[63]

---

[62]It is worth noting that the European Convention's formulation protects the right to 'respect' for private, family life etc, rather than freedom from interference with 'privacy'. It is doubtful whether this constitutes a significant limitation, see D Feldman, *Civil Liberties and Human Rights in England and Wales* (Oxford: Clarendon Press, 1993), 366–9. See too Professor Feldman's useful account of the decisions of the European Court of Human Rights under this article (*ibid*, 367–80).

[63]The implications of these limitations are unclear. See T Meron (ed), *Human Rights in International Law: Legal and Policy Issues* (Oxford: Clarendon Press, 1984); A Kiss, 'Permissible Limitations on Rights' in L Henkin (ed), *The International Bill of Rights: The Covenant on Civil and Political Rights* (New York: Columbia University Press, 1981). See too Y Ghai, 'Freedom of Expression' in R Wacks (ed), *Human Rights in Hong Kong* (Hong Kong: Oxford University Press, 1992), 390–6.

The juxtapositions of 'the rights' and 'or reputations of others' (Article 19, ICCPR) and 'reputation' and 'or rights of others' (Article 10, ECHR) suggest that the 'rights' contemplated include those that are infringed by publications which do not affect the individual's reputation, i.e., they would appear to include the right to prevent the public disclosure of private facts. There is precious little analysis of this question by the European Court of Human Rights or General Comments of the United Nations Committee on Human Rights.

In *Winer* v *United Kingdom*[64] the applicant complained of the absence of a remedy in English law for the publication of information that infringed his 'privacy'. He argued that such disclosures were not protected by Article 10 since they were not in the public interest. But he did not get very far. The Commission of Human Rights ruled his complaint inadmissible, observing that 'Whilst it is true that this state of the law gives greater protection to other individuals' freedom of expression, the applicant's right to privacy was not wholly unprotected, as was shown by his defamation action and settlement, and his own liberty to publish'. A cryptic conclusion which defies easy comprehension.

It is clear that the European Court of Human Rights will interpret the phrase 'prescribed by law' narrowly. In the *Sunday Times* case,[65] an appeal from the House of Lords on the question of whether the common law of contempt of court was a restriction 'prescribed by law', the court stated:

> First, the law must be adequately accessible: the citizen must be able to have an indication that is adequate in the circumstances of the legal rules applicable to a given case. Secondly, a norm cannot be regarded as a 'law' unless it is formulated with sufficient precision to enable the citizen to regulate his conduct — he must be able — if need be with appropriate advice to foresee, to a degree that is reasonable in the circumstances, the consequences which a given action may entail.[66]

The court held that despite the imprecision of the common law of contempt, it satisfied this test.[67] It seems likely, therefore, that

---

[64] Application No. 10871/84 (admissibility decision of 10 July 1986) European Commission of Human Rights 48 DR 154.
[65] *Sunday Times* v *United Kingdom* (1980) 2 EHRR 245.
[66] *Ibid*, para 49.
[67] A different conclusion was reached in the *Malone* case (involving official telephone tapping, see Chapter 3). The court held that the system of authorising taps was too vague to satisfy the test. See *Malone* v *United Kingdom* (1985) 7 EHRR 14, para 67. Cf *Klass* v *Federal Republic of Germany* (1980) 2 EHRR 214. See Wacks, *Personal Information* (note 1 above), 276–85.

limitations of free speech grounded on the law on breach of confidence would meet a similar fate.

The principles of legitimacy and proportionality will also be applied to limit the restrictions. The first requires that the restriction has a legitimate objective; vagueness of restrictions may undermine their legitimacy. The second requires that the restriction is 'necessary' for the legitimate objective pursued; if a less restrictive method is available, it should be adopted.[68]

The other important requirement of Article 10(2) of the ECHR is that any restrictions are 'necessary in a democratic society'. 'Necessary' has been held to mean that there is 'a pressing social need'. More is therefore required than that the restriction is 'reasonable' or 'desirable'.[69]

---

[68]See A Lester, 'Freedom of Expression: Relevant International Principles' in *Developing Human Rights Jurisprudence: The Domestic Application of International Human Rights Norms* (London: Commonwealth Secretariat, 1988), 39.
[69]*Handyside* v *United Kingdom* (1979–80) 1 EHRR 737.

2

Privacy and Press Freedom

Freedom of speech

Freedom of the press is inescapably bound up with the general question of free speech, a subject of vast and complex proportions the surface of which this chapter merely scratches.[1] Broadly speaking, justifications for free speech are either consequentialist or rights-based. The former normally draw on the arguments of Milton and Mill (from truth or democracy), while the latter conceive of speech as an integral part of an individual's right to self-fulfilment. When it comes to defending free speech these arguments tend invariably to be amalgamated, and even confused. So, for example, Thomas Emerson discerns four primary justifications which include *both* sorts of claim: individual self-fulfilment, attainment of the truth, securing the participation by members of society in social, including political, decision-making, and providing the means of maintaining the balance between stability and change in society.[2]

---

[1]See, in particular, F Schauer, *Free Speech: A Philosophical Enquiry* (Cambridge: Cambridge University Press, 1982); and Schauer, 'Reflections on the Value of Truth' (1991) 41 Case W Res L Rev 699 (Wacks, *Privacy II* (note 1 above), 407), to which subsequent references are made unless otherwise stated. See too E Barendt, *Freedom of Speech* (Oxford: Clarendon Press, 1985). On the legal regulation of the British media see G Robertson and A Nicol, *Media Law: The Rights of Journalists and Broadcasters*, 3rd ed (Harmondsworth: Penguin, 1992); and T Gibbons, *Regulating the Media* (London: Sweet & Maxwell, 1991).
[2]T Emerson, 'The Right of Privacy and Freedom of the Press' (1979) 14 Harv CR–CL L Rev 329, 331 (Wacks, *Privacy II* (Chapter 1 note 1 above), 377). See too J Raz, 'Free Expression and Personal Identification' (1991) 11 Oxford J Legal Stud 303; T Emerson, 'Toward a General Theory of the First Amendment' (1963) 72 Yale LJ 877; R Dworkin, 'Censorship and a Free Press' in *A Matter of Principle* (Cambridge, Mass: Harvard University Press, 1985); R Gavison, 'Too Early for a Requiem: Warren and Brandeis Were Right on Privacy vs Free Speech' (1992) 43 SC L Rev 437; S Fish, *There's No Such Thing as Free Speech* (Oxford: Oxford University Press, 1994); and D Feldman, *Civil Liberties and Human Rights in England and Wales* (Oxford: Clarendon Press, 1993), 580–632.

Supporters of 'privacy', on the other hand, rely almost exclusively on rights-based arguments. Thus, in his classic exposition, Alan Westin suggests that a right of privacy is essential to protect personal autonomy, allowing us to be free from manipulation or domination by others, to permit emotional release, to afford an opportunity for self-evaluation, and to allow limited and protected communication to share confidences and to set the boundaries of mental disturbance.[3]

Difficulties emerge at once. The extent to which the law may legitimately curtail speech that undermines an individual's 'privacy' is often presented as a contest between two heavyweights. But this may be mere shadow-boxing, if, as I shall suggest, with Emerson, that 'At most points the law of privacy and the law sustaining a free press do not contradict each other. On the contrary, they are mutually supportive, in that both are vital features of the basic system of individual rights.'[4]

This claim demands appropriate theoretical justification. In particular, the precise relationship between these competing rights and the 'basic system' is far from uncontentious. Tempting though it is, joining issue here would detract from the central focus of the present study. I resist, on the same ground, offering a sweeping exegesis on the subject of free speech. The chief concern of those turning these pages is, I assume, less to discover how many rounds 'privacy' can go with free speech, than to establish whether there is a contest at all.

This will not altogether let me off the hook for I shall have to suggest possible answers to at least three critical questions. First, when 'privacy' is 'balanced' against free speech, what is meant by 'privacy'? Secondly, how is free speech justified in circumstances when it appears to collide with 'privacy'? Thirdly, on what grounds is it thought that protecting individuals against the public disclosure of private information diminishes the freedom of the press?

The limited scope of this enquiry and the complexity of the issues should, however, be stressed. Even if I were able to resolve these problems, I am uncertain that the larger puzzle would be solved. But it may, I hope, be rendered a little less intractable. Moreover, my discussion concentrates on the press, though in the context of freedom of expression, and is alive to the narrow view of press freedom adopted in Britain which often neglects:

---

[3]See A Westin, *Privacy and Freedom* (London: Bodley Head, 1967), 339.
[4]Emerson, 'The Right of Privacy and Freedom of the Press' (note 2 above), 331.

... the rights of writers, publishers, and broadcasters to conduct their activities and purvey information and ideas, and to be protected when their scrutiny of government offends it. [Press freedom in the USA and Europe] means, also, the right of the public to a press which is independent of domination by government and private interests alike.[5]

In the United States the issue of press freedom is, of course, debated against the background of the First Amendment's injunction that 'Congress shall make no law ... abridging the freedom of speech, or of the press'. There are signs that, under the unfolding sway of the European Convention on Human Rights, English courts may embrace a more expansive understanding of this liberty.

The meaning of 'privacy'

As might be expected, in discussing the relationship between freedom of speech and 'privacy', courts and commentators employ the latter concept with little consistency. I have suggested that at the heart of the concern about 'privacy' lies the use or abuse of personal information about an individual. And that by confining the analysis of this and other issues to the control over such personal information, a more coherent means of reconciling the competing values might be found.[6] I define 'personal information' as 'those facts, communications, or opinions that relate to the individual and which are of such a nature that it would be reasonable to expect him to regard as intimate or sensitive, and therefore to want to withhold or at least to restrict their collection, use, or circulation'.[7] I then propose that by applying this objective test, courts might more easily 'balance' the protection of 'personal information', as defined, against other competing principles, including free speech.

Occasionally, within the voluminous literature, shafts of light appear; it is acknowledged that there is a need for greater clarity. Thus, after a detailed discussion of the 'public disclosure' tort, one writer concludes:

Privacy law might be more just and effective if it were to focus on identifying (preferably by statute) those exchanges of information that warrant protection at their point of origin, rather than continuing

---

[5]Feldman (note 2 above), 606.
[6]For the full argument, see Wacks, *Personal Information* (Chapter 1 note 1 above), 7–30; and R Wacks, 'The Poverty of "Privacy"' (1980) 96 LQR 73.
[7]Wacks, *Personal Information* (Chapter 1 note 1 above), 26.

its current, capricious course of imposing liability only if the material is ultimately disseminated to the public at large.... a careful identification of particularly sensitive situations in which personal information is exchanged, and an equally careful delineation of the appropriate expectations regarding how that information can be used, could significantly curtail abuses without seriously hampering freedom of speech. At the very least, this possibility merits considerably more thought as an alternative to the Warren-Brandeis tort than it has received thus far.[8]

Even Emerson suggests that there might be 'Another approach, and one that seems to me more fruitful' that would:

... place more emphasis on developing the privacy side of the balance. It would recognise the first amendment interests but it would give primary attention to a number of factors which derive ultimately from the functions performed by privacy and the expectations of privacy that prevail in contemporary society.[9]

The first such factor is:

... the element of intimacy in determining the zone of privacy. Thus, so far as the privacy tort [of 'public disclosure'] is concerned, *protection would be extended only to matters related to the intimate details of a person's life: those activities, ideas or emotions which one does not share with others or shares only with those who are closest. This would include sexual relations, the performance of bodily functions, family relations, and the like.*[10]

There are signs then that the pursuit of an elusive equilibrium between 'privacy' and free speech has induced some scepticism

---

[8]D L Zimmerman, 'Requiem for a Heavyweight: A Farewell to Warren and Brandeis's Privacy Tort' (1983) 68 Cornell L Rev 291, 362–4 (Wacks, *Privacy II* (Chapter 1 note 1 above), 504–6). Similar misgivings are expressed by R F Hixson, *Privacy in a Public Society: Human Rights in Conflict* (New York: Oxford University Press, 1987), ch 8.

[9]Emerson, 'The Right of Privacy and Freedom of the Press' (note 2 above), 343. See too T Emerson, *The System of Freedom of Expression* (New York: Random, 1970); and Emerson, 'Toward a General Theory of the First Amendment' (note 2 above).

[10]Emerson, 'The Right of Privacy and Freedom of the Press' (note 2 above), 343 (emphasis added).

towards the conventional approach.[11] This should not be surprising since a moment's reflection will reveal that attempting to weigh the relative merits of two less than coherent concepts is unlikely to yield satisfactory results.

The meaning of 'free speech'

Two closely associated difficulties arise. The first concerns the status of free speech; confusion sometimes arises between what might be called individual and community justifications. Secondly, who is actually served by protecting freedom of speech: the speaker or the audience?

Individual or community?
The individual justification is rights-based and argues for the interests in individual autonomy, dignity, self-fulfilment and other values that the exercise of free speech safeguards or advances. The community justification is consequentialist or utilitarian and draws on democratic theory or the promotion of 'truth' to support free speech as facilitating or encouraging the unfettered exchange of ideas, the dissemination of information and associated means of enlarging participation in self-government.

Freedom of speech and 'privacy' are often conceived as rights or interests of the individual, and (sometimes in the same breath) as rights or interests of the community as a whole. And, even more troubling, free speech is regarded as one and 'privacy' the other, thereby rendering any 'balancing' of the two problematic. In respect of the interests of the individual, they generally share the same concerns. Indeed, the social functions of 'privacy' are difficult to distinguish from those of freedom of expression, as mentioned above.

Treating both as individual 'rights' simplifies the issue. Support for such an approach might be sought in Ronald Dworkin's analysis.[12] For him, of course, a legal system contains, in addition to rules (which 'are applicable in an all-or-nothing fashion'), 'principles' and 'policies' which, unlike rules, have 'the dimension of weight or importance'. A principle provides a reason for deciding the case in a particular way, but

---

[11]See L Lusky, 'Invasion of Privacy: A Clarification of Concepts' (1972) 72 Colum L Rev 693, 709; T Gerety, 'Redefining Privacy' (1977) 12 Harv CR–CL L Rev 233, 268–71 (Wacks, *Privacy I* (Chapter 1 note 1 above), 234–7); and S Stoljar, 'A Re-examination of Privacy' (1984) 4 LS 67, 81.
[12]See generally, R Dworkin, *Taking Rights Seriously*, 2nd ed (Cambridge, Mass: Harvard University Press, 1977).

it is not a conclusive reason: it will have to be weighed against other principles in the system. It is 'a standard to be observed, not because it will advance or secure an economic, political, or social situation, but because it is a requirement of justice or fairness or some other dimension of morality'.[13] A 'policy', on the other hand, is 'that kind of standard that sets out a goal to be reached, generally an improvement in some economic, political, or social feature of the community'.[14] Principles describe rights; policies describe goals. It is part of Dworkin's argument for 'taking rights seriously' that rights have a 'threshold weight' against community goals; this is his theory of 'rights as trumps'. If we are to respect individual rights, he argues, they must not be capable of being demolished by some competing community goal. Where a genuine bout is fixed, we should beware of matching a heavyweight against a lightweight.

Free speech is, in Dworkin's view, a fundamental right related to the basic concept of human dignity and the background right to be treated with equal respect and concern. The right, in other words, is to be heard or read. This right 'trumps' the interest in suppressing speech where it might be considered necessary to protect the community.[15]

The extent to which we are 'fulfilled' by exercising (or at least by non-restriction of) our right to free speech is moot. How, for example, am I 'fulfilled' by publishing pornography?

Speaker or audience?
Theories of free speech that seek to protect the audience are generally arguments of policy (based on the importance of that freedom to the community). Theories that advance the interests of the speaker are generally arguments of principle which give primacy to the individual over the community.[16]

Dworkin suggests that free speech is likely to receive stronger protection when it is regarded as safeguarding, as a matter of principle,

---

[13]*Ibid*, 22.
[14]*Ibid, loc cit.*
[15]This formulation does run into certain difficulties, for 'it does not appear to provide any clear basis for distinguishing a free speech principle from general libertarian claims concerning, say, the choice of a dress or sexual life-style which might be favoured by individuals. Moreover, unlimited speech may well be contrary to a respect for human dignity. The restrictions imposed by libel and obscenity laws can easily be justified by reference to this value' (Barendt (note 1 above), 16).
[16]R Dworkin, 'Is the Press Losing the First Amendment?' in Dworkin (note 2 above), 386.

the rights of the *speaker*. And 'privacy' is, in its broad sense, also right-based rather than goal-based.[17] If this is correct, it would at least facilitate a greater symmetry in the balancing exercise.

Unfortunately it is not that simple. At first blush, this strategy would seem to provide a coherent basis for claiming that publications which harm other individuals cannot seriously be said to advance the speaker's or publisher's self-fulfilment. But who is to say whether or not certain forms of speech are instrumental in achieving this object?[18] Moreover, the argument 'suffers from a failure to distinguish intellectual self-fulfilment from other wants and needs, and thus fails to support a distinct principle of free speech'.[19] It is also founded on the principle of the free dissemination of *ideas* rather than *information*, which reduces its utility in the present context.[20] And, most embarrassingly, the argument is hard to deploy in defence of *press* freedom which appears to rest almost entirely on the interests of the community, rather than the individual journalist, editor, or publisher. What of the motive of the speaker? It would not be unduly disingenuous to postulate the possibility that profit may be of interest to newspaper editors and proprietors. And, as Barendt observes, a 'rigorous examination of motives to exclude speech made for profit would leave little immune from regulation'.[21] Nor does the audience necessarily care; a good read is a good read whether its author is moved by edification or greed.

The argument from truth

The essence of John Stuart Mill's celebrated argument from truth is that any suppression of speech is an 'assumption of infallibility' and that only by the unrestricted circulation of ideas can the 'truth' be

---

[17]Dworkin, 'Do We Have a Right to Pornography?', *ibid*, 350.
[18]A more sophisticated version of the theory is suggested by Scanlon who argues that government ought never to endanger the autonomy of individuals to determine rationally the validity of others' arguments, not on the basis of the argument from truth, but because of the rights of the individual as *listener*. See T Scanlon, 'A Theory of Freedom of Expression' (1972) 1 Philosophy and Public Affairs 204; and Scanlon, 'Freedom of Expression and Categories of Expression' (1979) 40 U Pitts L Rev 519. But, as Dworkin asks, how does this protect the rights of the *speaker*?
[19]Schauer, *Free Speech* (note 1 above), 56.
[20]'The value of the argument from autonomy is that it is an argument that is directed at *speech*, rather than at the entire range of interests that might with some minimal plausibility be designated "individual"' (*ibid*, 71).
[21]Barendt (note 1 above), 24.

discovered.[22] But this theory, taken to its logical conclusion, would prevent *any* inroads being made into the exercise of the right to speak (at least truthfully). Apart from Mill's questionable assumption that there is some objective 'truth', and his confidence in the prevalence of reason, his theory makes the legal regulation of disclosures of personal information (as well as several other forms of speech which cause harm) extremely difficult to justify. It asserts that freedom of expression is a social good because it is the best process by which to advance knowledge and discover truth, starting from the premise that the soundest and most rational judgment is arrived at by considering all facts and arguments for and against. This free market-place of ideas, Emerson argues, should exist irrespective of how pernicious or false the new opinion appears to be because 'there is no way of suppressing the false without suppressing the true'.[23]

But is the argument from truth relevant to the protection of 'privacy'? Schauer doubts whether truth is indeed ultimate and non-instrumental; does it not secure a 'deeper good' such as happiness or dignity?[24] If truth is instrumental, then whether more truth causes a consequential strengthening of this deeper good is a question of fact and not an inexorable, logical certainty from definition. For Schauer the argument from truth is an 'argument from knowledge',[25] an argument that the value in question is having people *believe* that things are in fact true. He formulates the argument in this way to concentrate not on the abstract truth of a proposition but how its propagation 'is directed towards human action'.[26]

One may fail to possess knowledge, or what Schauer calls 'justified true belief', in three ways: 'one's belief can be unjustified; one's belief can be false; and one can have no belief at all'.[27] He asks, 'Is it necessarily

---

[22]Scanlon considers the argument from truth a 'natural' (or non-instrumental) argument; see Scanlon, 'A Theory of Freedom of Expression' (note 18 above). See too W Bagehot, 'The Metaphysical Basis of Toleration', *Literary Studies*, vol 2 (New York: AMS Press 1973); J S Mill, *On Liberty* (London: Longman, 1913); J Milton, *Areopagitica and Of Education*, ed K M Lea (Oxford: Clarendon Press, 1973); and D A Richards, 'Free Speech as Toleration' in W J Waluchow (ed), *Free Speech: Essays in Law and Philosophy* (Oxford: Clarendon Press, 1994). In *International Brotherhood of Electricity Workers Local 501* v *NLRB* 181 F 2d 34, 40 (2d Cir 1950), Learned Hand CJ declared that 'truth will be most likely to emerge if no limitations are imposed upon utterances'.
[23]Emerson, 'Toward a General Theory of the First Amendment' (note 2 above), 882.
[24]Schauer (note 1 above), 706.
[25]*Ibid*, 707.
[26]*Ibid*, 708.
[27]*Ibid*, loc cit.

or generally the case that knowledge is better than ignorance?'[28] In many instances, new knowledge does not replace existing beliefs about a particular subject but adds to what was previously 'epistemological empty space'.[29] Thus, a gain in knowledge is simply an addition rather than substitution of the true for the false. In such cases, the concept of a market-place of ideas begins to collapse and one is left with the value of truth actually being contingent upon a theory which links truth to the aim to which it is instrumental. Schauer concludes that *this* theory depends upon a balancing exercise between members of a class or subclass; many increases in someone's knowledge are at the expense of someone else's well-being or dignity. He concedes that if we view society as a whole,

> ... more knowledge, as a class, will benefit the well-being or happiness or utility or dignity of the recipients of that knowledge, as a class, more than it will detract from the well-being or happiness or utility or dignity of the subjects of that knowledge, as a class.[30]

But if the class is subdivided, it becomes possible to identify subclasses within which the above tendency is reversed. Therefore, proceeding upon the assumption that knowledge is power, if, by law, we curtail the dissemination by A of information about B, then B is empowered at the expense of A who is relatively disempowered. The power struggle is therefore between possessors of information and the class of potential users of that information.

Schauer's approach liberates us from the straitjacket of the inviolability of free speech, though it is a fairly feeble constraint in Britain without explicit constitutional guarantees. His analysis seems also to accommodate the distinction in American defamation and common law privacy

---

[28]*Ibid, loc cit.* Gavison, addressing the argument from truth, claims that 'this particular rationale cannot support the many privacy-invading statements that do not concern ideas or attempt to explain the truth. To recall, the interest that is protected is an interest in not being discussed at all, not an interest in being known in an accurate way' (Gavison (note 2 above), 463).

[29]Schauer (note 1 above), 709. He gives the example of glancing at a publication at a supermarket counter and learning that somebody has lost 200 pounds on a diet of bat guano. This, he suggests, does not replace a previous belief so much as add to a 'stock of beliefs'.

[30]*Ibid*, 711.

jurisprudence between the public figure and the private individual.[31] His remarks on the balancing test between subclasses of society suggest a rejection of a 'personal information' approach:

> By focusing on actual relations between actual segments of the population, we can draw more sensible distinctions among, say, public figures, public officials, and private individuals, and *avoid distinctions that collapse social roles and focus on different categories of utterance.*[32]

Nevertheless support for a 'categories approach' may be drawn from Schauer's acceptance that certain increases in knowledge have no value at all.[33] On that assumption, the disclosure of personal information may be subject to control irrespective of the identity of the subject of the information. But where the subject is a public official, the test of public interest ought to be able to evaluate the relevance of that office to the argument from truth.[34]

---

[31]In the tort of defamation, this distinction derives from *New York Times* v *Sullivan* 376 US 254 (1964). In respect of the common law torts of privacy the logical starting-point is Warren and Brandeis's seminal essay where they state: 'Peculiarities of manner and person, which in the ordinary individual should be free from comment, may acquire a public importance, if found in a candidate for political office' (S D Warren and L D Brandeis, 'The Right to Privacy' (1890) 4 Harv L Rev 193, 215–16; Wacks, *Privacy II* (Chapter 1 note 1 above), 25–6). See Restatement (Second) of the Law of Torts, § 652D, comment h; *Rawlins* v *Hutchinson Pub Co.* 543 P 2d 988 (1975); and *Cassidy* v *American Broadcasting Companies* 377 NE 2d 126 (1978). However, the Supreme Court has thus far failed to distinguish between public and private figures in false-light privacy cases e.g., *Cantrell* v *Forest City Pub Co.* 419 US 245 (1974); *Time Inc* v *Hill* 385 US 374 (1967) and did not suggest that such a distinction was constitutionally relevant in *Cox Broadcasting Corporation* v *Cohn* 420 US 469 (1975).
[32]Schauer (note 1 above), 720 (emphasis added).
[33]*Ibid*, 711.
[34]Warren and Brandeis themselves conceded that the judgment of what is of legitimate public interest is predicated not only on the nature of the information but on the identity and the role of the individual concerned. Their definition of unjustified invasions of privacy was: 'matters ... which concern the private life, habits, acts and relations of an individual, and have no legitimate connection with his fitness for a public office ... or for any public or quasi public position ... and have no legitimate relation to or bearing upon any act done by him in a public or quasi public capacity' (note 31 above), 216.

Self-government

The argument that freedom of expression provides the tools for successful self-governance is an extension of the argument from truth.[35] As Alexander Meiklejohn puts it:

> The principle of the freedom of speech springs from the necessities of the program of self-government. It is not a Law of Nature or Reason in the abstract. It is a deduction from the basic American agreement that public issues shall be decided by universal suffrage.[36]

But, as in the case of the argument from truth, it must be queried how self-government is facilitated or advanced by the revelation of intimate private facts about, say, an individual's sexual proclivities? Is it 'speech' at all?[37]

In certain specific instances such information may be relevant to self-government. Where, for instance, the people acting through their democratically elected government consider a certain 'action' to be sufficiently antisocial to constitute a criminal offence, then it is in the interest of self-governance that offenders are apprehended and punished. Similarly, where an individual holds a public office, and thereby actually acts on behalf of the people, representing and implementing their political beliefs, any activity of that person which pertains directly to his fitness to perform that function is a legitimate interest of the community. As will become evident in Chapter 4, a public interest test is capable of supporting freedom of expression in these instances and thus the Meiklejohnian analysis should not be taken to justify unlimited freedom of speech in the 'privacy' arena.

---

[35]In *Castells v Spain* (1992) 14 EHRR 445 the European Court of Human Rights noted, at para 42, in relation to Article 10 of the European Convention on Human Rights, that freedom of expression 'constitutes one of the essential foundations of a democratic society and one of the basic conditions for its progress ... it is applicable not only to "information" or "ideas" that are favourably received or regarded as inoffensive or as a matter of indifference but also to those that offend, shock or disturb. Such are the demands of that pluralism, tolerance and broadmindedness without which there is no "democratic society"'.

[36]A Meiklejohn, *Political Freedom: The Constitutional Powers of the People* (Oxford: Oxford University Press, 1965), 27.

[37]For a perspicuous discussion of this difficult question, see Barendt (note 1 above), 37–77.

Press Freedom

Arguments from democracy are in full flower here. For Milton and Blackstone, it was the prior restraint of the press that represented the most sinister threat to freedom of speech. Blackstone declares:

> The liberty of the press is indeed essential to the nature of a free State; but this consists in laying no *previous* restraints upon publications, and not in freedom from censure for criminal matter when published. Every freeman has an undoubted right to lay what sentiments he pleases before the public: to forbid this, is to destroy the freedom of the press: but if he publishes what is improper, mischievous, or illegal, he must take the consequence of his own temerity.[38]

Both the conception of the press and the boundaries of its freedom are, however, considerably wider today. Thus the term 'press' normally extends beyond newspapers and periodicals, and includes the so-called electronic media of television and radio and perhaps even the Internet. Nor is the scope of press freedom restricted to prohibitions against 'prior constraint'.

The political justification for freedom of the press is an application of the argument from truth. Mill's second hypothesis, it will be recalled, is the 'assumption of infallibility' that specifies the conditions under which we are able to have confidence believing that what we think is true, actually is true. The safest way to achieve this, the argument runs, is to allow freedom to debate ideas, to subject them to contradiction and refutation. Interference with this freedom diminishes our ability to arrive at rational beliefs.

These are potent principles, even if they occasionally appear to be based on an idealised model of the political process in which individuals actively participate in government. On the other hand, a free press clearly has the potential to engender such interest and to facilitate its exercise. As Gibbons puts it:

> As a principle based upon democratic theory, freedom of speech derives its force much more from a sceptical tendency which stresses the fallibility of those in power, and displays a healthy attitude of incredulity towards the claims of authority. The need is for political

---

[38]W Blackstone, *Commentaries on the Laws of England*, 17th ed (1830), b 4, 151 (as quoted by Lord Denning MR in his dissenting judgment in *Schering Chemicals Ltd v Falkman Ltd* [1982] 1 QB 1, 17).

choices to be justified and for mistakes, with their potential for serious and wide-reaching consequences, to be avoided. In this task, the media have come to play a significant part, both in providing a forum for political debate and in helping to mould opinion.[39]

The attraction of the arguments from truth and from democracy is that they establish independent grounds for freedom of speech in a way that arguments based on the interests of the speaker do not.[40] But the press publishes a good deal that, even by the most magnanimous exercise of the imagination, is not remotely connected to these noble pursuits. Does this suggest that the press is entitled to no special treatment? Arguments to support special treatment for the press tend to fall on stony judicial ground in England. The Court of Appeal's strong rebuke of an editor who sought to justify his unlawful conduct captures the flavour:

I hope that Mr Molloy [the editor of the *Daily Mirror*] will acquit me of discourtesy if I say with all the emphasis at my command that I regard his assertion as arrogant and wholly unacceptable. Parliamentary democracy as we know it is based upon the rule of law. That requires all citizens to obey the law, unless and until it can be changed by due process. There are no privileged classes to whom it does not apply. If Mr Molloy and the *Daily Mirror* can assert this right to act on the basis that the public interest, as he sees it, justifies breaches of the criminal law, so can any other citizen. This has only to be stated for it to be obvious that the result would be anarchy.[41]

A stronger case for special treatment of the press can plainly be made where, unlike the *Daily Mirror* in this decision, the press offends decorum rather than the law. This (thinner) argument may then be made to turn on the importance to the political process of the publication of a *particular* report. Accounts of the private lives of government ministers, officials, politicians, and even perhaps royalty, could plausibly be claimed, under such a view, to warrant special treatment.[42] Here, the nature of the message, and not the medium of its propagation, is the focal point of concern.

---

[39]Gibbons (note 1 above), 16.
[40]*Ibid*, 16–17.
[41]*Francome* v *Mirror Group Newspapers Ltd* [1984] 1 WLR 892, 897 per Lord Donaldson of Lymington MR.
[42]This is not to underestimate the problem of determining which disclosures are indeed 'in the public interest'. See Chapter 4.

This undifferentiated argument for freedom of expression, whether exercised in the press or in the pub has much to commend it, for it avoids the difficulties in defining what is to be understood by the 'press'. Indeed, as Schauer puts it:

> We may wish to say that some forms of communication represent a constraint on governmental power even greater than that established by a general Free Speech Principle, but this powerful constraint would properly be keyed to political content, and not to the presence or absence of a printing press or transmitter.[43]

As a general rule, English law withholds from the press any privileged status or duties.[44] Indeed, even arguments for a 'right of reply' are sometimes regarded as inimical to press freedom in that it amounts to recognising the press as having distinct obligations.

Right of reply

The right of an individual to reply to misleading or inaccurate publications[45] about him appears to conflict not only with free speech, but also with the freedom of the newspaper proprietor to deal with his property as he chooses.[46] In respect of the former, Barendt questions whether a right of reply necessarily restricts this freedom.[47] A newspaper's freedom to speak (or more accurately, freedom not to speak):

> ... is not infringed merely because [the editor] is required by law to publish a proposition he does not agree with. It is only invaded if he is compelled to say or write something in circumstances in which it would appear to a reasonable bystander that he believes in its truth.[48]

---

[43]Schauer, *Free Speech* (note 1 above), 109.
[44]Exceptions inevitably exist, such as the right of the press to access to certain meetings, government officials and so on.
[45]The Calcutt Committee observed that 'there is no necessary correlation between the publication of an inaccurate story about an individual and an intrusion into his privacy'. However, a right to reply would always 'enhance individual freedom by allowing a person to respond' (Committee on Privacy and Related Matters, *Report of the Committee on Privacy and Related Matters*, Cm 1102, 1990, para 11.5).
[46]Feldman (note 2 above), 582–6.
[47]Barendt (note 1 above), 65, 69–70.
[48]*Ibid*, 65–6. In this regard, see Committee on Privacy and Related Matters (note 45 above), para 11.4.

A right of reply would not, on this argument, inhibit free speech if the reply were inserted into the newspaper in such a way as to make it clear that it was the correspondent's version of the truth, not necessarily shared by the editor. The right would, however, impede 'editorial freedom' (a secondary right to free expression), but Barendt argues that 'the weight of the free speech arguments' lies in favour of the right to the accurate representation of one's views, a right held not only by the individual, but by the community as well.[49]

On balance, the arguments in favour of a right to reply outweigh those against it, a position taken by the Calcutt Committee which considered it 'right that an individual who is the subject of a seriously inaccurate story should be able to seek a correction and an apology'.[50] Nevertheless, it rejected the proposal to enact a statutory right to reply; recommending that 'this problem should be tackled within the ambit of a code of practice'.[51] Clause 2 of the committee's proposed code of practice for the press provides that 'Individuals or organisations should be given a proportionate and reasonable opportunity to reply to criticisms or alleged inaccuracies which are published about them'.[52]

Notwithstanding its reluctance to recommend a statutory right, the committee regarded this clause as effectively creating a 'right to reply'.[53] This is clear from the comments of Sir David Calcutt QC in his *Review of Press Self-Regulation*[54] where he expressed dissatisfaction with the differences between the intended code of practice and the form it eventually took in the press industry's own code. Clause 2 of the latter, headed 'Opportunity to reply', reads, 'A fair opportunity for reply to inaccuracies should be given to individuals or organisations when reasonably called for'.[55] Calcutt criticised the narrower scope of the industry code on four grounds: that it provides merely an 'opportunity' rather than a 'right' to reply; that the clause covers only actual and not alleged inaccuracies; that it grants no 'opportunity' in cases of criticism; and, that 'a proportionate and reasonable opportunity to reply' has been replaced by a 'fair opportunity'.[56]

---

[49]Barendt (note 1 above), 70.
[50]Committee on Privacy and Related Matters (note 45 above), para 11.14. The committee rejected a requirement to publish a balancing point of view to counterpoise 'biased or unbalanced reporting', on the ground that it 'has little relevance to the protection of individual privacy' (para 11.7).
[51]*Ibid*, para 11.15.
[52]*Ibid*, app Q.
[53]The title of clause 2.
[54]Sir David Calcutt QC, *Review of Press Self-Regulation*, Cm 2135, 1993, para 3.49.
[55]For the press industry's code of practice, see app C, *ibid*.
[56]*Ibid*, para 3.49.

In his *Review*, Calcutt advocated the establishment of a statutory Press Complaints Tribunal to control the abuses of the press[57] with the power 'to require any publication to respond to its enquiries about complaints and to enforce publication of its adjudications (including, when appropriate, a requirement to publish an apology and correction)'.[58]

In the absence of even this limited right, the individual has little power to correct sensationalist reports which are inaccurate without necessarily being libellous.

The First Amendment

American courts and commentators have developed several theories of free speech, rights-based and consequentialist,[59] that seek to account for the exercise of free speech in all its protean forms. Nevertheless, though it would be artificial to conceive of the problems encountered by the efforts to reconcile 'privacy' and 'free speech' as a discrete question, the American law does appear to have developed the contours of a particular 'privacy/free speech' theory. In particular, there is a tendency to adopt a purposive construction of the First Amendment; to ask, in other words, what forms of speech or publication warrant protection by virtue of their contribution to the operation of political democracy. This is evident in the decisions which distinguish, with variable consequences, between 'public figures' and ordinary individuals. Indeed, the Supreme Court applied the principle adopted in the libel case of *Sullivan* to the 'privacy' case of *Hill* (see above). In the former decision, the court expressed its philosophy in unequivocal terms:

> ... we consider this case against the background of a profound national commitment to the principle that debate on public issues should be uninhibited, robust, and wide-open, and that it may well

---

[57]*Ibid*, point 9 of the summary (referring to the discussion by the Committee on Privacy and Related Matters of such a tribunal in the *Report* (note 45 above), paras 16.13–16.24).
[58]Para 16.16 of the *Report* (note 45 above). And see the fuller version in para 6.18 of the *Review* (note 54 above).
[59]See F Schauer, 'The Role of the People in First Amendment Theory' (1986) 74 Calif L Rev 761, 769–88. Professor Schauer finds rights-based and especially deontological theories (i.e., those that suggest free speech is a good *in itself* because, for example, it encourages self-fulfilment) to be unsound. But he is also critical of consequential theories (such as Meiklejohn's) which are premised on popular participation. He concludes that 'it is time to face up to the paternalism of the first amendment', implicit in which 'is the fact that a system of government has essentially been forced on us, and there is little we can do about it' (*ibid*, 788).

include vehement, caustic, and sometimes unpleasantly sharp attacks on government and public officials.[60]

The principal purpose of the First Amendment is, in this theorem, the protection of the right of all citizens to understand political issues in order that they might participate effectively in the operation of democratic government. This Meiklejohnian formula allows considerable scope for actions by private individuals who have been subjected to gratuitous publicity. In practice, however, it is frequently those who are in the public eye who (for this very reason) attract the attention of the tabloids. The difficult question which the theory is then required to answer is the extent to which such public figures are entitled to protection of aspects of their personal lives. And this, in turn, involves a delicate investigation of what features of a public figure's life may legitimately be exposed — in the furtherance of political debate.

Though the law seeks to distinguish between 'voluntary' and 'involuntary' public figures,[61] the application of this approach, except as a useful general rationale for the existence of the freedom of speech itself, provides uncertain guidance as to the respective rights and obligations in cases involving unwanted publicity. In the absence of an attempt to define the *kinds* of information in respect of which all individuals might *prima facie* expect to receive protection (even if such protection is subsequently to be outweighed by considerations of 'public interest') one of the central purposes of recognising an individual's interest in restricting information (the trust, candour and confidence it fosters) is diminished.[62]

Speech and action

The First Amendment explicitly protects 'speech' (though this has been given a fairly generous interpretation by the Supreme Court). Emerson argues that while expression is good in itself and should not be restricted, *action* may be susceptible to control for the general good. One ground for this dichotomy is that expression is normally less harmful than action. He argues that expression 'generally has less immediate consequences, is less irremediable in its impact'.[63]

---

[60]*New York Times* v *Sullivan* 376 US 254, 270 per Brennan J (1964). See too *Whitney* v *California* 274 US 357, 375–8 per Brandeis J (1927).
[61]Restatement (Second) of the Law of Torts, § 652D, comments e and f.
[62]Barendt (note 1 above), 23; and Schauer, *Free Speech* (note 1 above), 85–86.
[63]Emerson, 'Toward a General Theory' (note 2 above), 881.

But far from providing the main justification for the primacy of free speech, Stanley Fish argues that this duality suggests that such freedom should never be championed in the abstract but only as a result of a weighing of the consequences of the protection of that particular speech.[64] Fish's reasoning is based on the assertion that 'speech always seems to be crossing the line into action'.[65] In reality, then, the 'zone of constitutionally protected speech' — speech which has no provocative effect to anyone, which is mere abstract expression — is empty:

> ... when a court invalidates legislation because it infringes on protected speech, it is not because the speech in question is without consequences but because the consequences have been discounted in relation to a good that is judged to outweigh them.[66]

Hence speech is never protected *per se*, but compared 'in relation to a value — the health of the republic [or] the vigour of the economy'.[67] This in itself, he argues, provides strong support for a public interest balancing approach, which I examine in detail in Chapter 4 in the context of the action for breach of confidence.

Balancing

Numerous difficulties attend the attempt to formulate a coherent theory of free speech which is both sufficiently broad to capture the complexities of the exercise of the freedom, and sufficiently specific to account for its variable applications. Moreover, these attempts neglect the question of whether free speech is a policy or principle. The argument from democracy appears to attract considerably more support than the Millian or autonomy-based theories, but all provide at best only the most general guidance in respect of the legitimate controls on the public disclosure of personal information.

The matter could be pursued from the perspective of an interest-based theory which seeks to specify the particular interests of the parties involved in the disclosure. However, this approach raises numerous problems of its own (not dissimilar from the interest-based accounts of 'privacy'). In addition, while it is useful to distinguish, say, the 'personality' interests affected by the disclosure of private facts from the

---

[64]Fish (note 2 above), 106.
[65]*Ibid*, 105.
[66]*Ibid*, 106.
[67]*Ibid*, *loc cit*. The issue of whether flag-burning is a protected form of free expression is likely to continue to rage in the United States.

'reputational' interests that are affected by defamatory publications or the 'commercial' interests affected by breach of confidence, it fails to explain which species of information warrant protection in the face of the competing claims of free speech.

In mediating between the two interests the US Supreme Court has, despite the invitations extended by Justices Black and Douglas to adopt an 'absolutist' interpretation of the First Amendment, resorted to the process of 'balancing' by which the interest in free speech is weighed against other interests such as national security, public order, and so on. If such interests are found to be 'compelling' or 'substantial' or where there is a 'clear and present danger' that the speech will cause a significant harm to the public interest, the court will uphold the restriction of free speech.[68]

The dynamics of limitation

Emerson uses this phrase to describe the proposition that the public interest in the freedom of expression must fit in to a 'more comprehensive scheme of social values and social goals'.[69] So far the discussion has outlined the inapplicability of certain free speech justifications, allowing the right to privacy to escape unscathed. Where there is a genuine conflict between the two values, how is 'privacy' to be protected? Or, in other words, why should free speech be subordinated to the protection of personal information?

---

[68]English courts have occasionally followed suit; see, in particular, *Francome* v *Mirror Group Newspapers Ltd* [1984] 1 WLR 892; *Lion Laboratories Ltd* v *Evans* [1985] 1 QB 526 and *Cork* v *McVicar* (1984) *The Times*, 31 October 1984. See too *Secretary of State for Defence* v *Guardian Newspapers Ltd* [1985] 1 AC 339; *Attorney-General* v *Guardian Newspapers Ltd (No. 1)* [1987] 1 WLR 1248; *Stephens* v *Avery* [1988] 1 Ch 449, 456–7 per Sir Nicolas Browne-Wilkinson V-C. In respect of the newsworthiness of a particular publication, the Younger Committee took the view that 'because it is impossible to devise any satisfactory yardstick by which to judge, in cases of doubt, whether the importance of a public story should override the privacy of the people and personal information involved, the decision on this point can be made only in the light of the circumstances of each case. The question we have to answer, therefore, is who should make that decision.... We are in no doubt that the initial decision can only be made by those responsible for the publication: that is by the press themselves ... We do not think that this is the sort of duty that should be given to the courts' (Committee on Privacy, *Report of the Committee on Privacy*, Cmnd 5012, 1972, paras 187–8). In America, the Supreme Court, while obviously recognising the justiciability of the claim, has itself occasionally accepted the judgment of the press concerning what is and what is not newsworthy e.g., *Daily Times Democrat* v *Graham* 276 Ala 380, 162 So 2d 474 (1964); *Briscoe* v *Reader's Digest Association* 483 P 2d 34 (1971). This view is supported by a leading American theorist, Z Chafee, *Government and Mass Communication: A Report from the Commission on Freedom of the Press* (Chicago: Shoe String Press, 1965).
[69]Emerson, 'Toward a General Theory' (note 2 above), 887 and, generally, 887–93.

Emerson identifies three factors which diminish the need to protect freedom of expression absolutely. The first is where the injury to the individual is direct and peculiar to him, rather than one suffered in common with others. Secondly, the interest may be an intimate and personal one, embracing an area of privacy from which both the State and other individuals should be excluded. The third consideration is whether or not society leaves the burden of protecting the interest to the individual himself by, for example, recognising that he has a legal cause of action.

In the first two circumstances the harm in each case will probably be direct and irremediable, and hence almost approximating to an 'action'. Moreover, if the individual has the burden of establishing his case, the resources of the State are less likely to be marshalled into a coherent apparatus for the restriction of free speech. He suggests that 'so long as the interest of privacy is genuine, the conditions of recovery clearly defined and the remedy left to individual suit, it is most unlikely that the balance will be tipped too far toward restriction of expression'.[70]

Even against the background of the First Amendment, Emerson's approach is compelling. And no less so in the context of English law's constitutional silence on safeguards for free speech.[71] Our courts periodically recognise the importance of freedom of speech and of the press. In *Schering Chemicals Ltd* v *Falkman Ltd*, Lord Denning MR said:

> Freedom of the press is of fundamental importance in our society. It covers not only the right of the press to impart information of general interest or concern, but also the right of the public to receive it. It is not to be restricted on the ground of breach of confidence unless there is a 'pressing social need' for such restraint. In order to warrant a restraint, there must be a social need for protecting the confidence sufficiently pressing to outweigh the public interest in freedom of the press.[72]

Hoffmann LJ was recently even more emphatic:

---

[70]Emerson, *Toward a General Theory of the First Amendment* (New York: Vintage, 1966), 75.
[71]For a general discussion of the doctrine of freedom of expression in English law, see J Gardiner, 'Freedom of Expression' in C McCrudden and G Chambers (eds), *Individual Rights and the Law in Britain* (Oxford: Clarendon Press, 1994).
[72][1982] 1 QB 1, 22.

It cannot be too strongly emphasised that outside the established exceptions, or any new ones which Parliament may enact in accordance with its obligations under the Convention [for the Protection of Human Rights], there is no question of balancing freedom of speech against other interests. It is a trump card which always wins.[73]

He recognised, however, that 'a right of privacy may be a legitimate exception to freedom of speech'.[74] And Lord Denning MR in *Schering* went on to acknowledge that there are 'exceptional cases, where the intended publication is plainly unlawful and would inflict grave injury on innocent people or seriously impede the course of justice'.[75] Similarly, echoing Schauer's public sphere/private sphere distinction, Templeman LJ remarked that 'Blackstone was concerned to prevent government interference with the press. The times of Blackstone are not relevant to the times of Mr Murdoch'.[76]

In seeking to measure what is 'highly offensive' the American courts have developed what Prosser and Keeton call a '"mores" test'.[77] In the leading case of *Melvin* v *Reid*,[78] the plaintiff's past as a prostitute and defendant in a sensational murder trial was revealed in a film called *The Red Kimono*. She had, in the eight years since her acquittal, been accepted into 'respectable society', married, and moved in a circle of friends who were ignorant of her past. Her action for the invasion of her privacy caused by the defendant's truthful disclosures was sustained by the

---

[73]*R* v *Central Independent Television plc* [1994] Fam 192, 203.

[74]*Ibid*, 204. The case concerns the jurisdiction of the court to restrain publication of matters relating to the care of children. Hoffmann LJ pointed out that other countries to the European Convention 'have a right of privacy for grown-ups as well', adding that 'there may be room for constitutional argument as to whether ... it would not be more appropriate for the remedy to be provided by the legislature rather than the judiciary' (*ibid*). See J Gardiner, 'Another Step Towards a Right of Privacy?' (1995) 145 NLJ 225.

[75][1982] 1 QB 1, 18. This mirrors the approach of Article 10 of the European Convention on Human Rights. In *The Observer and the Guardian* v *United Kingdom* (1992) 14 EHRR 153, the European Court of Human Rights held that 'Article 10 of the Convention does not in terms prohibit the imposition of prior restraints on publication, as such' (para 60). For recent decisions on Article 10, see *Casado Coca* v *Spain* (1994) 18 EHRR 1; *Thorgeirson* v *Iceland* (1992) 14 EHRR 843; and *Chorherr* v *Austria* (1994) 17 EHRR 358.

[76][1982] 1 QB 1, 39. Feldman observes that to be prepared to punish an informant for his eventual disclosure but not to restrain that disclosure, is not only illogical but may in itself constitute 'prior restraint'. He suggests that it 'is undeniable that a person may be influenced in deciding whether to publish by the knowledge that he may make himself liable to criminal penalties or damages by doing so' (note 2 above, 556).

[77]W Prosser and W P Keeton, *The Law of Torts*, 5th ed (St Paul, Minn: West Publishing Co., 1984), 857.

[78]112 Cal App 285, 297 P 91 (1931).

California court (which had not hitherto recognised an action for invasion of privacy).[79]

In *Sidis v F-R Publishing Co.*, the plaintiff, a former child prodigy who, at 11, lectured in mathematics at Harvard, had become a recluse and devoted his time to studying the Okamakammessett Indians and collecting streetcar transfers. The *New Yorker* published an article, 'Where Are They Now? April Fool' written by James Thurber under a pseudonym. Details of Sidis's physical characteristics and mannerisms, the single room in which he lived, and his present activities were revealed by the article which acknowledged that he had informed the reporter who had tracked him down for the interview that he lived in fear of publicity and changed jobs whenever his employer or fellow workers learned of his past.

The New York District Court denied his action for invasion of privacy on the ground that it could find no decision 'which held the "right of privacy" to be violated by a newspaper or magazine publishing a correct account of one's life or doings ... except under abnormal circumstances which did not exist in the case at bar'.[80] On appeal,[81] the Second Circuit affirmed the dismissal of the privacy action, appearing to base its decision on a balancing of the offensiveness of the article with the public or private character of the plaintiff.

Indeed, in both *Melvin* and *Sidis* there is little attempt made to consider the extent to which the information divulged was 'private'. The conceptually vague notions of 'community customs', 'newsworthiness', and the 'offensiveness' of the publication, render these and many other decisions concerning 'public disclosure' singularly unhelpful in an area of considerable constitutional importance. And this is equally true of the attempts by the Supreme Court to fix the boundaries of the First Amendment in respect of publications which affect the plaintiff's 'privacy'. Thus, in *Time Inc v Hill*[82] the court held that the plaintiff's action for invasion of privacy failed where he and his family had been the subject of a substantially false report. The defendant had published a description of a new play adapted from a novel which fictionalised the ordeal suffered by the plaintiff when he and his family were held hostage in their home by a group of escaped prisoners.

---

[79]Where the account is fictionalised, the plaintiff may bring the action under the 'false light' tort. This tort is virtually indistinguishable from defamation or, as one writer puts it, 'belongs with defamation as its unacknowledged but not illegitimate offspring' (Gerety, 'Redefining Privacy' (note 11 above), 258.
[80]34 F Supp 19, 21 (SDNY 1938).
[81]113 F 2d 806 (2nd Cir 1940).
[82]385 US 374 (1967).

Adopting the test that it had applied in respect of defamation,[83] the Supreme Court held, by a majority,[84] that unless there was proof of actual malice (i.e., that the defendant knowingly published an untrue report) the action would fail. Falsity alone did not deprive the defendant of his protection under the First Amendment — if the publication was newsworthy. And, since the 'opening of a new play linked to an actual incident is a matter of public interest',[85] the plaintiff, because he was unable to show malice, failed. Yet the decision was not really concerned with the public disclosure of 'private information'[86] whether or not it was even a defamation action! This question is considered further in Chapter 3.

In so far as this issue has arisen in England, the conventional analysis has received a certain acceptance. It will be seen in Chapter 4 how the courts in cases of breach of confidence involving personal information have adopted a 'balancing' of the interests in confidentiality against the public interest in receiving certain information. Equally, in dealing with complaints concerning alleged invasions of 'privacy' by the press, the Press Council and Press Complaints Commission have attempted, with little success,[87] to strike a balance between these interests.

Restrictions on reporting

Anonymity in sex cases

One important statutory restriction of free speech in the name of 'privacy' is worth mentioning. The Sexual Offences (Amendment) Act

---

[83]*New York Times* v *Sullivan* 376 US 254 (1964).

[84]Fortas J dissented, 385 US 374, 411–420 (1967).

[85]*Ibid*, 388.

[86]'To me this is not "privacy" litigation in its truest sense,' per Harlan J, *ibid*, 476.

[87]The Press Council's decisions, though compared by a former chairman, Lord Devlin, to the methods used by 'generations of judges who produced the common law of England' (H P Levy, *The Press Council: History, Procedure and Cases* (London: Macmillan, 1967), xi) were frequently terse, unreasoned, and often difficult to understand. Successive royal commissions on the press have shown little sympathy for the council's claim that it is 'respected, feared and obeyed' (Committee on Privacy (note 68 above), paras 147 and 151). After the publication of the Kaye photographs, the *Sunday Sport*, in a front-page headline, left readers in little doubt of its view; it read 'Bollocks to the Press Council'. See too Royal Commission on the Press, *Final Report*, Cmnd 6810, 1977, para 20.75; Wacks, *Protection of Privacy* (Chapter 1 note 1 above), 106–9; and Wacks, *Personal Information* (Chapter 1 note 1 above), 164–6. For a comprehensive indictment of Press Council performance, practice and procedure, see G Robertson, *People Against the Press: An Enquiry into the Press Council* (London: Quartet Books, 1983).

1976 safeguards the anonymity of complainants of 'rape offences'. Such offences are defined in s. 7(2) to include 'rape, attempted rape, aiding, abetting, counselling and procuring rape or attempted rape, [incitement to rape, conspiracy to rape and burglary with intent to rape]'.[88] Rape itself is defined in s. 1 of the Sexual Offences Act 1956 as non-consensual sexual intercourse, either anal or vaginal, with a person, either male or female.[89]

The main provisions as to anonymity are contained in s. 4 of the 1976 Act which prescribes a 'two-tier' system of protection.[90] As soon as it is alleged that a rape offence has occurred, neither the name nor the address nor a still or moving picture of the complainant may be published during his/her lifetime if it is 'likely to lead members of the public to identify that person as an alleged victim of such an offence'.[91] The prohibition applies whether the allegation is made by the alleged victim or 'any other person'.[92] Once a person has been accused of a rape offence[93] the prohibition extends to 'matter likely to lead members of the public to identify a woman or man as the complainant in relation to that accusation during the person's lifetime'.[94]

The 'lifetime' protection does not lapse if the accused is subsequently acquitted, but at no time is it applicable to the reporting of criminal proceedings other than those directly related to the rape offence in question.[95]

These reporting restrictions may, under certain circumstances, be lifted. Section 4(2) provides that either the accused or 'another person against whom the complainant may be expected to give evidence' may apply to a judge of the Crown Court to have the restrictions lifted. The judge must be satisfied that the lifting is required both for the purpose of inducing persons to come forward as witnesses,[96] and to avoid the applicant's defence being substantially prejudiced.[97] Section 4(3) gives

[88]The words in square brackets were substituted by the Criminal Justice Act 1988, s. 158(6).
[89]Rape of a male was introduced by s. 142 of the Criminal Justice and Public Order Act 1994.
[90]See D Brogarth and C Walker, 'Court Reporting and Open Justice' (1988) 138 NLJ 909, 909–910 and 916. These provisions have been amended by the Criminal Justice Act 1988 and by the Criminal Justice and Public Order Act 1994.
[91]Sexual Offences (Amendment) Act 1976, s. 4(1)(a).
[92]Ibid, loc cit.
[93]As to what constitutes 'accused' see s. 4(6), ibid.
[94]Ibid, s. 4(1)(b).
[95]Ibid, s. 4(1). This provision, according to Brogarth and Walker, discourages 'false or malicious allegations of rape, since a prosecution of a woman for perjury can be fully publicised' (note 90 above), 910.
[96]Sexual Offences (Amendment) Act 1976, s. 4(2)(a).
[97]Ibid, s. 4(2)(b).

the judge a discretion at trial to remove or relax the restriction if it would 'impose a substantial and unreasonable restriction upon the reporting of proceedings at the trial and that it is in the public interest [to do so]'.

Section 4(4) allows a person convicted of a rape offence and who is appealing against conviction, to apply to the Court of Appeal for a direction that reporting restrictions should be lifted. The person must show both that the direction is needed for the purpose of obtaining evidence in support of the appeal and that he is likely to suffer substantial injustice if the direction is not given. Finally, s. 4(5A)[98] allows the complainant to consent to publicity in writing although consent is vitiated if it is proved that 'any person interfered unreasonably with the peace or comfort [of the complainant] with intent to obtain consent'.[99]

These provisions go a long way towards protecting the complainant's anonymity, and it is hard to see how the American decisions of *Cox Broadcasting Corp* v *Cohn*[100] and *The Florida Star* v *BJF*[101] could ever be followed in England. If the restrictions are flouted, any editor and any publisher of a newspaper or periodical in which the relevant matter is published, or in the case of its inclusion in a relevant programme, any body corporate engaged in providing the service containing the programme and any person with 'editorial' responsibilities, shall be guilty of an offence.[102]

More recently, the provisions of the 1976 Act have been extended by the Sexual Offences (Amendment) Act 1992 and the Criminal Justice and Public Order Act 1994.[103] Section 4 of the 1992 Act lays down special rules for offences under ss. 10–12 of the Sexual Offences Act 1956 (incest by a man or woman, and buggery). If the 'other party' to the offence is

---

[98]Inserted by the Criminal Justice Act 1988, s. 158(3).
[99]Sexual Offences (Amendment) Act 1976, s. 4(5B).
[100]420 US 469 (1975).
[101]491 US 524 (1989).
[102]Sexual Offences (Amendment) Act 1976, s. 4(5). It is a summary offence and the fine must not exceed level 5 on the standard scale.
[103]Section 168(1) and sch 9, para 52(2) of the 1994 Act. The offences to which the provisions apply are: intercourse with a mentally handicapped person by hospital staff etc (s. 128 of the Mental Health Act 1959), indecent conduct towards a young child (s. 1 of the Indecency with Children Act 1960); incitement by a man of his granddaughter, daughter or sister under the age of 16 to commit incest with him (s. 54 of the Criminal Law Act 1977), and any attempt or conspiracy or incitement of another to commit any of these offences. It includes also ss. 2–7, 9–12, 14–16 of the Sexual Offences Act 1956 which provide for the following offences: procurement of a woman by threats or by false pretences, administering drugs to obtain intercourse with a woman, intercourse with a girl under the age of 13, intercourse with a girl between the ages of 13 and 16, intercourse with a mentally handicapped person, procurement of a mentally handicapped person, incest by a man or by a woman, buggery, indecent assault on a woman, indecent assault on a man, and assault with intent to commit buggery.

Privacy and Press Freedom

himself or herself accused of committing the parallel offence, reporting
restrictions are not to apply, e.g., if the woman against whom incest by
a man is alleged to have been committed is herself accused of having
committed incest upon that man.[104]

Contempt of court

The reporting of legal proceedings is governed also by the law on
contempt of court. Section 4(1) of the Contempt of Court Act 1981
provides that 'a person is not guilty of contempt of court ... in respect
of a fair and accurate report of legal proceedings held in public,
published contemporaneously and in good faith'. But this is subject to
s. 4(2) which provides that a report may be postponed if that is necessary
to avoid a substantial risk of prejudice to the administration of justice.
In *R v Beck, ex parte Daily Telegraph plc*,[105] however, Farquharson LJ
refused to restrict the reporting of alleged sexual offences committed by
social workers against children in care notwithstanding that free
disclosure would involve a substantial risk of prejudice to the administration of justice. The balance tipped in favour of the public's right to
know 'what is going on'.[106] Similarly, in *R v Clerkenwell Metropolitan
Stipendiary Magistrate, ex parte The Telegraph plc*,[107] it was held that a court
had a discretionary power to hear representations from the press or the
news media when considering whether to make an order under s. 4(2)
of the 1981 Act.

Section 11 provides that a court may prohibit the publication of 'a
name or other matter' if that information has already been withheld
from the public in the proceedings before the court. The court must be
satisfied that the order is necessary in the public interest, not merely for
the protection of the individual.[108]

---

[104]The Sexual Offences (Amendment) Act 1992, s. 6(2), provides that where it is alleged
that a relevant offence has been committed, the fact that any person consented to the act
does not prevent that person being regarded as the person against whom the offence was
committed. Section 6(3) extends this provision to incest and buggery once a person has
been accused of such an offence.
[105][1993] 2 All ER 177.
[106]*Ibid*, 182 per Farquharson LJ.
[107][1993] QB 462.
[108]E.g., *R v Reigate Justices, ex parte Argus Newspapers Ltd* (1983) 5 Cr App R (S) 181. See also,
R v Socialist Worker Printers and Publishers Ltd, ex parte Attorney-General [1975] 1 QB 637
(order in respect of blackmail victims); *Attorney-General v Leveller Magazine Ltd* [1979] AC
440 (in respect of secret agents); *Birmingham Post and Mail Ltd v Birmingham City Council*
(1993) *The Times*, 25 November 1993 (DC).

Other statutory restrictions may be found in the Judicial Proceedings (Regulation of Reports) Act 1926; Children and Young Persons Act 1933, ss. 39, 49;[109] Administration of Justice Act 1960, s. 12;[110] Magistrates' Courts Act 1980, ss. 8, 71;[111] and the Criminal Justice Act 1987, s. 11.[112] At common law the court may, in addition, exclude the public from proceedings.[113]

Until the passing of the Criminal Justice Act 1988, restrictions ordered under the above provisions were not readily susceptible to challenge. Section 159 provides that 'a person aggrieved' may apply to the Court of Appeal for leave to appeal against an order under s. 4 or s. 11 of the Contempt of Court Act 1981;[114] any order restricting the access of the public to a trial;[115] and any order restricting the publication of any report of a trial.[116] Journalists come within the term 'person aggrieved' dispelling any doubts that they do not have *locus standi* to challenge a direction of a court.[117]

[109]See *R* v *Central Criminal Court, ex parte Crook* (1994) 159 JP 295 (CA).
[110]See *R* v *Central Independent Television plc* [1994] Fam 192.
[111]*R* v *Beaconsfield Justices ex parte Westminster Press Ltd* (1994) 158 JP 1055.
[112]Brogarth and Walker (note 90 above), 909.
[113]E.g., *R* v *Malvern Justices, ex parte Evans* [1988] 1 QB 540.
[114]Criminal Justice Act 1988, s. 159(1)(a).
[115]*Ibid*, s. 159(1)(b).
[116]*Ibid*, s. 159(1)(c).
[117]*R* v *Beck, ex parte Daily Telegraph plc* [1993] 2 All ER 177, 179 per Farquharson LJ.

3

Privacy and the Common Law

Introduction

It is one of the law's great ironies that, though rooted in the English law of confidence, the American 'privacy' torts have failed to germinate in England. Ever wary of the 'grand style' of judicial interpretation, founded on sweeping principles, English courts maintain a hard-nosed hostility towards legal rights allegedly immanent in the law. Yet this remedy, the equitable action for breach of confidence, remains the principal means by which to provide protection against the gratuitous publication of personal information and it is, therefore, the main subject of this chapter. But the victim of uninvited publicity may pursue other avenues. The law of tort may be of some assistance, especially in the light of recent developments in the action for the intentional infliction of emotional distress, which I briefly consider. I say little here about the tort of defamation on the simple ground that, although a defamatory imputation may result from the disclosure of intimate facts, the defence of justification effectively restricts liability to *false* statements. The gravamen of the complaint in a 'privacy' case is not that the information published is false, but that it has been published at all. Indeed, it is often its *truth* that wounds.

Breach of confidence

It is almost a quarter of a century since the Younger Committee concluded that the equitable remedy for breach of confidence offered 'the most effective protection of privacy in the whole of our existing law, civil and criminal'.[1] It requested the Law Commissions to clarify the law

---

[1] Committee on Privacy, *Report of the Committee on Privacy*, Cmnd 5012, 1972, para 87.

48

in legislative form which they did.[2] But Parliament has failed to act. Perhaps they were right. Few tears would be shed by Professor Jones who regarded the Law Commission's report in the following light:[3]

> At the end of the day the large question remains: is it desirable *at this time* to enact legislation on the lines suggested by the Law Commission, legislation which will, in some ways, petrify the development of this branch of the law? Certainly there are few signs in the last few years that the common law has failed to deal adequately with the problems which it has been required to solve. This area of the law is not crying out for reform. It is still in an embryonic state; and there may well be questions lurking unseen in the shadows.

This, of course, begs the question what are 'the problems which it has been required to solve'? In the years since these words were written, the ability of the remedy to address the problem of the protection of personal information might be questioned. In this regard, I have long argued that, though 'privacy' and 'confidence' often overlap, the action for breach of confidence provides an unsuitable means by which to safeguard 'privacy'. Has anything happened to undermine or, at least, to weaken this view?

I shall describe the principal features of the law of confidence,[4] and re-examine the question whether, even if the protection of 'privacy' and the protection of confidence are based on 'two alternative theories'[5] (the former being 'primarily designed to protect feelings and sensibilities'[6]), the action for breach of confidence may now have provided the courts with the means by which to protect an individual against unwanted publicity being given to his private life.

The elements of the action

It is little more than a truism that the leading cases[7] fail to establish with adequate clarity the circumstances in which (either direct or indirect) recipients of confidential information may be restrained from using or

[2]Law Commission, *Breach of Confidence*, Cmnd 8388, 1981; and Scottish Law Commission, *Breach of Confidence*, Cmnd 9385, 1984.
[3]G Jones, 'The Law Commission's Report on Breach of Confidence' [1982] CLJ 40, 47.
[4]For a lucid and comprehensive account see F Gurry, *Breach of Confidence* (Oxford: Clarendon Press, 1984).
[5]*Copley v Northwestern Mutual Life Insurance Co.* 295 F Supp 93, 95 (1968).
[6]*Ibid, loc cit.*
[7]In particular, *Prince Albert v Strange* (1849) 1 Mac & G 25; 41 ER 1171; *Morison v Moat* (1851) 9 Hare 241, 68 ER 492.

disclosing it. This may, in part, be a consequence of the action's frequently arising in the form of applications for interlocutory injunctions which call for speedy adjudication. More recent decisions recognise a wider equitable principle of 'good faith' or conscience on which to base the jurisdiction[8] but its precise scope is not easy to delineate.

In order to found a cause of action, three general requirements must be satisfied:

(a) The information itself must 'have the necessary quality of confidence about it'.[9] This requirement is normally satisfied by demonstrating that the information is 'not ... public property and public knowledge'.[10]

(b) The information must have been imparted in circumstances imposing an obligation of confidence. Such an obligation will normally arise when information is imparted—either explicitly or implicitly—for a limited purpose, and extends to any third parties to whom the information is disclosed, in breach of confidence, by the original confidant.[11]

(c) There must have been an unauthorised use of the information by the party who was under an obligation of confidence.

Each of these requirements will be briefly examined with particular reference to the protection of personal information.

The information
Although the vast majority of decisions involve trade secrets (including business[12] and technical secrets[13]), government secrets[14] and artistic and literary confidences,[15] as well as personal information, have all been the

---

[8]*Seager* v *Copydex Ltd* [1967] 1 WLR 922, 931 per Lord Denning MR; and *Fraser* v *Evans* [1969] 1 QB 349, 361 per Lord Denning MR.
[9]*Saltman Engineering Co. Ltd* v *Campbell Engineering Co. Ltd* (1948) 65 RPC 203, 215 per Lord Greene MR.
[10]*Ibid, loc cit.*
[11]*Lord Ashburton* v *Pape* [1913] 2 Ch 469.
[12]For instance *Thomas Marshall (Exports) Ltd* v *Guinle* [1979] 1 Ch 227, 248 where Megarry V-C considered the sort of information 'capable of being confidential'. In *Stephens* v *Avery*, Browne-Wilkinson V-C could see 'nothing either in principle or authority to support the view that information relating to sexual conduct cannot be the subject-matter of a duty of confidence' ([1988] 1 Ch 449, 455).
[13]For instance, *Ackroyds (London) Ltd* v *Islington Plastics Ltd* [1962] RPC 97 (invention of tool to manufacture plastic 'swizzle-sticks').
[14]*Attorney-General* v *Guardian Newspapers Ltd (No. 2)* [1990] 1 AC 109; *Attorney-General* v *Guardian Newspapers Ltd (No. 1)* [1987] 1 WLR 1248; *Attorney-General* v *Jonathan Cape Ltd* [1976] 1 QB 752; *Commonwealth of Australia* v *John Fairfax & Sons Ltd* (1980) 147 CLR 39.
[15]E.g., *Fraser* v *Thames Television Ltd* [1984] 1 QB 44 (idea for a television series).

subject of litigation. The main concern here is, of course, with personal information.

So, for example, in *Duchess of Argyll* v *Duke of Argyll*[16] the Duchess successfully sought an injunction to prohibit the Duke and a newspaper from publishing confidences she had reposed in her husband in the course of their marriage. Ungoed-Thomas J, relying largely on *Prince Albert* v *Strange*, held that such communications between spouses were protected against breach of confidence — notwithstanding the Duchess's subsequent adultery and divorce from the Duke. He declared, '... there could hardly be anything more intimate or confidential than is involved in [the relationship of marriage], or than in the mutual trust and confidences which are shared between husband and wife'.[17]

Similarly, in *Stephens* v *Avery*,[18] the information concerned the plaintiff's lesbian affair with a Mrs Telling. On application to strike out the plaintiff's pleadings as disclosing no cause of action at interlocutory stage, Browne-Wilkinson V-C stated, first, that grossly immoral conduct will not be protected[19] but that because of the inability in modern times to determine the mores of a nation, 'Only in a case where there is still a generally accepted moral code can the court refuse to enforce rights in such a way as to offend that generally accepted code'.[20] The Vice-Chancellor also recognised the test propounded by Megarry J in *Coco* v *A N Clark (Engineers) Ltd*[21] who doubted 'whether equity would intervene unless the circumstances are of sufficient gravity; equity ought not to be invoked merely to protect trivial tittle-tattle, however confidential'.[22] On the facts, the disclosure of intimate details regarding someone's sexual life was held by the Vice-Chancellor not to be trivial: 'I have the greatest doubt whether wholesale revelation of the sexual conduct of an individual can properly be described as "trivial" tittle-tattle'.[23] He added, 'I can see no reason why information relating to that most private sector of everybody's life, namely sexual

---

[16][1967] 1 Ch 302.
[17]*Ibid*, 322.
[18][1988] 1 Ch 449. See W Wilson, 'Privacy, Confidence and Press Freedom: A Study in Judicial Activism' (1990) 53 MLR 43.
[19]Following *Glyn* v *Western Feature Film Co.* [1916] 1 Ch 261.
[20][1988] 1 Ch 449, 454.
[21][1969] RPC 41.
[22]*Ibid*, 48.
[23][1988] 1 Ch 449, 454

conduct, cannot be the subject-matter of a legally enforceable duty of confidentiality'.[24]

In another decision concerning personal information, *Woodward* v *Hutchins*,[25] the exploits of pop stars and in particular the 'outrageous' behaviour of one of them aboard an aircraft was the subject of the action. There were no submissions in respect of the quality of the information revealed *per se* and Lord Denning MR proceeded on the basis that it was *prima facie* susceptible to the protection of a duty of confidentiality.

In *Lennon* v *News Group Newspapers Ltd*[26] the former wife of John Lennon sold the 'story' of her marriage to the ex-Beatle to the *News of the World* which commenced a serialisation of it. The articles disclosed intimate details of the relationship between the plaintiff and his ex-wife. The Court of Appeal denied an injunction on the ground that 'the relationship of these parties has ceased to be their own private affair'.

Similarly, in *Khashoggi* v *Smith*[27] the former housekeeper of the plaintiff, an affluent socialite who had attracted considerable publicity, disclosed intimate facts to the *Daily Mirror* concerning the plaintiff. But as there was an investigation proceeding into the alleged commission of an offence by the plaintiff, the Court of Appeal, on an interlocutory motion, refused to enjoin publication; there could be no confidence in information connected to the alleged offence.

Many disclosures assume the form of a photograph taken or used without the subject's consent. It is a problem that, though its contemporary form assumes rather different proportions, begins in the early days of photography. So in *Pollard* v *Photographic Co.*,[28] Mrs Pollard had her picture taken at the defendant's shop. An employee of the defendant used it in the shop window in the form of a Christmas card. There was some evidence that the employee may have been selling the cards for commercial gain (rather than using the card to advertise the services of the photographic company). North J held that a breach of confidence had occurred, declaring that '... where a person obtains information in the course of a confidential employment, the law does not permit him to make any improper use of the information so obtained'.[29] And he further emphasised that:

---

[24]*Ibid*, 455.
[25][1977] 1 WLR 760.
[26][1978] FSR 573.
[27](1980) 130 NLJ 168.
[28](1889) 40 ChD 345.
[29]*Ibid*, 349.

The customer who sits for the negative ... puts the power of reproducing the object in the hands of the photographer: and in my opinion the photographer who uses the negative to produce other copies for his own use, without authority, is abusing the power confidentially placed in his hands merely for the purpose of supplying the customer.[30]

This dictum supports the view that the law protects also a person's likeness,[31] but such a conclusion cannot be reached without an analysis of the following, second limb of the *Saltman* test.

The obligation of confidence

The recipient of information normally incurs an obligation of confidence by virtue of the relationship in the course of which the information is imparted. Such an obligation may arise, with or without a contract, in a variety of circumstances, ranging from marriage[32] to Cabinet meetings.[33]

It is generally the case that even in the absence of an explicit undertaking by the recipient of information to maintain its confidentiality, an obligation of confidence will be *imposed* upon him if the circumstances are such as to indicate that he knew or ought to have known that the information is to be treated as confidential.[34] Even where a third party receives confidential information, and, at the time he receives it, is unaware that he has acquired it as a result of a breach of confidence, he will, on being given notice of the breach, be *prima facie* subject to a duty of confidence. This is clear from the judgment of Megarry V-C in *Malone* v *Commissioner of Police for the Metropolis (No. 2)*:[35]

---

[30]*Ibid, loc cit.*
[31]See *Li Yau-wai* v *Genesis Films Ltd* [1987] HKLR 711 discussed below.
[32]*Duchess of Argyll* v *Duke of Argyll* [1967] 1 Ch 302.
[33]*Attorney-General* v *Jonathan Cape Ltd* [1976] 1 QB 752.
[34]The objectivity of the test was suggested, *obiter*, by Megarry J in *Coco* v *A N Clark (Engineers) Ltd* [1969] RPC 41, 48: 'It may be that that hard-worked creature, the reasonable man, may be pressed into service once more; for I do not see why he should not labour in equity as well as at law. It seems to me that if the circumstances are such that any reasonable man standing in the shoes of the recipient of the information would have realised that upon reasonable grounds the information was being given to him in confidence, then this should suffice to impose upon him the equitable obligation of confidence'.
[35][1979] 1 Ch 344, 361.

If A makes a confidential communication to B, then A may not only restrain B from divulging or using the confidence, but may also restrain C from divulging or using it if C has acquired it from B, even if he acquired it without notice of any impropriety.... In such cases it seems plain that however innocent the acquisition of the knowledge, what will be restrained is the use or disclosure of it after notice of the impropriety.

The key question, of course, is whether an obligation of confidence can arise in the absence of some pre-existing confidential relationship in which the plaintiff imparts confidential information to another. A negative answer to this enquiry would constitute a serious limitation on the action's viability as a tool by which to protect 'privacy'. I therefore consider it in the section below, 'Reappraising orthodoxy'.

Unauthorised use

For the plaintiff in a breach of confidence action to establish that the defendant has actually used or disclosed the confidential information, he must prove that the information was 'directly or indirectly obtained from [the] plaintiff, without the consent, express or implied, of the plaintiff'.[36] He does not have to show that the defendant has acted dishonestly or even consciously in using the information. Thus in *Seager* v *Copydex Ltd*[37] the defendant was held liable for 'unconscious plagiarism'[38] in using the plaintiff's idea for a carpet grip; the two parties had discussed — apparently in very general terms — the plaintiff's idea, but their negotiations broke down and the Court of Appeal found that the defendant honestly believed the idea to be his own.[39]

Whether the plaintiff need establish that he has suffered (or will suffer) detriment as a result of the breach of confidence is a matter of some uncertainty. While Megarry J (as he then was) in *Coco* v *A N Clark (Engineers) Ltd*[40] suggested that this might be a requirement of the action, the better view would seem to be that this factor ought to be conceived as relevant only to the determination of the appropriate remedy. In the context of public disclosure of personal information it

---

[36] *Saltman Engineering Co. Ltd* v *Campbell Engineering Co. Ltd* (1948) 65 RPC 203, 213 per Lord Greene MR.

[37] [1967] RPC 349.

[38] *Ibid*, 374.

[39] See too, *Terrapin Ltd* v *Builders' Supply Co. (Hayes) Ltd* [1967] RPC 375; (on appeal) [1960] RPC 128.

[40] [1969] RPC 41, 48; see too *Dunford & Elliott Ltd* v *Johnson & Firth Brown Ltd* [1978] FSR 143, 148 per Lord Denning MR.

would not, of course, always be easy to see how the plaintiff could realistically be said to have suffered any detriment in the strict sense of material disadvantage; though he almost certainly will have suffered injured feelings, embarrassment or distress.[41]

In principle, it ought not to matter whether the personal information disclosed was true or false or whether it lowered or enhanced the plaintiff's reputation (a view accepted by Knight Bruce V-C in *Prince Albert* v *Strange*[42] and by Megarry J in *Coco*[43]). There is no denying the fact that 'some people want privacy largely so that they can turn it to their own financial advantage'[44] and the detriment in such cases would not be different from the normal commercial confidence case. There is also much in Professor Cornish's view that:[45]

> It is tempting to say that liability ought to follow simply upon the breaking of the confidence without looking also for detriment. But one should remember that a very wide range of subject-matter is involved, and also that there is always some public interest in the freedom to use information. Restriction of that freedom accordingly requires sufficient reason.

The limits of the action

A number of obstacles beset the path of the law of confidence as a protector of 'privacy'. First is the apparent requirement, just mentioned, of a relationship of confidence between the person who confides the information and the person to whom it is confided. Such a relationship will not necessarily (or even normally) be present where the plaintiff's complaint is that personal facts have been published without his consent (e.g., by a newspaper which has obtained the information without any breach of confidence). But is it a prerequisite of the action? I examine this important matter below, and in Chapter 5.

---

[41]In *Attorney-General* v *Guardian Newspapers Ltd (No. 2)* [1990] 1 AC 109, 256, Lord Keith of Kinkel stated, *obiter*, 'I would think it a sufficient detriment to the confider that information given in confidence is to be disclosed to persons whom he would prefer not to know of it, even though the disclosure would not be harmful to him in any positive way'. Lord Goff of Chieveley wished to keep the question open (*ibid*, 281–2). See too *X* v *Y* [1988] 2 All ER 648, 657; *Li Yau-wai* v *Genesis Films Ltd* [1987] HKLR 711; and M Pendleton (1987) 17 HKLJ 362.
[42](1849) 2 De G & Sm 652, 697, 64 ER 293, 312.
[43][1969] RPC 41, 48; see, too, Scott J in *Cork* v *McVicar* (1984) *The Times*, 31 October 1984.
[44]W Cornish, *Intellectual Property: Patents, Copyright, Trade Marks and Allied Rights* 2nd ed (London: Sweet & Maxwell, 1989), para 8.035.
[45]*Ibid, loc cit.*

Secondly, the possible requirement that in order to succeed the plaintiff must show detriment may mean, in 'privacy' cases, that the only detriment suffered would be mental distress. This may suffice for the plaintiff to be awarded an injunction, but may deprive him of an award of damages. Thirdly, the plaintiff must establish that the information was inaccessible to the public, not in the 'public domain'; a requirement which sometimes produces artificial results in the context of 'privacy' claims.

Fourthly, the action is available only to the person to whom the obligation of confidence is owed, and it is only the person who has actual, imputed, or constructive knowledge that he is acting in breach of confidence who may be sued. It may not therefore normally assist a plaintiff who is subjected to unwanted press publicity. Fifthly, the application of the defence of 'clean hands' to a 'privacy' action results in the court refusing relief where, on a 'balance of perfidy',[46] the plaintiff has himself disclosed information which is of a greater order of impropriety than the revelation of which he complains or where he has himself exhibited little concern for the maintenance of the confidential relationship. Sixthly, the occasional application of the rule accepted in libel cases that an interlocutory injunction will not be granted against a defendant who intends to justify or plead fair comment, is inappropriate in cases involving breach of confidence, especially where personal information is concerned, for not only is the disclosure of a secret irrevocable, but, since compensation is unlikely to be awarded for mental distress (the plaintiff's usual injury in such cases), to leave the plaintiff to his remedy in damages is effectively to deprive him of effective relief.

It is not unreasonable to conclude that, in general terms, the action for breach of confidence is inadequate to deal with the archetypal 'privacy' complaint because the action is largely concerned with: (a) disclosure or use rather than publicity, (b) the source rather than the nature of the information, and (c) the preservation of confidence rather than the possible harm to the plaintiff caused by its breach.

These deficiencies are most effectively demonstrated by contrasting the action with the American tort of 'public disclosure of private facts' or

---

[46]*Duchess of Argyll* v *Duke of Argyll* [1967] 1 Ch 302, 331 per Ungoed-Thomas J.

what is called in the Restatement (Second) of the Law of Torts[47] 'publicity given to private life'.[48] The Restatement[49] defines the tort as follows:

One who gives publicity to a matter concerning the private life of another is subject to liability to the other for invasion of his privacy, if the matter publicized is of a kind that (a) would be highly offensive to a reasonable person, and (b) is not of legitimate concern to the public.

The tort has the following three elements:

(a) There must be *publicity*: to inform his employer or a small group that the plaintiff is, say, a homosexual, would not suffice.
(b) The information disclosed must be *private* facts: publicity given to matters of public record will not be actionable.
(c) The facts disclosed must be offensive to a reasonable man of ordinary sensibilities.

The American tort therefore differs in a number of respects from the equitable remedy for breach of confidence. Table 3.1 identifies the essential differences. The fundamental distinction lies, of course, in the fact that while the tort of unwanted publicity is based on the protection against the disclosure of certain information which is categorised as 'private', the action for breach of confidence rests on the more limited protection against disclosure of certain information which is categorised as 'confidential' and is subject to an obligation of confidence owed normally to the person who has confided it.

---

[47]Restatement (Second) of the Law of Torts, § 652D.
[48]But note that the American tort has generated less litigation than might have been anticipated, and in formulating certain, sometimes fundamental elements, there is a degree of imprecision and even speculation. Reports of the death of the tort may, however, be exaggerated. Compare D L Zimmerman, 'Requiem for a Heavyweight: A Farewell to Warren and Brandeis's Privacy Tort' (1983) 68 Cornell L Rev 291 (Wacks, *Privacy II* (Chapter 1 note 1 above), 433); and R Gavison, 'Too Early for a Requiem: Warren and Brandeis Were Right on Privacy vs Free Speech' (1992) 43 SC L Rev 437. Furthermore, some of the deficiencies of the tort may be partly explained by the existence of a remedy for breach of confidence.
[49]Restatement (Second) of the Law of Torts, § 652D.

Table 3.1: Public disclosure and breach of confidence compared

Public disclosure	Breach of confidence
Publicity given to 'private facts'	Use or disclosure of confidential information
Wide publicity generally required	Not required
Not required	Information must be imparted in circumstances imposing a duty of confidence
Facts disclosed must be 'highly offensive'	Not required, but 'trivial tittle-tattle' not protected
Disclosures in the public interest not actionable	Similar limitation obtains
Public figures may forfeit some protection	Similar limitation obtains
Anyone who is subject to unauthorised publicity may sue	Only the person to whom the duty of confidence is owed may sue
Anyone who publishes private facts without authority may be sued	Only the person who is subject to a duty of confidence may be sued

The American tort therefore protects the plaintiff against wide publicity being given to certain classes of information. The purpose of the law of confidence, on the other hand, though it requires the information to be 'confidential', is essentially to maintain the fidelity or trust that the plaintiff has reposed in the person to whom he has confided certain information (or, at any rate, who ought to recognise that he is violating such trust). The policy of the law is principally to promote the honesty which is important to commercial transactions. It is not therefore illogical that the action for breach of confidence should concentrate on the *source* rather than, as in the 'privacy' tort, the *content* of the information.

Moreover, there is no requirement in the law of confidence that the disclosure be 'highly offensive' (or indeed offensive at all) since its principal object is not to prevent harm to the plaintiff, but to ensure that information communicated in confidence (actually or constructively) will, in general, be protected. Under the American tort, I do not have a cause of action where the published information about me is, by reference to an objective standard, innocuous — even if its disclosure causes me embarrassment or distress. Where, however, I impart the *same* facts in the course of a confidential relationship, it is arguable that, because I might not have revealed them in the absence of an expectation of confidentiality, I should be able to prevent their disclosure by the action for breach of confidence.

In 'privacy' cases, therefore, the action for breach of confidence has the potential to protect a wider range of information relating to the plaintiff, subject, of course, to the existence of a relationship of confidence or, at any rate, circumstances in which the defendant knew or ought to have known that he was acting in breach of confidence. This is consistent with the law's objective in protecting the interest in the maintenance of confidential relationships. And even if the revelations made in breach of confidence were innocuous it would not be unreasonable for the confider to fear that possible future disclosures may be less trivial.

Similarly, whereas the 'privacy' tort requires wide publicity,[50] in the case of breach of confidence the plaintiff will have a legitimate objection if disclosure is made in breach of confidence to a single individual.

Reappraising orthodoxy

Prior relationship
The Law Commission concluded that 'An obligation of confidence will arise when the circumstances of the relationship [between confider and confidant] import it'.[51] And this principle figured in the Commission's draft Bill.[52] An obligation of confidence was only to be imposed if the confidant had agreed to treat the information as confidential in the form of an express undertaking or in circumstances where, by conduct in relation to the confider, or by virtue of the relationship between them,

---

[50] *Peterson* v *Idaho First National Bank* 367 P 2d 284 (1967). Cf *Beaumont* v *Brown* 257 NW 522 (1977).
[51] *Breach of Confidence* (note 2 above), para 4.2.
[52] *Ibid*, app A.

such an undertaking on the part of the confidant could be inferred.[53] The Commission could not state any clear overreaching principle to guide the courts,[54] but it must be noted that at the time of formulating its recommendations there were no authorities in which a prior relationship between the confider and confidant was absent.

Since then, however, a number of decisions have illuminated the grounds upon which the action is based. Can a plausible case now be established to support the proposition that the action is predicated not upon a prior relationship between the parties but on the principle of unconscionability?

To answer this question (and so to present the strong case against my earlier position) I shall examine a number of decisions since the Law Commission's Report, in particular, *Francome* v *Mirror Group Newspapers Ltd*,[55] *Stephens* v *Avery*,[56] *Attorney-General* v *Guardian Newspapers Ltd (Nos 1 and 2)*,[57] and *Franklin* v *Giddins*.[58]

In *Franklin* (which was considered by the Law Commission),[59] the defendant occasionally lent a hand at the plaintiff's orchard, subsequently set up his own rival orchard and then, surreptitiously, stole budwood cuttings from the plaintiff's premises. The cuttings provided the defendant with information regarding a new strain of nectarines that the plaintiff had cross-bred. Dunn J did not consider the obligation of confidence to be predicated upon a relationship between the parties during the course of which the information was divulged from confider to confidant. He found himself 'quite unable to accept that a thief who steals a trade secret, with the intention of using it in commercial

---

[53] *Ibid*, clause 3(1)(a) and (b).

[54] The Commission was content to restate its comments in its Working Paper: 'No one can say with any assurance how a particular issue will be decided in the future' (Law Commission, *Breach of Confidence* (Working Paper No. 58), Cmnd 5012, 1972, para 5.2).

[55] [1984] 1 WLR 892.

[56] [1988] 1 Ch 449.

[57] *Spycatcher (No. 1)* [1987] 1 WLR 1248 and *Spycatcher (No. 2)* [1990] 1 AC 109.

[58] [1978] 1 QdR 72, and see W J Braithwaite, 'The Secret of Life: A Fruity Trade Secret' (1979) 95 LQR 323.

[59] The Law Commission stressed that its terms of reference 'are not directed to the protection of privacy as such' (*Breach of Confidence* (note 2 above), para 2.1). However, it was explicitly asked to consider whether the law in this area protected information 'unlawfully obtained' (*loc cit*). It was in response to this question that it concluded, 'it is very doubtful to what extent, if at all, information becomes impressed with an obligation of confidence by reason solely of the reprehensible means by which it has been acquired' (para 4.10). Implicit in this statement is the further conclusion that *Franklin* could not be taken as authority, in England at least, that the law was moving to receipt-based conscionability principles.

competition with its owner, to the detriment of the latter, and so uses it, is less unconscionable than a traitorous servant'.[60]

Though I earlier characterised this decision as an infringement of the plaintiff's property in his budwood,[61] this now seems a rather restrictive interpretation. There is, I think, justification for reading the judgment as the beginning of the demise of the need for a relationship for the imposition of an obligation of confidence.[62]

The limitations of the decision must, however, be immediately acknowledged. The information was of a wholly commercial nature and, more importantly, the cutting — the carrier of the information — was obtained unlawfully from the plaintiff's orchard. This point is considered below. Suffice it to observe here that the result could well have been very different if the defendant had stumbled upon the cutting lying on a road near the plaintiff's orchard.[63]

In *Stephens*, though on the facts there clearly was a strong prior relationship between the plaintiff and Mrs Telling, the Vice-Chancellor, in response to the defendant's submission that there must be such a relationship for the duty of confidence to be imposed, stated that 'the basis of the equitable intervention to protect confidentiality is that it is unconscionable for a person who has received information on the basis that it is confidential subsequently to reveal that information'.[64] These sentiments have been explicitly restated by Lord Goff:

> ... a duty of confidence arises when confidential information comes to the knowledge of a person (the confidant) in circumstances where he has notice, or is held to have agreed, that the information is confidential, with the effect that it would be just in all the circumstances that he should be precluded from disclosing the information to others.[65]

---

[60][1978] 1 QdR 72, 80.

[61]Wacks, *Personal Information* (Chapter 1 note 1 above), 255–6.

[62]As suggested by Braithwaite (note 58 above). He considers it authority for the proposition that an individual who surreptitiously obtains confidential information (as distinct from learning through a confidential disclosure) will be subject to an obligation of confidence.

[63]The Law Commission specifically reviewed *Franklin* under the heading 'Can information initially become impressed with an obligation of confidence by reason only of the reprehensible means by which it has been acquired?' (*Breach of Confidence* (note 2 above), Part IV, Section C). As remarked above (note 59), this unwillingness to discuss the case in relation to the wider issue may be a result of the Commission's terms of reference.

[64][1988] 1 Ch 449, 456.

[65]*Spycatcher (No. 2)* [1990] 1 AC 109, 281.

Kaye v *Robertson,*[66] which has become, as already mentioned, something of a *cause célèbre,* involved the use of the plaintiff's photograph, taken by newspaper reporters while he was convalescing in a private room of a hospital from which they were expressly barred. Breach of confidence was not pleaded (presumably because counsel shared my own reservations about the limits of the action)[67] but, apart from the question of a prior relationship between the parties, the case has much in common with *Pollard* v *Photographic Co.*[68] Both concern the unauthorised use of the plaintiff's likeness, though in *Kaye* the plaintiff's objection is to the unauthorised publicity, while in *Pollard* it is against the defendant's commercial use.[69]

The absence of a relationship between the parties has not inhibited the Hong Kong courts from imposing liability for breach of confidence. In *Lam* v *Koo and Chiu,*[70] the Hong Kong Court of Appeal held that a medical researcher was under a duty of confidence in respect of a questionnaire that had been prepared by a 'rival' research team and which, by the appellant's admission, he had used in formulating his own questionnaire. It is unfortunate that there is no clear evidence as to how the appellant obtained access to the respondents' questionnaire. Penlington JA, commenting upon the trial judge's finding that the appellant had obtained the information 'surreptitiously', remarked:

> ... he did somehow come into possession of the document, and he must have known it was confidential because of the amount of work which had gone into its preparation. It had not been given to him by the persons whose information it was and again he must have realised he was not entitled to use it.[71]

This dictum takes the law considerably further than both *Franklin* and *Francome* for in those decisions the 'surreptitious taker' acted contrary

---

[66][1991] FSR 62. See B S Markesinis, 'Our Patchy Law of Privacy — Time to Do Something About It' (1990) 53 MLR 802; P Prescott, '*Kaye* v *Robertson* — A Reply' (1991) 54 MLR 451; Markesinis, 'The Calcutt Report Must Not Be Forgotten' (1992) 55 MLR 118; and D Feldman, *Civil Liberties and Human Rights in England and Wales* (Oxford: Clarendon Press, 1993), 387–8.

[67]Scott LJ, writing extrajudicially, after having noted that the breach of confidence action was not argued before the court in *Kaye*, could only ask 'Why not?' See L Clarke (ed), *Confidentiality and the Law* (London: LLP, 1990), xxiii.

[68](1889) 40 ChD 345.

[69]See M P Thompson, 'Confidence in the Press' [1993] Conv 347; *Li Yau-wai* v *Genesis Films Ltd* (note 41 above).

[70]Civil Transcript No. 116 (1992).

[71]*Ibid*, 30.

to law (theft and an offence contrary to the Wireless Telegraphy Act 1949, respectively). In *Lam*, Penlington JA emphasised that the finding of 'surreptitious obtaining' did not extend as far as theft which, he said 'cannot be supported by the evidence'.[72] But if surreptitious taking extends to the mere fact that the appellant 'did somehow come into possession' of the questionnaire with the knowledge that it was confidential, the Hong Kong Court of Appeal appears (by accident or design) to have grasped the nettle and embraced the notion of receipt-based liability, albeit under cover of surreptitiousness rather than unconscionability.

But caution is required. First, the actual finding, at first instance, that the information was imparted in circumstances imposing an obligation of confidence (the second *Saltman* limb) was not challenged upon appeal.[73] Secondly, the rival teams of researchers worked at the same university which implies a 'course of dealing' between the parties during which the appellant arguably became aware that the question-naire was confidential. This could, to some extent, approximate to a relationship of confidence on orthodox principles.

The case is plainly not one of a stranger stumbling across a diary in the street. Nevertheless the judgment demonstrates the utility of the breach of confidence action where the strict requirement of a prior relationship is relaxed. It does not, however, remove all the obstacles in the path of the protection of 'privacy', for the finding that the appellant knew that the information contained in the questionnaire was confiden-tial was derived less from the nature of the information than from his personal experience, and the limited relationship between the parties.

Kaye exemplifies the difficulties associated with predicating the action for breach of confidence upon a relationship between the parties. The archetypal 'invasion of privacy' complaint is not, of course, based on a direct relationship between the victim and the wrongdoer; indeed this is the primary objection to the American tort of breach of confidence which centres upon the fiduciary nature of certain relationships and prohibits the disclosure of information imparted within them.[74] Thus it has been argued that this tort is capable (at least in the context of the relationship between employer and employee) of assuming the (frayed) mantle of Warren and Brandeis's public disclosure tort as a means of

---

[72] *Ibid*, 29.
[73] One is bound to ask why not? The decision of the trial judge represented a significant divergence from existing authority.
[74] See S L Fast, 'Breach of Employee Confidentiality: Moving Toward a Common-Law Tort Remedy' (1993) 142 U Pa L Rev 431.

protecting 'privacy'. This interpretation of the tort[75] suggests that it affords protection to any unauthorised disclosure within a non-public relationship 'that goes beyond mere friendship, family, or confessor-confidant',[76] such relationship which must be 'customarily understood to carry an obligation of confidence'.[77]

An approach of this kind (apart from inviting the problems under discussion) is plainly too narrow. How would it assist the victim against the disloyal friend in *Stephens*, or against the newspaper reporters in *Kaye*?

Constructive knowledge

If the principle of unconscionability is indeed at the heart of the action, the insistence on the need for a prior relationship between confider and confidant may be explained as the threshold of the circumstantial evidence that the plaintiff must establish in order to show that the recipient's conscience has been pricked by the confidential nature of the information. The question therefore becomes one of standard of proof: under what circumstances will *constructive* knowledge be attributed to a confidant — that he has received information he is expected to keep secret when such knowledge cannot be said to exist in fact? In *Coco* Megarry J said:

> It seems to me that if the circumstances are such that any reasonable man standing in the shoes of the recipient of the information would have realised that upon reasonable grounds the information was being given to him in confidence, then this should suffice to impose upon him the equitable obligation of confidence.[78]

This dictum pertains both to the confidant and to third-party recipients. In the case of the latter, however, the court has never required any kind of relationship directly between confider and third party, nor between confidant and third party, though, as conceded above, there has in fact been a relationship between confider and confidant in all but two of the cases.[79]

---

[75]Relying upon *Vassiliades* v *Garfinckel's* 492 A 2d 580 (DC 1985).
[76]Fast (note 74 above), 452.
[77]*Ibid, loc cit.*
[78][1969] RPC 41, 48.
[79]Namely, *Franklin* (note 58 above) and *Francome* (note 55 above).

In *Li Yau-wai* v *Genesis Films Ltd*[80] the plaintiff, an insurance salesman, allowed his photograph to be taken by the defendant film company upon the understanding that it would facilitate his being considered for casting in a future film. Instead, the defendant used the photograph as a prop in a 'ribald comedy', causing the plaintiff considerable embarrassment. The court held that, in addition to liability in defamation, the defendant owed the plaintiff an obligation of confidence in respect of the photograph and, accordingly, the unauthorised use constituted breach of that obligation. Rhind J applied the reasoning of North J in *Pollard* v *Photographic Co.* to find that the photograph had the necessary quality of confidence about it, adding that '... where a person makes himself accessible to be photographed by another in circumstances where one would expect confidentiality to be respected, a duty of confidence on the part of the person taking the photograph will arise'.[81]

The court applied Megarry J's objective test to determine the second limb of the traditional test of actionability: was the information imparted in circumstances importing an obligation of confidence? It was satisfied that 'any officious bystander would emphatically pronounce that when Genesis took Mr Li's photograph, Genesis knew that it was only supposed to use it for casting purposes'.[82] The application of the standard of the reasonable man to impose upon the defendant an obligation of confidence represents a significant development, especially because the actual intentions of the parties had to be drawn by inference rather than by reference to a specific remark made or the nature of their relationship. It demonstrates the potential of the unconscionability test in protecting 'privacy'.

In the case of a third party, his obligation to keep information secret is parasitic upon there being an obligation owed to the confider by a confidant.[83] *A fortiori*, a relationship between the confider and confidant is required, without which third-party obligations cannot attach. This third-party obligation points the way to the future development of the action. The law attaches such a duty in respect of the confidences of a person whom the third party has not even met because a duty of confidence has arisen at the primary level between confidant and confider. Why then should that duty *at the primary level* require a prior relationship? Why, in other words, should the court be satisfied that the

---

[80][1987] HKLR 711. See Pendleton (note 41 above).
[81][1987] HKLR 711, 719.
[82]*Ibid, loc cit.*
[83]See Gurry (note 4 above), especially 269–83.

third party acted unconscionably according to a lower standard of proof than it applies to the confidant?

The principle of unconscionability does indeed admit of a lower standard of proof. Could this provide the basis for the protection against unauthorised publicity by the law of breach of confidence? If, as is suggested above, the rationale of the law *is* unconscionability, then there would seem to be no obvious obstacle in the way of attaching an obligation to a person by virtue merely of receipt of information whose *nature* is such that the person, on the principles of constructive knowledge, is taken to have realised that he may not divulge it to another. This is the mechanism by which personal information may be protected from transactions which take place outside of a relationship between the person who is the subject of that information and he who disseminates it.[84] Do the authorities support this contention?

Re-reading the cases

In *Stephens* the Vice-Chancellor noted that '... the relationship between the parties is not the determining factor. It is the acceptance of the information on the basis that it will be kept secret that affects the conscience of the recipient of the information'.[85] This remark, though plainly *obiter* (there was a close relationship between the plaintiff and Mrs Avery) explicitly recognises that the requirement of a relationship is not a rule of law but merely a means of proving to an acceptably high standard that the information is received *on the basis that it will be kept secret*.

Is this a (belated) creative leap towards Younger? If, as I formerly argued, the action is generally concerned to protect the *source* rather than the *nature* of the information, such decisions (or at least their reasoning) may legitimately be so regarded. Thus on the basis of *Stephens* and *Spycatcher (No. 2)*, Wilson adopts this view because for him the basis of the jurisdiction for breach of confidence in cases of personal information is the protection of 'the integrity of certain types of relationship',[86] whereas in cases of commercial confidences it is the

---

[84]This must be read in the light of the fundamental principle that the only person who may call for the fulfilment of the obligation of confidence is the person to whom that obligation is owed (*Fraser v Evans* [1969] 1 QB 349). The Law Commission observed that 'the mere fact that a person has an interest in the secrecy of information does not of itself give that person a right to sue' (*Breach of Confidence* (note 2 above), para 5.9). This is discussed below.
[85][1988] 1 Ch 449, 456.
[86]Wilson (note 18 above), 49.

protection of 'the pre-existing rights of the plaintiff'.[87] He refers to Ungoed-Thomas J's view in *Argyll* that 'the protection of confidential communications between husband and wife is not designed to intrude into [the marital] domain but to protect it, not to break their confidential relationship but to encourage and preserve it'.[88]

This was how I, too, understood the decisions.[89] But a more faithful reading might suggest that, though in both instances clear relationships between the parties existed,[90] the courts were chiefly concerned with unconscionable conduct. Thus the question of a relationship becomes a sufficient but not a necessary condition of liability. It is, in other words, an important factor in determining whether the evidence supports the inference that the recipient of the information either knew or ought reasonably to have known that the information was subject to a duty of confidence. But it is not a requirement of the action.

In *Francome*[91] the nature of the information unlawfully intercepted was not considered by the court for it was an interlocutory application by the defendant newspaper to discharge an injunction restraining it from publishing until trial extracts from the recordings of the telephone conversations between the plaintiff and his wife. It is clear, however, that the information was such that both sides were aware of its value: the plaintiff in destroying his reputation, the newspaper in profiting from a scoop concerning alleged illicit activities by one of Britain's leading jockeys. On a conventional analysis, it is possible, if slightly artificial, to consider Mr Francome (the plaintiff) as the confider and his wife, the confidant. But here there is an important factor: the confidant has herself committed no breach of confidence.

How then could a third-party (the tapper) be held liable? To what does the parasite of third-party liability attach? The court directed itself to the *mens rea* of the tapper. Could it be said that his conscience was pricked? The answer, according to the Court of Appeal was emphatically in the affirmative. The only basis upon which such a conclusion could have been reached was the tacit assumption that a person who unlawfully listens to another's telephone conversation acquires information that was intended to be received by no one other than the person on the end of the line. A tapper is, by definition, on notice, either

[87]*Ibid*, 50.
[88]*Duchess of Argyll* v *Duke of Argyll* [1967] 1 Ch 302, 330.
[89]Wacks, *Personal Information* (Chapter 1 note 1 above), 87 and 97.
[90]As Wilson puts it: 'the obligation imposed was clearly indebted to a "special" relationship between the confider and confidant' (note 18 above), 49.
[91][1984] 1 WLR 892.

explicitly (and it seems difficult to avoid the conclusion that he knows precisely the confidential nature of the information) or implicitly (on the ground that he ought reasonably to know).

This decision is difficult to square with orthodoxy. Wilson asserts that 'In the absence of . . . a relationship the courts have nevertheless shown themselves ready to intervene to protect a confidence where it would advance or support a particular right of the plaintiff'.[92] Such rights, he suggests, are 'socially based'.[93] But this begs the question. If Mr Francome's 'right' not to have his telephone tapped (and his conversation overheard) had not been recognised by the court, he would have had no legal right at all. And Wilson's reference to the dictum in *Argyll* must be read in the light of Lord Keith's observation in *Spycatcher (No. 2)* that '. . . as a general rule, it is in the public interest that confidences should be respected, and the encouragement of such respect may *in itself* constitute a sufficient ground for recognising and enforcing the obligation of confidence'.[94]

Thus while the scope of the action has manifestly enlarged, this has occurred on the basis of principles that have long supplied its equitable underpinning.[95] And the limitations that I earlier identified[96] led me to conclude, *inter alia*, that in the absence of a relationship of confidence between the person who confides the information and the confidant, no duty of confidence can be born. So, I suggested, a newspaper may publish with impunity personal information which it has obtained without a pre-existing relationship of confidence. If this is indeed the law it would represent a formidable restriction of the utility of the action, and a powerful argument in support of the enactment of specific 'privacy' legislation.

It does not follow, of course, that were the action capable of accommodating these kinds of activities, the case for explicit legislation would be defeated, though it would weaken it. What then is the status of the argument that a duty arises on discovery or receipt of obviously confidential information?

---

[92] Wilson (note 18 above), 54.

[93] *Ibid*, 52.

[94] [1990] 1 AC 109, 256 (emphasis added).

[95] See G Jones 'Restitution of Benefits Obtained in Breach of Another's Confidence' (1970) 86 LQR 463. Even in 1970, Jones identifies a general principle of unconscionability in cases such as *Seager* v *Copydex Ltd* [1967] RPC 349. He argues: 'The plaintiff's right is based upon the broad equitable principle that the defendant . . . shall not *knowingly* take advantage of the plaintiff's confidence' (*ibid*, 492, emphasis added).

[96] See Wacks, *Personal Information* (Chapter 1 note 1 above), 100–34. I there consider what I call the structural, functional, doctrinal, and (with scant regard for elegance) the 'functional-structural' problems in applying the action to protect 'privacy'.

In *Spycatcher (No. 2)*, Lord Goff remarked that the duty of confidentiality, as currently defined, embraced the situation 'where an obviously confidential document is wafted by an electric fan out of a window into a crowded street, or where an obviously confidential document, such as a private diary, is dropped in a public place, and is then picked up by a passer-by'.[97] He then, rather cryptically, continued:

> I have however deliberately avoided the fundamental question whether, contract apart, the duty [of confidentiality] lies simply 'in the notion of an obligation of conscience arising from the circumstances in or through which the information was communicated or obtained'.[98]

Although the latter comment (and that there was in fact a relationship of confidence) suggests that these observations were *obiter*, the importance of the first dictum hardly requires pointing out. It plainly contemplates attaching a duty of confidence to a person who receives information that is *obviously confidential* by virtue only of the *nature of the information*. Hence the reasonable man who stumbles across a private diary would clearly apprehend that the information unintentionally imparted to him should not be passed on to others.

Moreover, the court's willingness in *Francome* (at the interlocutory stage) to recognise a duty of confidence imposed by virtue of receipt of confidential information *simpliciter* is significant. Indeed, *Francome* demonstrates that the traditional distinction between the obligation imposed on a confidant within a relationship of confidence with the confider, and the obligation on a third party whose conscience may be pricked simply by notice, is, at least on certain facts, difficult to sustain. It looks like a straightforward acceptance of a duty based on unconscionable behaviour *per se*.

The decision does, however, have its limits. First, it was an interlocutory hearing. And, secondly, the court appears to condemn the *manner* in which the information was obtained, rather than its *nature*. In respect of the first matter, the Master of the Rolls warned:

> It is of paramount importance that everyone should understand the exercise on which ... we are engaged. There is to be a speedy trial at which the rights of the parties will be determined.... It is not our

---

[97] [1990] 1 AC 109, 281.
[98] *Ibid, loc cit,* citing *Moorgate Tobacco Co. Ltd* v *Philip Morris Ltd (No. 2)* (1984) 156 CLR 414, 438 per Deane J.

function to decide questions of law or fact which will be in issue at the trial.[99]

Yet, though the force of *Francome* may be reduced by its interlocutory setting, the court was nevertheless faced with clear authority that in the case of telephone tapping, no cause of action would lie. And while one presumes that in awarding an injunction, it was influenced by the fact that the plaintiff's remedy of damages, if the article were published before trial, was a fairly hollow one, the court explicitly addressed the conflicting authority on the point. It was obviously persuaded that there was a reasonable prospect of the plaintiff's substantive claim succeeding at trial.

It will be recalled that in *Malone*,[100] on the other hand, the Vice-Chancellor declined an injunction to protect an individual whose telephone had been tapped by the police who had acted according to law under directions from the Home Secretary. In his view, 'However secret and confidential the information, there can be no binding obligation of confidence if that information is blurted out in public or is communicated in other circumstances which negative any duty of holding it confidential'.[101] He added, 'It seems to me that a person who utters confidential information must accept the risk of any unknown overhearing that is inherent in the circumstances of communication'.[102]

This reasoning was, however, distinguished by the Court of Appeal in *Francome*. Fox LJ observed:

> Sir Robert Megarry V-C was only dealing with a case of authorised tapping by the police.... Illegal tapping by private persons is quite another matter since it must be questionable whether the user of a telephone can be regarded as accepting the risk of that in the same way as, for example, he accepts the risk that his conversation may be overheard in consequence of the accidents and imperfections of the telephone system itself.[103]

Despite this backsliding, straws remain for the traditionalist to clutch at. It might, for example, be contended that the true rationale of

---

[99][1984] 1 WLR 892, 894–5.
[100]For a discussion of the case, see Wacks, *Personal Information* (Chapter 1 note 1 above), 276–85.
[101][1979] 1 Ch 344, 375, quoting from *Coco v A N Clark (Engineers) Ltd* [1969] RPC 41, 47–8.
[102]*Ibid, loc cit.*
[103][1984] 1 WLR 892, 900.

Francome and *Franklin* is that the court will not condone the improper or unlawful obtaining of information.[104] It is tempting to distinguish between such conduct and the innocent finding of a diary or, indeed, lawful telephone tapping. How might *Franklin* have been decided if the defendant had innocently found the budwood cutting on a path? George Wei argues that the concept of 'illegality of means' provides the best explanation of these two decisions,[105] and he proposes a number of factors that the court ought to take into account including the legality of the means used to acquire the secret information, the standards and practices of the relevant industry, and the general circumstances of the case.[106] But, apart from those circumstances which have a bearing on the reasonable man's knowledge of the obligation of confidence, the means of taking should not be directly relevant when imposing a duty of confidence.[107]

In any event the distinction drawn by Fox LJ in *Francome* rests on the *quality of the information*. The information in *Malone* was information in the public domain; the conversations in *Francome* were not. Moreover, in *Francome* there was no breach of duty apart from the eavesdropping of a 'third party'. On what other ground could the telephone conversations be protected than that the conscience of the recipient was pricked by the confidentiality of the information?

If telephone conversations are an acceptable category of *confidential information* it requires, of course, only a limited exercise of the legal imagination to extend protection to the victim of the zoom lens for, 'In principle, there cannot be any distinction between eavesdropping on telephone conversations and intruding on private occasions by the use of long-range cameras or binoculars'.[108]

This at once raises the prospect of vexatious litigation, for if the traditional test is to be supplanted by criteria defining when information is confidential, how is the law to regulate the circumstances in which the information is imparted? Ultimately this is a matter of policy. And the guardian of policy is whether that information is in the public domain, the question to which I now turn.

---

[104]The Law Commission's view on this matter was almost entirely based on *Malone* and is therefore questionable in the light of *Francome*. See paras 4.7–4.10 of *Breach of Confidence* (note 2 above).
[105]G Wei, 'Surreptitious Takings of Confidential Information' (1992) 12 LS 302, 308.
[106]*Ibid*, 315.
[107]See Wacks, *Personal Information* (Chapter 1 note 1 above), 169–71.
[108]P Milmo, 'Confidence and Privacy' (1993) 143 NLJ 1647.

Public domain

That information is generally available or accessible is better regarded as a factor negating the obligation of confidence *ab initio*, than as a defence to an action for breach of confidence. In the commercial context, the classic formulation of the test is, as expounded in *Saltman*, that the information is public property and public knowledge. This has been refined by concepts like the springboard doctrine. Hence, in a typical trade case, *O Mustad & Son v Dosen*,[109] the defendant, allegedly in breach of confidence, informed a rival company about details of the plaintiffs' process for making fish hooks (the defendant having formerly worked for the plaintiff firm). The details had to some extent been revealed by the plaintiffs in their patent. In Lord Buckmaster's view:

> Of course, the important point about the patent is not whether it was valid or invalid, but what it was that it disclosed, because after the disclosure had been made by the plaintiffs to the world, it was impossible for them to get an injunction restraining the defendants from disclosing what was common knowledge. The secret, as a secret, had ceased to exist.[110]

In the case of personal information, the test sits a little less comfortably, though much of the confusion has arisen as a consequence of an incomplete analysis of the commercial doctrines or of the factual circumstances of the particular decisions in issue. The apparent difficulty of applying the test in a non-technical context emerges from *Spycatcher (No. 1)*,[111] and in particular the comments of Sir John Donaldson MR in the Court of Appeal where he stated:

> I accept that to the extent that these publications have been read the information to which they related has become public knowledge, but not that it has entered the public domain, so losing the seal of confidentiality, because that only occurs when information not only becomes a matter of public knowledge, but also public property.[112]

He added:

> The only post-July 1986 publication which *could* render confidential information public property is that revealed in the Australian

---

[109][1963] RPC 41.
[110]*Ibid*, 43.
[111][1987] 1 WLR 1248.
[112]*Ibid*, 1275.

proceedings or in the United Kingdom Parliament. On the hypothesis that the government would otherwise successfully establish its right to confidentiality at the trial, it will be able to require the court to treat all other publications as tainted by the fact that Mr Wright was their source and so incapable of becoming public property.[113]

July 1986 was the date when the government first attempted to enjoin publication in Britain of information concerning the revelations in *Spycatcher*. The Master of the Rolls's reasoning might therefore be formulated as follows:

(a)   Peter Wright may be subject to a duty of confidentiality (if such is proved in law).
(b)   At the time the government first attempted to restrain publication of the information it was not in the public domain.
(c)   The only releases which might be held to have caused the information to enter the public domain are those which are the subject of the main action.
(d)   If, therefore, a possible right of action is denied at the interlocutory stage owing to revelations made since the right was first attempted to be exercised, the court will allow the breach to defeat the action to prevent the breach.

His lordship was concerned to maintain the plaintiff's rights at the interlocutory stage. The critical element is that the revelations which the court would not allow to be considered to be in the public domain were revelations made *after* the government sought to exercise its rights. Until then the public was unaware of the *Spycatcher* allegations apart from the reports of the Australian litigation. As in *Francome*, any other reasoning would have left the government with a hollow right at trial, for the disclosure would have been permitted, and the plaintiff's only remedy would be in damages. Indeed, at trial, none of the judges who heard the substantive action had any doubt that the information was indeed in the public domain. And in the second *Spycatcher* action Lord Goff remarked that 'On any sensible view the information contained in the book was, at the date of trial, in the public domain'.[114]

More difficult is *Schering Chemicals Ltd* v *Falkman Ltd*.[115] Here, the court, in effect, imposed on the second defendant a blanket duty not to

---

[113]*Ibid*, 1275–6.
[114][1990] 1 AC 109, 290.
[115][1982] 1 QB 1.

disclose matters which he had learned as an interviewer for the course which Schering had provided to counteract adverse publicity which had surrounded their pregnancy-testing drug. The court appeared to annihilate the public domain test to determine liability and instead to treat it as one of the factors to be taken into account in the 'public interest' balancing exercise. (See Chapter 4.)

However, *Schering* may be read as an application of the springboard doctrine, i.e., that someone who acquires confidential information may not take advantage of that information even if it subsequently enters the public domain.

The springboard doctrine

The scope of the principle is well expressed by Roxburgh J in *Terrapin Ltd* v *Builders Supply Co. (Hayes) Ltd*:[116]

> ... a person who has obtained information in confidence is not allowed to use it as a springboard for activities detrimental to the person who made the confidential communication, and springboard it remains even when all the features have been published or can be ascertained by actual inspection by any member of the public.[117]

But the obvious problem with this expression of the doctrine is that it appears to nullify the public domain test, i.e., that information obtained *prima facie* under an obligation of confidentiality can never be used even if it is subsequently published. This places the recipient of the information in a worse position than anyone else. And it contradicts *O Mustad & Son* v *Dosen* which specifically acknowledges the inability of the courts to enforce a duty of confidence in respect of information available to the public at large. Attempts to reconcile *Mustad* and *Terrapin* have not been especially successful (see below).

There is much to be said for Gurry's view that emphasis be placed on the 'inaccessibility of the information to the public':

> What the courts are protecting, therefore, is essentially an original *process of mind* which produces inaccessible information, and the protection operates against anyone who, by taking unfair advantage

---

[116][1967] RPC 375.
[117]*Ibid*, 391. See Gurry (note 4 above), especially 245–52.

of the information which has been disclosed to him, saves himself the time, trouble, and expense of going through the same process.[118]

And it is worth recalling that Roxburgh J in *Terrapin* was considering the specific argument that, although the defendant had received information concerning the plaintiff's building units, publication by the plaintiff of brochures released the information into the public domain. Roxburgh J maintained:

> The brochures are certainly not equivalent to the publication of the plans, specifications, other technical information and know-how. The dismantling of a unit might enable a person to proceed without plans or specifications, or other technical information, but not, I think, without some of the know-how, and certainly not without taking the trouble to dismantle. I think it is broadly true to say that a member of the public to whom the confidential information had not been imparted would still have to prepare plans and specifications. He would probably have to construct a prototype, and he would certainly have to conduct tests. Therefore, the possessor of the confidential information still has a long start over any member of the public.[119]

This approach may be used to explain *Schering*. Support may be drawn from a remark by Shaw LJ:

> To extend the knowledge or to revive the recollection of matters which may be detrimental or prejudicial to the interests of some person or organisation is not to be condoned because the facts are already known to some and linger in the memories of others.[120]

In other words, although the information in *Schering* had, at some time, been accessible in the press and on television, the defendant, by virtue of his position 'inside the story', had a permanent advantage over all others since, even though the public could rekindle and augment their knowledge concerning the affair from existing media sources, the

---

[118]Gurry, *ibid*, 247.
[119][1967] RPC 375, 391.
[120][1982] 1 QB 1, 28.

defendant was one step ahead in terms of the time, money and effort required to perform the requisite investigation.[121]

The cases which have (vainly) sought to reconcile *Mustad* with *Terrapin*, do so on the basis of the identity of the author of the disclosure. In *Mustad* the confider itself released the information and this fact was used in *Cranleigh Precision Engineering Ltd v Bryant*[122] and in *Speed Seal Products Ltd v Paddington*,[123] concerning disclosure by a third party and the confidant respectively, to hold that in such cases the information would not be held to have entered the public domain. The underlying principle appears to be that no man may profit from his own wrong.

In *Spycatcher (No. 2)* the House of Lords explored the reach of this principle.[124] For Lord Goff, *Cranleigh* involved merely an extension of the springboard doctrine and, accordingly, the reasoning in *Speed Seal* (the identity of the discloser) which was widely thought to be embodied in *Cranleigh*, 'cannot, to my mind, be supported'.[125] He was unequivocal:

> I have to say, however, that I know of no case ... in which the maxim [no man may profit from his own wrong] has been invoked in order to hold that a person under an obligation is not released from that obligation by the destruction of the subject-matter of the obligation, on the ground that that destruction was the result of his own wrongful act.[126]

On the other hand, Lord Griffiths[127] explicitly maintained that the obligation of confidence owed by Peter Wright to the Crown could not be destroyed by a deliberate act of disclosure by Wright (and, hence, that the *Sunday Times*, as third parties with knowledge of Wright's

---

[121]The Law Commission described *Schering* as an 'unfortunate and paradoxical result' (*Breach of Confidence* (note 2 above), para 6.67). The effect of the decision, taken to its logical conclusion, is that information once acquired in confidence could not be used by the acquirer even though the information was, at the time of acquisition, in, or subsequently entered, the public domain.

[122][1966] RPC 81.

[123][1985] 1 WLR 1327.

[124]See Y Cripps, 'Breaches of Copyright and Confidence: The Spycatcher Effect' [1989] PL 13.

[125][1990] 1 AC 109, 285.

[126]*Ibid*, 286.

[127]*Ibid*, 271.

obligation, should not be permitted to publish future serialisations of *Spycatcher*).[128] Cripps calls this a 'major departure from orthodoxy'.[129]

Lord Goff's appears to be the better view and, although *obiter*, supports Gurry's approach as to the nature and scope of the springboard doctrine. It certainly provides a more logical foundation for the public domain test.[130] Lord Griffiths's approach, perhaps, may legitimately be confined to the secret-service context.[131]

Public domain and privacy

Does the test work when it is personal information that is disclosed? I expressed doubts in my earlier work.[132] And some of these misgivings persist, but, in practical terms, the concept of the public domain and the associated springboard doctrine have operated reasonably successfully in non-commercial contexts.

Consider again the telephone-tapping cases of *Francome* and *Malone*. The former involved the interception of telephone conversations by a private individual, the latter by the police in the exercise of its statutory powers. In exercising their discretion as to what kind of disclosure constitutes a statement to the public (and thus one which is in the public domain and hence unprotectable), the courts may be interpreted as concluding that while it is wholly unreasonable to regard the unlawful tapping of one's telephone conversation by a private individual as an everyday risk of using the telephone, it is not unreasonable to consider it so if the listener is an arm of the State acting in pursuance of its lawful authority. In other words the question of public domain is pressed into service to decide whether the conduct in question occurs in circumstances in which it is reasonable to expect to be unobserved. Being naked in one's garden is different from parading naked in a public highway. The question in both situations is whether the risk of having personal information divulged to others is a natural, reasonable, and foreseeable

---

[128]Lord Jauncey of Tullichettle concurred with Lord Griffiths's reasoning but stopped short of restraining the *Sunday Times* from future serialisation. He considered that such an injunction would be illogical in the face of the various other newspapers which were capable of serialising *Spycatcher* (*ibid*, 293–4).
[129]Cripps (note 124 above), 17.
[130]The Law Commission adopts a standpoint identical to that taken by Gurry in respect of the interpretation and scope of the springboard doctrine (*Breach of Confidence* (note 2 above), paras 4.24–4.31).
[131]'It would make a mockery of the duty of confidence owed by members of the Security and Intelligence Services if they could discharge it by breaching it' ([1990] 1 AC 109, 271).
[132]E.g., Wacks, *Personal Information* (Chapter 1 note 1 above), 59–68.

consequence of that conduct. If it is, the information is in the public domain and cannot be the subject of a duty of confidence.

Yet problems linger. Earlier, I suggested that the principal complaint in breach of confidence cases is one of *disclosure*, whereas with 'privacy' the wrong involves *publicity*.[133] This distinction has since been adopted in the consultation paper published by the Lord Chancellor's Department.[134] Thus, as pointed out in both the paper and the Law Commission's report (and mentioned above), once information has entered the public domain it can no longer be protected from further disclosures to the public at large, even by someone formerly obliged to keep the information secret.[135] The Law Commission gives two examples to illustrate the difficulty. The first[136] concerns information imparted by a patient to his doctor in confidence and which is later revealed to a small, local newspaper by the latter. If the story, initially published to a limited audience in breach of confidence, is taken up by a national newspaper, does the patient lose his right to restrain the national paper from republishing, to a far wider audience, information which is already in the public domain?[137]

The second example[138] relates to the assiduous researcher who combs through back copies of newspapers to compile a list of facts regarding a particular person, all of which, individually, at some stage, were known to the public (and thus did enter the public domain), but as a collective article cannot be said to be 'generally' known.[139] The researcher may be restrained by application of the springboard doctrine, as explained above. If the extraction of information, though accessible to the public, requires 'a significant expenditure of labour, skill or money'[140] then the information cannot be said to be in the public

---

[133]See Wacks, 'The Poverty of "Privacy"' (1980) 96 LQR 73, 82.

[134]*Infringement of Privacy*, Lord Chancellor's Department, Scottish Office, 1993.

[135]Upon the formulation of the springboard doctrine advanced above. If *Schering* is strictly followed, the complainant would be saved from repeated disclosures by the confidant (see above).

[136]*Breach of Confidence* (note 2 above), para 5.12.

[137]The Law Commission remarks, 'The patient's real complaint is based, not on considerations of confidentiality, but on the ground that his medical history is a private matter that should be protected by a right of privacy' (*ibid, loc cit*).

[138]*Ibid*, para 6.68.

[139]As in the infamous American decision, *Sidis* v *F-R Publishing Co.* 113 F 2d 806 (2d Cir 1940), in which a former child prodigy was denied a remedy to prevent his past from being dug up in an article compiled exclusively from information in the public domain.

[140]Clause 2(2) of the draft Bill in *Breach of Confidence* (note 2 above), app A.

domain, and the complainant may well be able to restrain its disclosure.[141] I grapple again with this difficulty in Chapter 5.

Conclusion

The action for breach of confidence manifestly provides considerable adventitious protection to personal information. It is, however, too extravagant to assert that since *Stephens* 'discrete areas of law which enjoy no obvious thematic unity have been united and organised by a new moral principle — privacy'.[142] At best, these cases point to a growing recognition of the principle of unconscionability. We are not yet able to greet a new dawn of 'privacy' protection. But, on a practical level, the action goes some way towards equipping the courts with a useful means by which to restrain several forms of conduct which are most likely to *cause* an invasion of 'privacy'.[143]

In short, '... the early emphasis in breach of confidence actions was to protect the secrecy of information confided by one person to another ... the law seems to be moving beyond this, to afford protection to secret information *which may not have been confided to anyone'*.[144]

Perhaps the Law Commission underestimates the ability of equity to treat the right of confidence as one *in rem* where the recipient is held to owe an obligation by virtue of the nature of the information he receives. It is true that equity acts *in personam*. But the nature of certain information puts a reasonable man on notice that confidential or personal information would not have been revealed to him unless he undertook to keep it secret. The courts need therefore to begin to

---

[141]For a criticism of the Law Commission's change of heart (from its original proposals in its Working Paper (note 54 above), para 103) see Wacks, *Personal Information* (Chapter 1 note 1 above), 63–8.

[142]Wilson (note 18 above), 54.

[143]In *Spycatcher (No. 2)* Lord Keith stated that 'The right to personal privacy is clearly one which the law should in this field [of breach of confidence] seek to protect' ([1990] 1 AC 109, 255).

[144]M P Thompson in *Confidentiality and the Law* (note 67 above), 73.

identify types of information which carries with it (like a health warning) a clear obligation of confidence.[145]

Intentional infliction of emotional distress

In *Wilkinson* v *Downton*,[146] the defendant, as a practical joke, told the plaintiff that her husband had been injured whilst returning from a day at the races and was lying in a pub with broken legs. The plaintiff fell seriously ill as a result, and sought damages for, *inter alia*, mental anguish and for her consequent illness. The jury found that the defendant meant the words to be acted upon, that they were acted upon and that he knew the words to be false, and a sum of £100 was awarded to compensate the plaintiff for her loss and damage. Wright J held:

> The defendant has ... wilfully done an act calculated to cause physical harm to the plaintiff — that is to say, to infringe her legal right to personal safety, and has in fact thereby caused physical harm to her. That proposition without more appears to me to state a good cause of action, there being no justification alleged for the act. This wilful *iniuria* is in law malicious, although no malicious purpose to cause the harm which was caused nor any motive of spite is imputed to the defendant.[147]

The decision therefore establishes that 'doing an act calculated to cause physical harm is actionable if physical harm results'.[148] The plaintiff must, of course, show that the defendant's act would cause harm to a person of ordinary firmness, and that the act caused the harm,

---

[145]Such an approach would also obviate another barrier to the use of the action in the protection of 'privacy': the requirement that the obligation of confidence is owed only to the confider (*Fraser* v *Evans* [1969] 1 QB 349). It is sometimes suggested that the action would be unable to provide a remedy to a father whose child's body is photographed after, say, a disaster at a football match: a harrowing example that materialised at Hillsborough. By protecting 'information pertaining to the health of one's family', a remedy might be available. This is the definition proposed in the Lord Chancellor's consultation paper where privacy is taken to include matters appertaining to 'A natural person's health, personal communications and family and personal relationships and a right to be free from harassment and molestation' (*Infringement of Privacy*, note 134 above, para 5.22). Another route to protection in such cases is via the cause of action for the intentional infliction of emotional distress, see below.

[146][1897] 2 QB 57.

[147]*Ibid*, 58–9.

[148]N J Mullany and P R Handford, *Tort Liability for Psychiatric Damage* (Sydney: Law Book Co., 1993), 284 and, generally, ch 14.

and is not too remote. Liability will attach even if the act would not affect a person of ordinary sensibilities if the plaintiff can prove that the defendant was aware of the plaintiff's special susceptibility.[149] As to remoteness, Wright J explicitly recognised that recovery for nervous shock at that time was 'without precedent'.[150]

Might this action assist a victim of unwanted publicity? Could the principle be applied in circumstances where the defendant is a newspaper, and the act which causes the plaintiff's physical harm is not a false statement but an article revealing personal information about the plaintiff?

Several matters need to be addressed. In particular, it is obviously important to determine how far the general proposition advanced in *Wilkinson* may be extended beyond *false* statements. Also, the meaning of the words 'wilfully done an act calculated to cause physical harm' needs to be ascertained. And other elements of the action require clarification.

Conduct other than false statements

Judgments following *Wilkinson* v *Downton* reveal that the broad principle there enunciated is applicable not merely to false statements but to threats,[151] and other conduct.[152] In *Bradley* v *Wingnut Films Ltd*,[153] for instance, the plaintiff, the holder of an exclusive right to burial in a plot in a certain cemetery, sought an injunction against the defendant film company to prevent the plot being shown as a backdrop to a particular scene of a 'comedy horror' film. The burial plot appeared in the film for a total of only 14 seconds and it was not possible to read the words on the tombstone marking the site. The plaintiff pleaded, *inter alia*, the intentional infliction of emotional distress as a cause of action having been 'shocked and upset' by the association of the burial site

---

[149]E.g., *Timmermans* v *Buelow* (1984) 38 CCLT 136.

[150][1897] 2 QB 57, 61. Times have, of course, changed. The Privy Council's decision to refuse to allow recovery for the negligent infliction of nervous shock in *Victorian Railways Commissioner* v *Coultas* (1888) 13 App Cas 222 was not followed in *Dulieu* v *White & Sons* [1901] 2 KB 669.

[151]*Khorasandjian* v *Bush* [1993] QB 727 and see below.

[152]See Winfield and Jolowicz, *Tort*, 14th ed (London: Sweet & Maxwell, 1994), 74–5; F A Trindade, 'The Intentional Infliction of Purely Mental Distress' (1986) 6 Oxford J Legal Stud 219, 230–1. In *A* v *B's Trustees* (1906) 13 SLT 830, the plaintiff landlady suffered nervous shock when she came across a lodger who had committed suicide in her bathroom.

[153][1993] 1 NZLR 415. I am indebted to Geoffrey Robertson QC for drawing my attention to this case.

with the film. Although the plaintiff's claim on this ground was rejected (for reasons considered below), Gallen J clearly proceeded on the basis that the film's depiction of the cemetery plot constituted conduct sufficient to found an action under *Wilkinson v Downton*.[154]

The importance of the distinction between false statements and other conduct is that it is far easier to establish the defendant's requisite state of mind for the former than for the latter. In *Bradley*, the court specifically adverted to the relative unimportance of the burial plot in the scene in question and considered that the conduct of the defendant could not therefore be taken to have been calculated to produce harm to the plaintiff. Thus the issue of how the defendant caused the plaintiff's harm directly affects the ease with which the plaintiff can prove that the emotional distress was 'intentionally' inflicted as a matter of law.[155]

The defendant's state of mind

The defendant's act must be wilful; that is to say either intentional or reckless.[156] Recklessness lies between that standard and negligence.[157] The second requirement is that the defendant's act, in the words of Wright J, be 'so plainly calculated to produce some effect of the kind which was produced that an intention to produce it ought to be imputed'.[158] The ease with which the plaintiff is able to prove that the defendant's conduct was 'plainly calculated' to cause physical harm depends on the nature of the act. As suggested above, this will be more difficult in the case of conduct other than overt, direct statements. In *Bradley* Gallen J took the view that,

> There is no evidence in this case to suggest that the defendant intended in the ordinary sense of that word, to cause any distress to the plaintiff or his family in filming the sequence under consideration and in context I do not think that the consequences were so

[154]*Ibid*, 420–2.
[155]'As regards the conduct which precipitates the physical harm, it may take any form.... What matters is not the kind of conduct but its likely effect on the plaintiff' (Mullany and Handford (note 148 above), 289).
[156]Restatement (Second) of the Law of Torts, § 8A, comments that conduct is intentional when the actor either desires to cause particular consequences or knows that they are certain or substantially certain to result from the act.
[157]*Ibid*, § 500. In *Abramzik v Brenner* (1967) 65 DLR (2d) 651, 654, Culliton CJC said, 'There can be no doubt that an action will lie for the wilful infliction of shock, or a reckless disregard as to whether or not shock will ensue from the act committed'.
[158]*Wilkinson v Downton* [1897] 2 QB 57, 59.

foreseeable in terms of the plaintiff's distress bearing in mind the position occupied by the tombstone in the film and its lack of relation to the action, that the damage even if proven could be said to have been intentional.[159]

Though the meaning of the term 'calculated' is far from clear, the boundaries of liability are reasonably plain. 'Calculated' cannot be restricted to *intention*, because in *Wilkinson* itself, the defendant's intention was to play a prank and presumably neither desired the harm nor considered it certain or substantially certain to follow from his statement. Moreover, in order to preserve the distinction between the intentional infliction of 'physical harm' and the corresponding action in negligence, it should not be sufficient for the consequences of the defendant's conduct merely to be reasonably foreseen. The defendant must intend, or at least be reckless as to, the consequences. '"Calculated" seems to mean something between "intended" and "foreseeably likely"'.[160]

The nature of the harm

As a matter of principle there is nothing to prevent a plaintiff recovering under *Wilkinson* v *Downton* for injury to the person *simpliciter*. In fact, however, the decisions have all concerned 'nervous shock'.[161] There is a vital distinction between a transient shock, however severe, which is called 'emotional distress', on the one hand, and the subsequent development of physical symptoms as a result of the initial shock, on the other. Only in the latter event is recovery allowed.[162] As Lord Wilberforce has stated, 'nervous shock' is a 'hallowed expression',[163] but

---

[159][1993] 1 NZLR 415, 422.
[160]Mullany and Handford (note 148 above), 288. However, this view has been questioned. Winfield and Jolowicz (note 152 above), 75, cite *Slatter* v *British Railways Board* (1966) 110 SJ 688 in support of the proposition that a negligent act could entail liability under *Wilkinson* v *Downton*. But negligence liability and the rule in *Wilkinson* v *Downton* should be distinguished, for many of the arguments which support a restrictive approach to compensation for the former are weak when applied to the latter. This is examined in greater detail below. In respect of intentional infliction of emotional distress the American Restatement (Second) of the Law of Torts, § 312, uses the formulation 'likely to result' in harm to the plaintiff.
[161]See *Janvier* v *Sweeney* [1919] 2 KB 316; *Burnett* v *George* [1992] 1 FLR 525; and *Khorasandjian* v *Bush* [1993] QB 727.
[162]Lord Ackner recently reiterated that, 'Mere mental suffering, although reasonably foreseeable, if unaccompanied by physical injury, is not a basis for a claim for damages' (*Alcock* v *Chief Constable of South Yorkshire Police* [1992] 1 AC 310, 401).
[163]*McLoughlin* v *O'Brian* [1983] 1 AC 410, 418.

modern usage prefers 'recognisable psychiatric illness'.[164] In *Bradley*,[165] Gallen J said:

> I accept that on the authorities to which I was referred, it is necessary for the plaintiff to establish something more than a transient reaction, however initially severe. This must translate itself into something physical and having a duration which is more than merely transient.[166]

What of secondary victims? There is authority for the view that the principle in *Wilkinson v Downton* may be extended to compensate those who suffer shock but who were not the primary victim of the defendant's act. In the New Zealand decision of *Stevenson v Basham*,[167] Herdman J applied *Wilkinson* to allow the plaintiff to recover for nervous shock caused when she overheard somebody threatening to burn her husband out of his home. This case must, however, be approached with caution; the court found as a fact that the defendant *knew* that his primary victim's wife was in the house. But there is the possibility that proceeding under *Wilkinson* allows recovery by a wider number of people than for the strictly regulated negligence action.[168] In the words of Bray CJ in *Battista v Cooper*:[169]

> ... there is no reason for restricting the category of plaintiffs who can recover for physical injury from an intentional tort to those who could recover in the same circumstances if the tort were a negligent one, and every reason, in my opinion, for widening it.[170]

If this is to occur, it would remove a significant hurdle mentioned above in respect of the equitable remedy for breach of confidence. The plaintiff's right in such actions is *in personam*. This normally means that the obligation may be enforced only by the person to whom it is owed.[171] A liberal approach to the range of persons qualifying as 'secondary

---

[164]*Hinz v Berry* [1970] 2 QB 40, 42 per Lord Denning MR.
[165][1993] 1 NZLR 415.
[166]*Ibid*, 421.
[167][1922] NZLR 225. See also, e.g., *Johnson v Commonwealth* (1927) 27 SR (NSW) 133.
[168]The House of Lords in *Alcock* refused to extend the exceptions to the 'aftermath doctrine' beyond marital and filial ties.
[169](1976) 14 SASR 225.
[170]*Ibid*, 230.
[171]*Fraser v Evans* [1969] 1 QB 349.

victims' would enable a plaintiff to restrain the publication of a newspaper article that discloses intimate information about, for instance, his girlfriend or grandmother.[172]

The future of the cause of action

It has been suggested in the light of the paucity of cases decided upon the *Wilkinson* principle, that it 'may well be a dying cause of action'.[173] At the time that view was expressed, *Wilkinson* had been followed in only one English decision: *Janvier* v *Sweeney*.[174] In that case, in order to gather information that the plaintiff might have about 'certain letters purporting to be written by Major X', a private detective visited the plaintiff and announced, 'I am a detective inspector from Scotland Yard, and represent the military authorities. You are the woman we want, as you have been corresponding with a German spy.' This statement caused the plaintiff to suffer a severe shock leading to physical incapacity for which she successfully recovered. Bankes LJ was in no doubt that *Wilkinson* v *Downton* was good law.[175]

Whatever the relevance today of *Wilkinson*, it is plain that, since *Dulieu* v *White & Sons*,[176] the action for the *negligent* infliction of nervous shock has developed significantly. As already mentioned, it is not easy to categorise rigidly the varying degrees of foresight into negligence or recklessness, and this has engendered the view that *Wilkinson* should be, and has been, subsumed within the ever-expanding tort of negligence. In relation to *Wilkinson* and *Janvier*, '... it is true only in a limited sense to say that the physical harm was intentional, for although the acts themselves were intentional in both cases, there was no evidence that the defendants intended the plaintiffs to become ill'.[177] The facts of *Wilkinson* certainly fall within current negligence principles, but at the time of the decision recovery upon the basis of mere foreseeability of nervous shock was precluded by the Privy Council's decision in *Victorian Railways Commissioners* v *Coultas*.[178]

---

[172]Or others, i.e., categories outside the recognised marital/filial exception to the 'aftermath doctrine' in negligence actions.
[173]Mullany and Handford (note 148 above), 290.
[174][1919] 2 KB 316.
[175]*Ibid*, 324.
[176][1901] 2 KB 669.
[177]A L Goodhart (1943) 7 MLR 86, 88 (book review). See Mullany and Handford (note 148 above), 290–2.
[178](1888) 13 App Cas 222.

In any event, *Wilkinson* may have received a shot in the arm from the recent decision of the Court of Appeal in *Khorasandjian* v *Bush*.[179] The defendant launched a campaign of harassment against the plaintiff after their relationship broke down. Persistent unsolicited telephone calls were accompanied by threats of violence. The plaintiff was faced with the difficulty that, although the experience caused her considerable stress, it did not give rise to a recognisable psychiatric illness. Acknowledging the fact of her suffering, and that it was not in law sufficient to found an action under *Wilkinson* v *Downton*, Dillon LJ[180] stated:

> But there is, in my judgment, an obvious risk that the cumulative effect of combined and unrestrained further harassment such as [the plaintiff] has undergone would cause such an illness. The law expects the ordinary person to bear the mishaps of life with fortitude and ... customary phlegm; but it does not expect ordinary young women to bear indefinitely such a campaign of persecution as that to which the defendant has subjected the plaintiff. Therefore, in my judgment, on the facts of this case and in line with the law as laid down in *Janvier* v *Sweeney*, the court is entitled to look at the defendant's conduct as a whole and restrain those aspects on a *quia timet* basis also of his campaign of harassment which cannot strictly be classified as threats.[181]

This suggests that the court will protect the plaintiff in circumstances where there is only a risk, albeit an obvious one, of nervous shock *later* resulting from the cumulative effect of the defendant's conduct.[182] It is possible to reconcile *Khorasandjian* with existing authority; the principle merely being applied to the special concerns of *quia timet* injunctions rather than the usual action for damages. But it is also possible to take the view that the Court of Appeal, in 'practical reality',[183] extended

---

[179][1993] QB 727.
[180]With whom Rose LJ agreed, Peter Gibson J dissenting. See, *ibid*, 740–6.
[181]*Ibid*, 736.
[182]See J Bridgeman and M A Jones, 'Harassing Conduct and Outrageous Acts: A Cause of Action for Intentionally Inflicted Mental Distress?' (1994) 14 LS 180, 192–201.
[183]*Ibid*, 196.

Wilkinson to cases of purely emotional distress in situations where an injunction is being sought.[184]

This leads inevitably to the possibility of awarding damages for emotional distress under *Wilkinson v Downton*, though it is important to recall the recent restatement by the House of Lords of the requirement in negligence actions for something more than purely mental distress.[185]

Returning to the question of the desirability of maintaining an action for the intentional infliction of emotional distress distinct from negligence liability, the policy arguments which have led the courts to reject recovery for mental distress in negligence cases are less persuasive when applied to the intentional tort:[186]

> There may be good policy reasons for limiting claims for 'nervous shock' arising from *negligent* conduct to harm that can be categorised as genuine psychiatric illness or disorder, based on the fear of opening up the sphere of liability to a potentially vast category of plaintiffs. But where without any legitimate purpose or excuse the defendant *intends* to inflict mental distress there can be no justification for the law refusing to grant a plaintiff protection from this form of antisocial behaviour.

If this view were indeed adopted, the action for the intentional infliction of emotional distress would closely resemble the American tort of 'extreme outrage'.[187] This action ordinarily compensates the plaintiff for 'nervous shock', though the Restatement makes it clear that it is not limited to 'bodily harm', and where the conduct is sufficiently extreme and outrageous, recovery may be allowed for emotional distress alone.[188]

Protecting 'privacy'

The greatest obstacle to the application of *Wilkinson v Downton* is the need to prove that the act in question is calculated to cause physical

---

[184]In *Burnett v George* [1992] 1 FLR 525, the Court of Appeal, on facts not dissimilar to those in *Khorasandjian*, refused to apply *Wilkinson v Downton*. Arnold P stated that molestation or interference is not an actionable wrong unless 'there be evidence that the health of the plaintiff is being impaired by [such conduct] calculated to create such impairment, in which case relief would be granted by way of an injunction to the extent that it would be necessary to avoid that impairment of health' (*ibid*, 527).

[185]*Alcock v Chief Constable of South Yorkshire Police* [1992] 1 AC 310.

[186]Bridgeman and Jones (note 182 above), 196.

[187]See Restatement (Second) of the Law of Torts, § 46.

[188]*Ibid*, § 46, comment k.

harm. The plaintiff may, at most, be able to show that the defendant's conduct is negligent, and it is clear that the courts will not allow recovery for mental distress in a negligence action.[189]

Would it be open to a plaintiff to prevent publication of her photograph, surreptitiously taken in her home while she was sunbathing, on the ground that it would cause emotional distress? It is strongly arguable that such conduct is calculated to cause harm; it can at least be said that the journalist is reckless as to the potential consequences of his action. Accordingly, on the authority of *Khorasandjian*, she should be able, at the very least, to enjoin the photograph from being published if she can satisfy the court that there is an 'obvious risk' that the cumulative effect of having her scantily clad image published would be to cause her psychiatric illness. This approach need not represent a departure from orthodoxy; it is simply a question of what degree of proof of likelihood of 'nervous shock' the courts will require to satisfy the notion of 'obvious risk'.

There is also the possibility, as yet unsupported by authority, that for the intentional tort under *Wilkinson*, the court will be prepared to award damages for purely emotional distress. But what constitutes a meritorious case? Perhaps only where there is distress caused by a *course of conduct* by the defendant or where the mental distress is serious.[190] There are difficulties, however, with both. In the former, isolated instances of extreme behaviour would not be caught by the action. In the latter, limiting recovery to objective states of mind would overlook different subjective reactions of individuals to the same stimulus.

There is merit in the suggestion, albeit in a slightly different context, that:

> ... the very vagueness of the applicability of a molestation tort could be seen as one of its strengths, for the focus is clearly on the actual parties to the action and their relationship. In assessing whether the acts done by the defendant were calculated to cause harm to the plaintiff and whether such harm did, or was likely, to ensue, the defendant's knowledge of his victim will be highly material.... Flexibility enables the court to make common-sense judgments based

---

[189]See *Alcock* [1992] 1 AC 310.
[190]Bridgeman and Jones (note 182 above), 198–201. The concentration upon conduct would be in conformity with the American approach discussed above which distinguishes between mere insult and 'extreme and outrageous conduct'.

on a determination of when intrusive and unpleasant conduct exceeds the bounds of what society will tolerate and poses a risk of damage to an individual's fundamental right to freedom from injury.[191]

Similar considerations apply to the infliction of emotional distress.

Defamation

It will be recalled that among the four 'privacy' torts in American law is 'publicity which places the defendant in a false light in the public eye'. Whether or not this is properly conceived as a matter of 'privacy', it underlines the association between defamation and 'privacy'. Indeed, the argument is not infrequently heard that an action in defamation provides a means of protecting the plaintiff's 'privacy'.

In respect of the American law, Nimmer[192] claims that the libel standard adopted in *New York Times* v *Sullivan*[193] was wrongly applied in *Time Inc* v *Hill*[194] because the Hill family (the account of whose ordeal was falsely reported) were not defamed by the account of their experience.[195] But it does not follow from this argument that the interests protected by the 'false light' tort are sufficiently distinguishable from those that underpin defamation to justify separate treatment. He suggests that the 'false light' category ought to be dealt with in the same way as 'public disclosure' cases.

The 'false light' category seems to be both redundant (for almost all such cases might equally have been brought for defamation) and only tenuously related to the protection of the plaintiff against aspects of his private life being exposed. The Younger Committee recognised that 'placing someone in a false light is an aspect of defamation rather than of privacy',[196] and several commentators raise the question 'whether

---

[191]M Brazier, 'Personal Injury by Molestation — An Emergent or Established Tort' [1992] Fam Law 346, 347–8.
[192]M B Nimmer, 'The Right to Speak from *Times* to *Time*: First Amendment Theory Applied to Libel and Misapplied to Privacy' (1968) 56 Calif L Rev 935.
[193]376 US 254 (1964).
[194]385 US 374 (1967).
[195]See Chapter 2.
[196]Committee on Privacy (note 1 above), para 70.

this branch of the tort is not capable of swallowing up and engulfing the whole law of defamation'.[197]

It has been said that 'the fundamental difference between a right to privacy and a right to freedom from defamation is that the former directly concerns one's own peace of mind, while the latter concerns primarily one's reputation'.[198] This, however, is not a distinction that has ever been a sharp one, and not only has the jurisdiction of defamation been enlarged, but (more to the point) recovery has been allowed for invasion of privacy in several American decisions where the plaintiff has been depicted in a 'false light' and it is the plaintiff's reputation, rather than his 'privacy', that would appear to be affected. While defamation is concerned with *false* statements, the falsity or otherwise of the disclosure is irrelevant in an action for public disclosure. A plaintiff who is faced with a *true* statement by which he is embarrassed may obtain relief by bringing his action under the public disclosure tort (provided, it seems, that there is the requisite publicity). In Prosser's view, the tort protects his reputation.[199] But this seems mistaken, for the rationale behind the tort of public disclosure is 'not merely to prevent inaccurate portrayal of private life, but to prevent its being depicted at all'.[200] Moreover, even though the disclosure of sensitive information actually portrays the plaintiff in a *favourable* light, there is no reason why he should in principle be barred from recovery.

---

[197]W Prosser and W P Keeton, *The Law of Torts*, 5th ed (St Paul, Minn: West Publishing Co., 1984), 813; J W Wade, 'Defamation and the Right of Privacy' (1962) Vand L Rev 1093; J Skelly Wright, 'Defamation, Privacy and the Public's Right to Know: A National Problem and a New Approach' (1968) 46 Tex L Rev 630; F Davis, 'What Do We Mean By "Right to Privacy"?' (1959) 4 SD L Rev 1; and H Kalven, 'Privacy in Tort Law: Were Warren and Brandeis Wrong?' (1966) 31 Law & Contemp Probs 326 (Wacks, *Privacy II* (Chapter 1 note 1 above), 31). See too F S Haiman, *Speech and Law in a Free Society* (Chicago: University of Chicago Press, 1981), 85–6. In comparing 'defamation' and 'privacy', however, there are several difficulties, not least of which is the fact that these writers share only the most general conceptions of both issues. For example, Davis (*ibid*, 8) regards the two as 'identical' since they are both concerned largely in protecting the plaintiff's mental feelings. Wade (*ibid*, 1124) expresses a similar view, but appears to regard disclosure and 'false light' as offending the plaintiff's reputation. W Prosser, 'Privacy' (1966) 48 Calif L Rev 383, 401 (Wacks, *Privacy II* (Chapter 1, note 1 above), 65) and E Bloustein, 'Privacy as an Aspect of Human Dignity: An Answer to Dean Prosser' (1964) 39 NYU L Rev 962, 993 (Wacks, *Privacy II* (Chapter 1, note 1 above), 120), both identify an overlap, but of different interests. If one conceives (as Prosser does) the interest protected by the tort of public disclosure as reputation, the overlap becomes even more substantial.

[198]*Themo* v *New England Newspaper Publishing Co.* 27 NE 2d 753, 755 (1940).

[199]Prosser, 'Privacy' (note 197 above), 398.

[200]S D Warren and L D Brandeis, 'The Right to Privacy' (1890) 4 Harv L Rev 193, 218 (Wacks, *Privacy II* (Chapter 1 note 1 above), 28).

On the other hand, if the statement is false, the tort of 'false light' might have been committed, and here too Prosser, more plausibly, suggests that it is the plaintiff's reputation that is affected. But, since the 'false light' cases appear to be equally actionable in defamation, it is arguable that the overlap between defamation and privacy might be thought 'substantial enough to make an approach via privacy superfluous'.[201]

The suggestion is sometimes made that by modifying the defence of justification many of the actions brought to vindicate the plaintiff's loss of 'privacy' might be accommodated within the tort of defamation. The proposal is that in order for the defence to succeed, the defendant ought to be required to show not only that the statement is true, but that its publication is in the public interest — the position which obtains in several Australian and American jurisdictions and in the Roman-Dutch law in Sri Lanka and South Africa. Such a proposal was, of course, open to Warren and Brandeis to have adopted, though Brandeis might then 'have been marked as a Lorentz, certainly not an Einstein of legal thought'.[202] But since they regarded the principles of the law of defamation as 'radically different' from those underlying the protection of 'privacy', this modification would hardly be consistent with their general thesis. In any event, even if the law of defamation were to be so modified,[203] many actions would still not succeed where the plaintiff's reputation has not, in fact, been affected by the private facts disclosed.

The plaintiff who proceeds against the publisher of defamatory material normally invites even greater publicity. This may well be the right price to be paid in a society that prizes free speech. But where his complaint is that private facts have been disclosed, the salt of a libel action may simply be too much for his wound to take.

Circumstances may occasionally arise in which disclosure of private facts carries the defamatory innuendo that the plaintiff consented to its

---

[201]Kalven (note 197 above), 332. 'Practically all the cases [i.e., 'false light' cases] ... are covered by the existing remedies of defamation and injurious falsehood and it seems as if the American concept of privacy has been grafted on to these traditional causes of action *ex abundanti cautela*' (G Dworkin, 'The Common Law Protection of Privacy' (1964–67) 2 U Tas L Rev 418, 426). See also Committee on Privacy (note 1 above), para 70; Prosser, 'Privacy' (note 197 above), 401; and, Bloustein (note 197 above), 993.

[202]P Freund, 'Privacy: One Concept or Many?' (1971) 13 Nomos, 182.

[203]The suggestion has been made on several occasions and rejected; most recently by the Committee on Defamation (Chairman: Faulks J), *Report of the Committee on Defamation*, Cmnd 5909, 1975, para 137 et seq. Other attempts to reform the law of libel have appeared (including in 1990, a number of measures announced by the Lord Chancellor to simplify procedure).

publication. In *Tolley v J S Fry and Sons Ltd*,[204] a caricature of the well-known amateur golfer, Cyril Tolley, was used, without his permission, to promote the defendant's chocolates. The House of Lords held that readers would assume that he had prostituted his amateur status in the cause of advertising. Such an innuendo is rarely present, and Greer LJ in the Court of Appeal acknowledged the limitation of the law:

> I have no hesitation in saying that in my judgment the defendants in publishing the advertisement in question, without first obtaining Mr Tolley's consent, acted in a manner inconsistent with the decencies of life, and in doing so they were guilty of an act for which there ought to be a legal remedy.[205]

The defendant in *Corelli v Wall*[206] published and sold postcards depicting, without her permission, imaginary events in the plaintiff's life. The court rejected the argument that publication was libellous. It was also argued 'that the plaintiff as a private person was entitled to restrain the publication of a portrait of herself which had been made without her authority and which, although professing to be her portrait was totally unlike her'.[207] This could not be supported by any authority. Clearly there must be some defamatory imputation before liability will be imposed. As Greer LJ put it, immediately after the dictum just quoted:

> ... unless a man's photograph, caricature, or name be published in such a context that the publication can be said to be defamatory within the law of libel, it cannot be made the subject-matter of complaint by action at law.[208]

In any event, few 'privacy' cases present such facts. In *Kaye v Robertson*[209] (though an argument based on malicious falsehood succeeded in preventing the newspaper from stating that the plaintiff had consented to the intrusion) the court did not regard the publication as defamatory.

---

[204][1931] AC 333.
[205][1930] 1 KB 467, 478. For some other instances where libel assisted victims of the advertising agencies, see Wacks, *Protection of Privacy* (Chapter 1 note 1 above), 168.
[206](1906) 22 TLR 532.
[207]Winfield claims the decision cannot be regarded as authority for the view that a plaintiff can never obtain an injunction in an action for libel against a defendant who publishes a bad portrait of him (P Winfield, 'Privacy' (1931) 47 LQR 23, 32).
[208]*Tolley v J S Fry and Sons Ltd* [1930] 1 KB 467, 478. But this goes too far. See *Pollard v Photographic Co.* (1889) 40 ChD 345, discussed above.
[209][1991] FSR 62.

4

Privacy and the Public Interest

It is a truism that the limits to the right of 'privacy' are drawn by the right to publish information that is in the public interest, a matter canvassed in Chapter 2. Far less certainty, however, attends the question of what constitutes the 'public interest' and the circumstances under which private facts may be disclosed in its name. This chapter attempts first to examine the matter in respect of the action for breach of confidence. When may information, *prima facie* subject to an obligation of confidentiality, be published because it is in the public interest so to do? The answer must be sought against the background of the principle of free speech; restrictions of the free circulation of ideas and information call for compelling reasons.

The march of the action for breach of confidence into the sphere of personal information, described in Chapter 3, invites an appraisal of the defence of public interest: is it a sufficiently flexible mechanism for the exercise of the court's discretion to enforce the equitable obligation of confidence? The second half of the chapter considers the approach adopted by the American courts in 'privacy' litigation.

Breach of confidence and the public interest

The status of the concept

It is trite law that the action for breach of confidence is circumscribed by a public interest test.[1] Less clear is the precise nature of the test: whether

---

[1] See Y Cripps, 'The Public Interest Defence to the Action for Breach of Confidence and the Law Commission's Proposals on Disclosure in the Public Interest' (1984) 4 Oxford J Legal Stud 361; and, Law Commission, *Breach of Confidence*, Cmnd 8388, 1981, paras 4.36–4.53.

its absence constitutes a substantive requirement of the action, or whether it operates as a defence to what would otherwise be a protected confidence. This analysis turns in large part upon the conceptual basis of the action itself. If, as was argued in Chapter 3, the action is grounded in equitable considerations, the nature of the public interest test falls to be treated in like manner.[2]

In attempting to reconcile the maintenance of confidentiality, on the one hand, with the public interest in the dissemination of information on the other, English courts have applied a balancing act similar to that employed in American 'privacy' decisions. I argued in my earlier work[3] that since the action for breach of confidence involves different interests, it requires the application of different considerations. In particular, the fact that the plaintiff has entrusted the information to a confidant, whether or not its disclosure is regarded as being in the public interest, ought to be given considerably more weight than is manifest in recent English cases. Suppose, for instance, that Sidis had confided in his doctor or lawyer or spouse.[4] Even as a (recently resurrected) 'public figure', it is arguable that his action for breach of confidence against the party divulging this information would have given rise to a different evaluation of the interests concerned, and, *a fortiori*, if he were a 'private' figure. In the case of public figures, moreover, I suggested that, since they are more likely to attract publicity concerning their private lives, the court ought to confer even greater protection to the information that they impart in the course of a confidential relationship. Certainly it should be no less than that which is accorded to private figures.

It would perhaps be unreasonable to expect the English courts to have formulated a systematic, or even a precise, analysis of these different considerations in the context of 'personal information' breach of confidence litigation for, as Ungoed-Thomas J conceded in *Duchess of Argyll* v *Duke of Argyll*,[5] 'If this were a well-developed jurisdiction doubtless there would be guides and tests to aid in exercising it'. But the courts have, in extending the scope of the public interest defence, exhibited a somewhat lopsided approach to the reconciliation of confidentiality and the dissemination of information. In the process the legitimate expectations of those who divulge information in the course of a relationship of confidence have been eroded. This is not to suggest

---

[2]Cripps outlines five separate conceptual bases: equity, contract, property, tort and 'an action *sui generis*' (*ibid*, 362–7).
[3]See Wacks, *Personal Information* (Chapter 1 note 1 above), 129–30.
[4]*Sidis* v *F-R Publishing Co.* 113 F 2d 806 (2d Cir 1940).
[5][1967] 1 Ch 302. A conspicuous exception is the recent case of *X* v *Y* [1988] 2 All ER 648.

that the recent expressions of judicial support for the principle of the public right to know are to be disparaged, but the reasonable expectations of confiders of information warrant more careful and perhaps more sympathetic evaluation.

This approach is evident in the majority's judgment in *Schering Chemicals Ltd v Falkman Ltd*[6] where the Court of Appeal attached greater importance to the preservation of confidence than to the circulation of information in the public interest. It is, however, unfortunate that it was faced with information which had already become public knowledge, a factor which, along with the repugnance with which both Shaw and Templeman LJJ clearly viewed the breach of faith involved, may reduce slightly the force of the majority's argument. But it does represent a more balanced view (and this is true, to some extent, even of Lord Denning's dissenting judgment) of the competing interests in issue than is exhibited in other decisions concerning information relating to the plaintiff personally. In the absence of a confidential relationship, it may be that the approach adopted in cases such as *Woodward v Hutchins*,[7] *Lennon v News Group Newspapers Ltd*,[8] *Khashoggi v Smith*,[9] and *Lion Laboratories Ltd v Evans*[10] is an entirely proper one, but where the court is faced with a newspaper that wishes to publish information which it has obtained in breach of confidence, different issues arise. Some acknowledgement of this is evident in *Francome v Mirror Group Newspapers Ltd*[11] in which the Master of the Rolls issued a firm warning to the media which were, in his view, 'peculiarly vulnerable to the error of confusing the public interest with their own interest. Usually these interests march hand in hand, but not always'.[12]

Admittedly this case involved the use of 'reprehensible means' (telephone tapping) to obtain the information which was offered to the newspaper for sale, and it is therefore probable that the court was less disposed to deny an injunction than it might have been if faced with facts of a *Woodward* variety.[13] Yet the observation that the defendants would not be 'substantially prejudiced, if they have to wait until after

---

[6][1982] 1 QB 1.
[7][1977] 1 WLR 760.
[8][1978] FSR 573.
[9](1980) 130 NLJ 168.
[10][1985] 1 QB 526.
[11][1984] 1 WLR 892.
[12]*Ibid*, 898. See too the Vice-Chancellor's dictum in *Stephens v Avery* [1988] 1 Ch 449, 456.
[13]'The fact that coincidentally publication would be a criminal offence which the defendants say they are prepared to commit strongly reinforces the case for an injunction' (*Francome* [1984] 1 WLR 892, 902 per Stephen Brown LJ).

the trial of the action'[14] suggests a more general application of this consideration to cases involving information relating to the plaintiff. This aspect of the decision is further considered in Chapter 5.

The essence of any equitable action is that the court may *recognise* the plaintiff's equitable right yet refuse to grant a remedy to protect it. Unlike the common law position, protection does not follow recognition *as of right*; equitable remedies are discretionary. Accordingly, if the obligation of confidence never came into existence '... the courts would be deprived of the opportunity to exercise the discretionary features of their equitable jurisdiction'.[15] Moreover, as Cripps points out,[16] if the obligation were struck down *ab initio* by the public interest element of the information in question, a court of equity could not assess the appropriateness of damages in lieu of the granting of an injunction preventing disclosure.[17]

For these reasons, it is submitted that the public interest qualification acts as a defence in that it operates to bar the enforcement of the right rather than to deny its existence.[18] The Law Commission, however, with specific reference to the judgment of Lord Widgery CJ in *Attorney-General v Jonathan Cape Ltd*,[19] felt unable to draw such a conclusion. In that case the Lord Chief Justice considered that it was for the plaintiff to show: '(a) that ... publication would be a breach of confidence; (b) that the public interest requires that the publication be restrained, and (c) that there are no other facts of the public interest contradictory of and

---

[14]*Ibid*, 898 per Donaldson MR.

[15]Cripps (note 1 above), 363.

[16]*Ibid*, 363–4.

[17]See s. 50 of the Supreme Court Act 1981 for the modern-day embodiment of Lord Cairns's Act. In *Church of Scientology of California v Kaufman* [1973] RPC 627, 658, Goff J did not feel that the successful invocation of the public interest defence could deprive the plaintiff of its remedy in damages. This, it is contended, is strong evidence for the rejection of the test as a substantive requirement. 'He simply refused to grant an injunction to enforce the obligation of confidence' (Cripps, *The Legal Implications of Disclosure in the Public Interest* (Oxford: ESC Publishing, 1986), 43).

[18]The acceptance of this view leads to a further difficulty recognised by the Law Commission in respect of the observations of the courts in this area: '(1) whether they relate to the proper scope of the public interest in being informed of the subject-matter of an action for breach of confidence, which, to determine whether the defendant is liable for the breach, has to be weighed by the court against the public interest in the preservation of the obligation; or (2) whether they refer to the extent to which the public interest in being so informed should be taken into account by a court in determining whether or not to grant an interlocutory injunction; or (3) whether they are concerned with the extent to which such public interest is a factor to be considered by the court in determining in its discretion whether to grant a final injunction, irrespective of any claim which the plaintiff may make for damages' (*Breach of Confidence* (note 1 above), para 4.49).

[19][1976] 1 QB 752.

more compelling than that relied upon'.[20] The Commission cited this dictum as authority for the view that the disclosure of the information *not* being in the public interest is a 'positive requirement of the action'[21] and, hence, on the basis of the jurisprudence in this area, concluded that whether the test constituted a defence was a 'further uncertainty'.[22]

It is arguable, however, that Lord Widgery CJ's remarks pertain more to the burden of proof of the public interest test than to its legal rationale. It is, admittedly, unusual to cast the legal burden of disproving a defence in civil matters upon the plaintiff,[23] but this may well be due to the importance of free speech which would otherwise be subjugated in a successful action for breach of confidence. As the Commission put it:

> ... the law on breach of confidence ... is a not insubstantial check on freedom of speech. ... If Lord Widgery's test is applicable to the action for breach of confidence in all circumstances this check may be more acceptable in that it only operates if the plaintiff can show that it is justified on a balance of the public interests involved.[24]

I return to this question below.

What is in the public interest?

In *Gartside* v *Outram*,[25] Wood V-C declared:

> ... there is no confidence as to the disclosure of an iniquity. You cannot make me the confidant of a crime or a fraud, and be entitled to close up my lips upon any secret which you have the audacity to disclose to me relating to any fraudulent intention on your part: such a confidence cannot exist.[26]

The court therefore declined to impeach the actions of a former clerk to the plaintiff who informed certain individuals that they had been defrauded by his ex-employer. On the other hand, in *Weld-Blundell* v *Stephens*[27] the defendant's partner in a firm of chartered accountants

---

[20]*Ibid*, 770.
[21]*Breach of Confidence* (note 1 above), para 4.42.
[22]*Ibid*, para 4.53.
[23]This, of course, is the requirement in criminal evidence.
[24]*Breach of Confidence* (note 1 above), para 4.44.
[25](1856) 26 LJ Ch 113.
[26]*Ibid*, 114.
[27][1919] 1 KB 520.

negligently published libellous statements, made by the plaintiff, to those who had been defamed. The plaintiff successfully recovered damages, Warrington LJ commenting that he could see 'no reason founded on public policy or any other ground why an agent should be at liberty to disclose evidence of a private wrong committed by his principal'.[28] The Court of Appeal saw *Gartside* as an example of the Court of Chancery declining to exercise its equitable discretion and leaving the plaintiff to his remedy at law because he came to court with 'unclean hands'.[29]

It is possible to reconcile *Gartside* and *Weld-Blundell* on their facts, a position reinforced by Viscount Finlay's remarks on the latter in the House of Lords when he recognised that 'There may, of course, be cases in which some higher duty is involved. Danger to the State, or public duty may supersede the duty of the agent to his principal'.[30]

In *Initial Services Ltd v Putterill*,[31] Lord Denning MR dismissed the suggestion that the public interest defence was confined only to cases where the party seeking enforcement of the obligation of confidence had been guilty of an actual or contemplated crime or fraud:[32]

> ... I do not think that it is so limited. It extends to any misconduct of such a nature that it ought in the public interest to be disclosed to others.... The exception should extend to crimes, frauds and misdeeds, both those actually committed as well as those in contemplation, provided always — and this is essential — that the disclosure is justified in the public interest.[33]

He qualified this principle by imposing a requirement that, even where the information in question does relate to matters in which there is a legitimate public interest:

> The disclosure must ... be to one who has a proper interest to receive the information.... There may be cases where the misdeed is of such

---

[28] *Ibid*, 535.
[29] Cripps (note 17 above), 31, considers this to be inconsistent with Wood V-C's proprietary analysis in *Gartside v Outram* (1856) 26 LJ Ch 113, 116: 'The real ground of the jurisdiction, as it is properly put, is founded first upon property'.
[30] [1920] AC 956, 965–6.
[31] [1968] 1 QB 396.
[32] A suggestion of Bankes LJ in *Weld-Blundell v Stephens* [1919] 1 KB 520, 527.
[33] [1968] 1 QB 396, 405.

a character that the public interest may demand, or at least excuse, publication on a broader field, even to the press.[34]

This point receives further elaboration below. Suffice it to say that it may be a potent counter-argument against those who regard the action for breach of confidence when applied to personal information as an unjustifiable restriction on free speech. As *Francome* demonstrates, the competing public interest of having confidences preserved may be upheld notwithstanding that the court orders the information to be disclosed to interested parties.[35]

In *Woodward*, an archetypal 'privacy' case, the plaintiffs, three pop stars, were denied the injunction they sought to restrain their press agent revealing information relating to various 'outrages' committed by them. Lord Denning MR stated:

> If a group of this kind seek publicity which is to their advantage, it seems to me that they cannot complain if a servant or employee of theirs afterwards discloses the truth about them. If the image which they fostered was not a true image, it is in the public interest that it should be corrected.[36]

The Master of the Rolls went on to state that in cases involving confidential information, the public interest in maintaining the confidence must be balanced against the public interest in knowing the truth.[37] In this case, he held, the balance came down in favour of the truth being told despite the breach of confidence that had been committed: 'As there should be "truth in advertising", so there should be truth in publicity. The public should not be misled.'[38]

The Court of Appeal's conception of the 'public interest' is curious. While there may well be a public interest in the truth being told about a fraudulent or dishonest businessman,[39] the same can hardly be said for the private proclivities of pop singers. Moreover, the extravagant or

---

[34]*Ibid*, 405–6.

[35]Donaldson MR commented: 'Assuming that the tapes reveal evidence of the commission of a criminal offence or a breach of the rules of racing — and I stress that this is an assumption — it may well be in the public interest that the tapes and all the information to be gleaned therefrom be made available to the police or the Jockey Club' ([1984] 1 WLR 892, 899).

[36][1977] 1 WLR 760, 762–3. See R Wacks, 'Pop Goes Privacy' (1978) 31 MLR 67.

[37][1977] 1 WLR 760, 764.

[38]*Ibid, loc cit.*

[39]As in *Initial Services Ltd v Putterill* [1968] 1 QB 396.

hyperbolic claims made in public relations literature (by no means restricted to entertainers) ought not to operate to destroy the claims of such public figures to maintain the confidentiality of those aspects of their lives upon which such publicity has little or no bearing.

A similar approach was adopted by the Court of Appeal in *Lennon* v *News Group Newspapers Ltd*.[40] The former wife of John Lennon sold the 'story' of her marriage to the ex-Beatle to the *News of the World* which began to serialise it. The articles disclosed intimate details of the relationship between the plaintiff and his ex-wife. The court denied an injunction on the ground that 'the relationship of these parties has ceased to be their own private affair'.[41] Lord Denning MR said that since neither of them had much regard for the sanctity of marriage, the confidential nature of that relationship had ceased to exist. Yet the same description could be attached to the marriage between the Duke and Duchess of Argyll. Nor can the cases be distinguished on the possible ground that here 'each of [the parties] is making money by publishing the most intimate details about one another'[42] for in publishing his disclosures in the newspaper the Duke had hardly acted gratuitously. In *Lennon*, as in *Woodward*, the Master of the Rolls was unwilling to restrain the publication of confidential information where the plaintiff had courted publicity in respect of his private life.

The Court of Appeal in *Khashoggi* v *Smith*[43] refused an injunction where the former housekeeper of the plaintiff disclosed intimate facts to the *Daily Mirror* concerning the plaintiff, a wealthy socialite who had attracted considerable publicity. Here, however, there was an investigation proceeding into the alleged commission of an offence by the plaintiff. The court, on an interlocutory motion, refused to enjoin publication on the principal ground that there could be no confidence in information concerning the commission of alleged offences. Significantly, it recognised that if it were concerned 'only with the question of whether or not the intended disclosures regarding Mrs Khashoggi's private life were permissible, different questions would or at least might arise'. This presumably suggests that in the absence of the criminal investigation, the court would have examined the question, which arose in *Woodward*, of the extent to which a former employee may disclose intimate facts concerning his or her former employer. Yet it is not easy to see how the Court of Appeal could have distinguished its decision in

---

[40] [1978] FSR 573.
[41] *Ibid*, 574 per Lord Denning MR.
[42] *Ibid*, 575.
[43] (1980) 130 NLJ 168.

Woodward, for the principal motive in both cases was the financial one of selling to a newspaper secrets gained in the course of a relationship of trust. In other words, the action for breach of confidence that failed to assist the plaintiff in *Woodward* would be unlikely to have assisted Mrs Khashoggi — even if she had *not* been the subject of a criminal investigation.

Moreover, the fact that Mrs Khashoggi was herself negotiating with the *Daily Mirror* for the sale of her memoirs did not, in the view of the court, deprive her of any right to confidentiality to which she would otherwise be entitled. This appears to be a relaxation of Lord Denning's strict view in *Woodward* that the plaintiffs had foregone their right to the protection of private facts about them because they had themselves courted publicity. Yet it would be somewhat artificial to compare Mrs Khashoggi to three famous entertainers — whatever the extent of her fame or notoriety — and, in any event, since her memoirs were at the time of the hearing no more than a future prospect, the court could hardly be expected to attach any greater importance to them as evidence of her attitude to obtaining a 'favourable image'.[44]

In *Fraser* v *Evans*[45] Lord Denning MR further modified his *Woodward* balancing test with specific reference to the public interest. Though the *ratio* of the case was that an obligation of confidence may be enforced only by the person to whom it is owed, the Court of Appeal was nevertheless willing to consider the question of the public interest defence and to introduce a test of considerably wider ambit and flexibility than had hitherto been propounded. The Master of the Rolls remarked:

> ... the court will in a proper case restrain the publication of confidential information. The jurisdiction is based, not so much on property or on contract, but rather on the duty to be of good faith. No person is permitted to divulge to the world information which he has received in confidence, unless he has *just cause or excuse* for doing so.[46]

As Cripps[47] suggests, the 'just cause or excuse' formula may have increased the range of factors to be taken into account when assessing

[44]*Woodward* [1977] 1 WLR 760, 763 per Lord Denning MR. This aspect of the *Khashoggi* case must be examined in the light of *Times Newspapers* v *Mirror Group Newspapers Ltd* [1993] EMLR 443, where the Court of Appeal reasoned that the content of a book intended for publication could not be the subject of an obligation of confidentiality.
[45][1969] 1 QB 349.
[46]*Ibid*, 361 (emphasis added).
[47]Cripps (note 17 above), 39.

whether publication is to be enjoined. But Lord Denning MR cast doubt on the universal applicability of his new formulation, in *Hubbard* v *Vosper*,[48] by reverting to the public interest expression of the test. This ambiguity, it is submitted, is more a question of form than substance. In *Church of Scientology of California* v *Kaufman* Goff J adopted the 'just cause or excuse for breaking confidence'[49] test but reasoned that it comprised both a 'narrow basis' — the public interest test in *Hubbard* and *Putterill* — and a 'wider basis': *Fraser* v *Evans*.[50] This bifurcation was adopted by Megarry V-C in *Malone*,[51] but one must be wary of drawing any general conclusions from his application of the test.

The significance of the motives and beliefs of the 'public informer' is discussed below. In *Malone* it was necessary for the Vice-Chancellor to excuse the actions of the police in tapping the plaintiff's telephone, even though they were, to some extent, on 'fishing expeditions' which *might* have satisfied their suspicions of iniquity. Hence, Sir Robert eschewed the 'narrow basis' and adopted the 'wider' one because '. . . that is not confined to misconduct or misdeeds. There may be cases where there is no misconduct or misdeed but yet there is a just cause or excuse for breaking confidence'.[52]

In other words, if Megarry V-C had accepted only the narrow basis, it would not have justified the police's measures if the information subsequently revealed did not disclose misconduct on the part of Malone.

In *British Steel Corporation* v *Granada Television Ltd*,[53] Granada Television broadcast a programme seeking to show that the huge losses being incurred by British Steel at the time were due to mismanagement and poor quality control. This information, which Granada knew to be confidential, had been passed to them by an unknown person. It is important to note that the only contended issue was an order granted to British Steel that Granada disclose its source. In spite of this, the Law Lords took it upon themselves to consider the public interest test, and the majority view was the traditional one. As Lord Wilberforce stressed:

There is an important exception to the limitations which may exist upon the right of the media to reveal information otherwise restricted.

---

[48][1972] 2 QB 84.
[49][1973] RPC 627, 649.
[50]*Ibid, loc cit.*
[51]*Malone* v *Commissioner of Police for the Metropolis (No. 2)* [1979] 1 Ch 344, 376–7.
[52]*Ibid*, 377.
[53][1981] AC 1096.

That is based on what is commonly known as the 'iniquity rule'. It extends in fact beyond 'iniquity' to misconduct generally.... It must be emphasised that we are not in this field in the present case; giving the widest extension to the expression 'iniquity' nothing within it is alleged in the present case. The most that it is said the papers reveal is mismanagement and government intervention.[54]

Uncertainties surrounding the nature and scope of the public interest test have, to a large extent, been clarified by the *Lion Laboratories* case.[55] This concerned Intoximeters manufactured by the plaintiff to be used to breath-test drivers suspected of being over the prescribed alcohol limit.[56] Two ex-employees of the plaintiff had disclosed internal memoranda to a newspaper relating to their concern about the accuracy of the device in calibration tests. At first instance, Leonard J granted the plaintiff an interlocutory injunction. The Court of Appeal, without hesitation, discharged the injunction on the ground that the information contained in the memoranda concerned matters in the public interest.

In the course of his judgment, Stephenson LJ highlighted four points. First, he emphasised that the courts were concerned only with what was *in* the public interest not what was *of* interest to the public.[57] Secondly, he recognised that the media have their own private interest in increasing circulation.[58] Thirdly, he said that the public interest is not always best served by disclosure to the press. Fourthly, and most significantly, the court rejected the defendants' submission that the public interest test was confined to cases of iniquity. Stephenson LJ expressed the view that iniquity was 'merely an instance of just cause or excuse for breaking confidence'[59] and accordingly there was no need

---

[54]*Ibid*, 1169. However, Lord Salmon (dissenting) foreshadowed the approach in *Lion Laboratories Ltd v Evans* [1985] 1 QB 526 when he declared, 'No doubt crime, fraud and misconduct should be laid bare in the public interest; and these, of course, did not occur in BSC. There was however much else, even more important in all the circumstances, which called aloud to be revealed in the public interest' ([1981] AC 1096, 1191). Among the factors which Lord Salmon identified was the fact that BSC was a nationalised undertaking and thus any losses would affect the public purse (*ibid*, 1185).

[55][1985] 1 QB 526.

[56]See Y Cripps, 'Alcohol Measuring Devices and Breaches of Copyright and Confidence' [1985] CLJ 35.

[57][1985] 1 QB 526, 537 (citing Lord Wilberforce's remarks in *British Steel* [1981] AC 1096, 1168: 'there is a wide difference between what is interesting to the public and what it is in the public interest to make known').

[58]In terms of personal information, this might be described as an injudicious understatement.

[59][1985] 1 QB 526, 538 (citing Lord Denning MR's formulation in *Fraser v Evans* [1969] 1 QB 349, 362).

to show misconduct on the part of the plaintiff. He believed that the just cause or excuse in the instant case was 'the public interest in admittedly confidential information'.[60] The decision represents 'a deeper inroad into actions for breach of confidence ... than any previous case on the public interest defence',[61] but an important feature of this case is that the alleged inaccuracy of the Intoximeter could have had an effect on 'the life, and even the liberty, of an unascertainable number of Her Majesty's subjects'.[62]

In X v Y,[63] an employee of a health authority leaked the names of two practising doctors who had contracted AIDS. The information was given to a newspaper reporter in return for the payment of a sum of money. The plaintiffs, the health authority, obtained an order restraining the newspaper from publishing or using the information. The newspaper nevertheless published an article implying that there were doctors in the health service who were continuing to practise despite having contracted AIDS and suggesting that the DHSS wished to suppress this information. The newspaper intended to publish a further article identifying the doctors. The plaintiffs sought, *inter alia*, an injunction restraining the newspaper from disclosing the identity of the doctors.

The court granted a permanent injunction; it held that the public interest in preserving the confidentiality of hospital records identifying actual or potential AIDS sufferers outweighed the public interest in the freedom of the press to publish such information because victims should not be deterred by fear of discovery from coming forward for treatment. Protecting the confidentiality of the names of sufferers would not stifle the free and informed public debate about the disease. Moreover, as Rose J put it:[64]

---

[60] *Ibid*, 537.

[61] Cripps (note 56 above), 39.

[62] [1985] 1 QB 526, 546 per Stephenson LJ. In *Spycatcher (No. 2)*, Lord Goff explicitly embraced the *Lion Laboratories* approach. He said that, although the 'defence of iniquity' was originally 'narrowly stated, on the basis that a man cannot be made "the confidant of a crime or a fraud".... It is now clear that the principle extends to matters of which disclosure is required in the public interest' ([1990] 1 AC 109, 282).

[63] [1988] 2 All ER 648. In addition to the action for breach of confidence, the case involved also a breach of an injunction which prohibited publication of the confidential information. The defendants were convicted of contempt of court and fined £10,000 for the 'deliberate and florid use of information which the injunction prohibited' (*ibid*, 666 per Rose J). The defendants were not, however, compelled to disclose the source of the information because the plaintiffs had failed to prove that disclosure was necessary for the prevention of crime within s. 10 of the Contempt of Court Act 1981.

[64] *Ibid*, 661.

The risk of identification is only one factor in assessing whether to permit the use of confidential information. In my judgment to allow publication ... would be to enable both defendants to procure breaches of confidence and then to make their own selection for publication. This would make a mockery of the law's protection of confidentiality when no justifying public interest has been shown.

The plaintiffs were not, of course, the doctors themselves and there is no evidence of a relationship of confidence between them and the 'mole'. Nevertheless it is likely that they would have had a cause of action against the newspaper on the basis that an obligation of confidence is imposed where a third party knew or ought to have known that the information is to be treated as confidential.[65]

Factual influences on the public interest test

The following considerations would seem to be relevant:[66]

    (a) To whom was the information given?
    (b) Is the plaintiff a 'public figure'?
    (c) Was the plaintiff in a public place?
    (d) Is the information in the public domain?
    (e) Did the plaintiff consent to publication?
    (f) How was the information acquired?
    (g) Was it essential for the plaintiff's identity to be revealed?
    (h) Was the invasion a serious one?

In addition to these issues, the following are among those that have played in the courts with some effect on the outcome of breach of confidence actions.

The defendant's motives and beliefs
The tabloids rely heavily upon members of the public 'selling' information concerning either themselves or, more pertinently in the present context, others. Accordingly, the motive of the informant has the potential to be a crucial factor in the application of the public interest test. In *Initial Services Ltd* v *Putterill* Lord Denning MR qualified his general public interest test with reference to informants disclosing

---

[65]*Coco* v *A N Clark (Engineers) Ltd* [1969] RPC 41, 48. See Chapter 3.
[66]See Wacks, *Protection of Privacy* (Chapter 1 note 1 above), 98–106. See too Cripps (note 1 above), 373–87.

information 'out of malice or spite or ... for reward'.[67] He thought such to be 'a different matter. It is a great evil when people purvey scandalous information for reward.'[68]

It is only in *Schering* that weight is attached to this proposition. As already argued, the case presents several difficulties in its treatment of the public domain issue[69] but paramount to the Court of Appeal was the public interest defence and, in particular, the majority view that the informant Elstein had acted with improper motives. Shaw LJ warned that 'The law of England is indeed, as Blackstone declared, a law of liberty; but the freedoms it recognises do not include a licence for the mercenary betrayal of business confidences'.[70]

Yet Lord Denning MR, who in *Initial Services* had supported the importance of motive, thought it 'quite unfair to accuse [Elstein], on the present evidence, of a flagrant breach of duty, or of being a traitorous adviser seeking to make money out of his misconduct'.[71] It is arguable that this is his conclusion *on the facts* and not on legal principle,[72] but in the light of his comments in *Woodward*, it is hard to escape the conclusion that he did dismiss motive as a matter of law. Indeed, with regard to the latter, 'It is difficult to imagine a clearer case of a person purveying "scandalous information for reward"'.[73] Yet the Master of the Rolls discerned a public interest in there being truth in publicity.[74]

Further problems arise from *Malone*, primarily because the factual context concerned the exercise by the police of their executive powers. Cripps warns that Megarry V-C's views are to be treated 'with some caution'[75] because he was 'careful to limit his comments to the particular facts of the case and hence to the special considerations involved in telephone tapping at the behest of the police'.[76] The Vice-Chancellor took as his starting-point the observation that 'The detection and

---

[67][1968] 1 QB 396, 406.

[68]*Ibid, loc cit.*

[69]See Chapter 3.

[70][1992] 1 QB 1, 27. Templeman LJ was equally explicit on the matter: 'It is important in the present case that, if the injunction is withheld, the court will enable a trusted adviser to make money out of his dealing in confidential information' (*ibid*, 40).

[71]*Ibid*, 16.

[72]'Lord Denning ... openly disregarded the fact that the defendant had been paid for his disclosures' (Cripps, note 1 above, 374).

[73]See *ibid, loc cit.*

[74]*Woodward* v *Hutchins* [1977] 1 WLR 760, 763–4.

[75]Cripps (note 1 above), 378.

[76]*Ibid, loc cit.*

prosecution of criminals, and the discovery of projected crimes, are important weapons in protecting the public'.[77] He then went on to limit the implication of this statement (that all confidences could be disclosed if they furthered the aim of 'crime prevention') in two ways.

First, the information could not be used for any purpose other than the prevention and detection of crime, and secondly, the informant must have had reasonable grounds for believing that the disclosure of the information would facilitate such a purpose.[78] As to the latter, it is obviously for the court and not for the informant to decide what matters are in the public interest to be disclosed in breach of confidence. As to the first limitation, it is most doubtful whether the court would censure the disclosure of information revealing criminal behaviour on account of the professedly opportunistic attitude of the informant.

The correct approach, it is submitted, is to disregard the motive of the informant. The public interest test should focus on the value of the information to the public. If the community has a legitimate interest in preserving confidences (against which must be balanced the interest in free speech), taking account of the motive of the informant effectively introduces a further value of preventing the transfer of information for money. If the recipient is willing to pay, it is difficult to see what comprises this third value. Moreover, this 'value' cannot be a factor in assessing the other two. The interest in protecting confidences springs from commercial and social considerations. Access to information rests on the (often competing) needs of a free society. Upon what basis are the motives of the informant to be evaluated?[79]

Following *Lion Laboratories*, it is, in any event, unlikely that the defendant's motives will be taken into account. In his definition of the public interest balancing test, Stephenson LJ said:

There is confidential information which the public may have a right to receive and others, in particular the press ... may have a right and even a duty to publish, even if the information has been unlawfully

---

[77][1979] 1 Ch 344, 377.

[78]*Ibid, loc cit.*

[79]'If there is a public interest in the receipt of certain information then that public interest ought not to be said to be diminished, extinguished or, indeed, affected by a defendant's ulterior motives for publication' (Cripps, note 1 above, 377). The learned author rightly acknowledges that this argument may have less force in relation to the 'just cause or excuse' formulation of the defence.

obtained in flagrant breach of confidence and *irrespective of the motive of the informer*.[80]

The timing of the disclosure

In *Initial Services Ltd* v *Putterill*, Lord Denning MR observed:

> In [*Weld-Blundell* v *Stephens*], Bankes LJ rather suggested that the exception is limited to the proposed or contemplated commission of a crime or a civil wrong. But I should have thought that was too limited. The exception should extend to crimes, frauds and misdeeds, *both those actually committed as well as those in contemplation*, provided always ... that the disclosure is justified in the public interest.[81]

As a general rule the timing of the disclosure is not relevant, but there are certain exceptions. In *Schering*, Shaw LJ remarked that the public no longer had an interest in the drug Primodos and its side-effects because the drug had been taken off the market by the plaintiff. He believed that 'Neither the public nor any individual stands in need of protection from its use at this stage in the history'.[82] Similarly, the timing of the disclosures played a crucial role in *Attorney-General* v *Jonathan Cape Ltd* where the Attorney-General sought, unsuccessfully, to restrain the publication of the first volume of the diaries of the late Richard Crossman. The diaries disclosed Cabinet discussions and other governmental confidences, but Lord Widgery CJ held that the public interest defence must be subject to a limit of time. The events described in the diaries were a decade old, and the Lord Chief Justice found it hard to believe that 'the publication at this interval of anything in volume one would inhibit free discussion in the Cabinet of today, even though the

---

[80] [1985] 1 QB 526, 536 (emphasis added). Stephenson LJ drew upon the formulation of the balancing test of Lord Fraser in *British Steel Corporation* v *Granada Television Ltd* which he considered 'so apt that I follow the judge in quoting it' (*ibid*, 539): 'The answer to the question therefore seems to me to involve weighing up the public interest for and against publication.... The informer's motives are, in my opinion, irrelevant' (*British Steel* [1981] AC 1096, 1202).
[81] [1968] 1 QB 396, 405 (emphasis added). Note that the *Initial Services Ltd* v *Putterill* formulation has now been superseded as far as the scope of the public interest test is concerned. See *Lion Laboratories*, discussed above.
[82] [1982] 1 QB 1, 27.

individuals involved are the same, and the national problems have a distressing similarity with those of a decade ago'.[83]

The recipient of the disclosure

The court is reluctant to allow the public interest defence to become a 'mole's charter'.[84] One of the methods used to circumscribe the scope of the defence is that disclosure, though in the public interest, ought to be sanctioned only when it is made to an appropriate body (and this will normally not include the press). Reference has been made to Lord Denning's comments in *Initial Services*[85] and their approval by Stephenson LJ in *Lion Laboratories*.[86] In the latter decision, Griffiths LJ was at pains to explain why this was an appropriate occasion for disclosure to the press and not to the Home Office:

> The public stance of the Home Office is that there is no risk of a false conviction as a result of the use of the machine. The Home Office is an interested and committed party. Of course I do not suggest that the Home Office would deliberately shut their eyes to evidence that the machine, or the manufacturers, might not be as reliable as they thought; but civil servants are human, and beauty lies in the eye of the beholder. I think in all the circumstances that the *Daily Express* is not to be criticised for thinking that the impact of the revelations in their newspaper would be more likely to galvanise the authorities into action than a discreet behind-doors approach.[87]

In *Francome* the Court of Appeal, though declining to lift an injunction prohibiting the defendants from publishing allegations of breaches of the rules of horse-racing by the plaintiff, supported such disclosure being made to the police or the Jockey Club. As Stephenson LJ put it:

---

[83][1976] 1 QB 752, 771. It has been mentioned above that the Law Commission thought that Lord Widgery's test served to 'make more acceptable' the fact that the action for breach of confidence was a 'not insubstantial check on freedom of speech' (see text after note 17 above). The Commission went on to comment that the time factor, in the personal information sphere: 'would enable a court to hold that the balance of interest lay in favour of protecting the confidence; the claim of the individual to have this information kept secret may well with the passage of the years become stronger, while a claim on behalf of the public to have access to it may in time tend to be less compelling' (*Breach of Confidence* (note 1 above), para 4.44).
[84]*Lion Laboratories* [1985] 1 QB 526, 553 per Griffiths LJ.
[85]See note 34 above.
[86]See text after note 58 above.
[87][1985] 1 QB 526, 553.

In the instant case, pending a trial, it is impossible to see what public interest would be served by publishing the contents of the tapes which would not equally be served by giving them to the police or to the Jockey Club. Any wider publication could only serve the interests of the *Daily Mirror*.[88]

The burden and standard of proof

The comments of Lord Widgery CJ in *Jonathan Cape* and their interpretation by the Law Commission have been considered above.[89] The ambiguities which the Law Commission identified concern which party should bear the burden of proof of the public interest defence, and not whether the defence is a defence at all but a mandatory requirement of the action for breach of confidence. *Lion Laboratories* has gone a long way towards resolving this problem, at the interlocutory stage at least. The court laid to rest the suggestion that the standard of proof for actions for breach of confidence was the same as that for libel actions, i.e., if the public interest defence was raised then no interlocutory injunction should be granted, the plaintiff being left to his damages at trial.[90]

Stephenson LJ, agreeing with the remarks of Sir David Cairns in *Khashoggi*, said that 'To be allowed to publish confidential information, the defendants must do more than raise a plea of public interest; they must show *"a legitimate ground for supposing it is in the public interest for it to be disclosed"'*.[91] This was translated into a 'serious defence of public interest which may succeed at the trial'.[92]

In respect of the burden of proving the defence at trial, the authorities point to a distinction between private and public actions for breach of confidence. *Jonathan Cape* concerned an action between the State and an individual and this may explain why Lord Widgery CJ placed the burden of proof upon the plaintiff, whereas in decisions such as *Fraser*, the public

---

[88][1984] 1 WLR 892, 898.

[89]See text at note 17 above. The final conclusion of the Law Commission was that it was: 'A further uncertainty in the light of *Cape's* case ... whether, as Lord Widgery there held, it is for the plaintiff to satisfy the court that the balance of the public interest lies in favour of protecting confidence or whether, as previously widely accepted, it is for the defendant to raise the issue of public interest as a defence' (*Breach of Confidence* (note 1 above), para 4.53).

[90]See the comments of Lord Denning MR in *Hubbard* v *Vosper* [1972] 2 QB 84, 96; and in *Fraser* v *Evans* [1969] 1 QB 349, 360–1; and of Roskill LJ in *Khashoggi* v *Smith* (1980) 130 NLJ 168.

[91][1985] 1 QB 526, 538 (emphasis added).

[92]*Ibid*, 539.

interest defence failed because the *defendant* had not been able to make out a ground for publication. As Lord Goff pointed out in *Spycatcher (No. 2)*:

> In cases concerned with government secrets . . .[93] it is incumbent upon the Crown, in order to restrain disclosure of government secrets, not only to show that the information is confidential, but also to show that it is in the public interest that it should not be published. . . . The reason for this additional requirement in cases concerned with government secrets appears to be that, although in the case of private citizens there is a public interest that confidential information should as such be protected, in the case of government secrets the mere fact of confidentiality does not alone support such a conclusion, because in a free society there is a continuing public interest that the workings of government should be open to scrutiny and criticism. From this it follows that, in such cases, there must be demonstrated some other public interest which requires that publication should be restrained.[94]

In cases involving personal information, it would appear that the burden of proof rests upon the defendant to show why the protection of confidence should be overridden in favour of the public interest in receiving the information. But even this may be subject to exceptions as is illustrated by comparing *Williams* v *Williams*[95] with *Distillers Co. (Biochemicals) Ltd* v *Times Newspapers Ltd*.[96] In the former, Lord Eldon LC, referring to the attempt by the plaintiff to prevent the disclosure of an unpatented eye medicine, was not of the opinion 'that the court ought to struggle to protect this sort of secrets in medicine'.[97] In *Distillers*, however, the information in question concerned the harmful side-effects of the notorious drug thalidomide on unborn children. At first instance, Talbot J phrased the defence in such a way as to leave no doubt that he thought it was for the defendant to prove that there is 'a

---

[93]Lord Goff refers to Lord Widgery CJ in *Jonathan Cape* [1976] 1 QB 752, 770, and to Mason J in *Commonwealth of Australia* v *John Fairfax & Sons Ltd* (1980) 147 CLR 39, 51–3.
[94][1990] 1 AC 109, 283.
[95](1817) 3 Mer 157, 36 ER 61.
[96][1975] 1 QB 613.
[97](1817) 3 Mer 157, 160, 36 ER 61, 62.

competing public interest which overrides the plaintiffs' private rights and the public interest arising out of discovery'.[98]

Distillers represents the better approach. The burden of proof should always rest upon the defendant in 'private' confidence actions. If there are very strong public interest considerations going against the plaintiff (such as the interest society has in the free circulation of information likely to lead to advances in medicine), apart from the omnipresent interest in free speech, this should result in the evidential threshold being lowered, making it easier for the defendant to prove his defence. In stricter terms of evidence, the plaintiff should have to adduce a greater weight of evidence in rebuttal. In its draft Bill, however, the Law Commission proposes the *Jonathan Cape* test for the tort of breach of confidence:

> Having regard to the importance in our view of the free circulation of information, we think it in principle right that the plaintiff should be required to establish that the balance of the public interest lies in his particular case in protecting the confidentiality of the relevant information.[99]

This conclusion resulted in clause 11 of the bill. Subclauses (1)(a) and (2) control the evidential burden of the defendant, whilst subclause (1)(b) imposes the legal burden on the plaintiff. Clause 11(2) provides:

> For the purposes of subsection (1) a defendant raises the issue of public interest in relation to a disclosure or use of information if he satisfies the court that, in view of the content of the information, there was, or (in the case of an apprehended disclosure or use) will be, at the time of the disclosure or use a public interest involved in the information being so disclosed or used.

This is an unattractive solution, for the reasons suggested below. These proposals accord value to certain forms of free speech which have no intrinsic worth, a matter considered in Chapter 2.

---

[98][1975] 1 QB 613, 623. The reference to discovery indicates what may well have dominated the minds of the judges who dealt with the case up to the House of Lords. The information which *The Times* sought to publish had been passed to them as a result of a discovery order by the court in the action between Distillers and the users of thalidomide. One of the competing public interests was therefore the administration of justice, a consideration not unlikely to be defended by the guardians of that very justice.
[99]*Breach of Confidence* (note 1 above), para 6.82.

The American law[100]

It is widely acknowledged that the American 'newsworthiness' defence has effectively demolished the private-facts tort.[101] In *Sidis* v *F-R Publishing Co.*,[102] the court declared that 'at some point the public interest in obtaining information becomes dominant over the individual's desire for privacy'.[103] The privilege is defined in the Restatement (Second) of the Law of Torts as extending to information 'of legitimate concern to the public';[104] a conclusion which is reached by weighing the competing interests of the public's 'right to know' against the individual's right to keep private facts from the public's gaze.[105] This may be decided by the judge, as a matter of law or, more often, by the jury as a question of fact. The test embodied in the Restatement, reads as follows:

> In determining what is a matter of legitimate public interest, account must be taken of the customs and conventions of the community; and in the last analysis what is proper becomes a matter of the community mores. The line is to be drawn when the publicity ceases to be the giving of information to which the public is entitled, and becomes a morbid and sensational prying into private lives for its own sake, with which a reasonable member of the public, with decent standards, would say that he had no concern.[106]

The categories of information which is newsworthy have steadily expanded as the courts become increasingly conscious of the free speech implications of censoring accurate reporting.[107] This trend is exemplified by the change of position of the courts from the cases of *Melvin* v *Reid*[108] and *Briscoe* v *Reader's Digest Association*[109] (where it was held that the clear identification of the subject of a newspaper publication by

---

[100]See J P Elwood, 'Outing, Privacy, and the First Amendment' (1992) 102 Yale LJ 747; D L Zimmerman, 'Requiem for a Heavyweight: A Farewell to Warren and Brandeis's Privacy Tort' (1983) 68 Cornell L Rev 291 (Wacks, *Privacy II* (Chapter 1 note 1 above), 433); and generally, Restatement (Second) of the Law of Torts, § 652D, comments d, g.

[101]Kalven questions whether the newsworthiness defence 'is not so overpowering as virtually to swallow the tort' (H Kalven, 'Privacy in Tort Law — Were Warren and Brandeis Wrong?' (1966) 31 Law & Contemp Probs 326, 336; Wacks, *Privacy II*, (Chapter 1 note 1 above), 41).

[102]113 F 2d 806 (2d Cir 1940).

[103]*Ibid*, 809.

[104]Restatement (Second) of the Law of Torts, § 652D (b) and comment h.

[105]*Diaz* v *Oakland Tribune Inc* 188 Cal Rptr 762, 771 (Cal Ct App 1983).

[106]Restatement (Second) of the Law of Torts, § 652D, comment h.

[107]Elwood (note 100 above), 755–6.

[108]112 Cal App 285, 297 P 91 (1931).

[109]483 P 2d 34 (1971).

name served little independent public purpose, and was struck down), to decisions such as *Ross* v *Midwest Communications Inc*[110] and the Supreme Court ruling in *Cox Broadcasting Corporation* v *Cohn*[111] (in which such disclosure was held to be protected by the newsworthiness defence).[112]

Sexual matters (understandably) dominate. It may therefore be instructive to examine the American jurisprudence in this area, especially the scope of the newsworthiness defence. In *Sipple* v *Chronicle Publishing Co.*,[113] an ex-marine became the subject of intense media interest when he foiled an assassination attempt on President Ford. The *San Francisco Chronicle* revealed that Sipple was a prominent member of the gay community, which indeed was true, but he brought an action under the tort of private-facts disclosure because he claimed that he had always kept his homosexuality private from his relatives. The court dismissed Sipple's action on two grounds. First, the information was already in the public domain, and, secondly, it held that the facts disclosed were newsworthy because the exposé was motivated by the wish to combat the stereotyping of homosexuals as 'timid, weak and unheroic' and to discuss the potential biases of the President (one newspaper had suggested that the President's reticence in thanking Sipple was on account of the latter's homosexuality).[114]

In *Diaz* v *Oakland Tribune Inc*, a newspaper article revealed that the first female student body president of a Californian college was a transsexual. The court held that Diaz's transsexuality was a private fact[115] and also that, although Diaz was involved in a public controversy (in that she accused the college of misuse of student funds), the disclosure was irrelevant to that issue and, accordingly, not newsworthy.[116] The court emphasised that the purpose of First Amendment

---

[110]870 F 2d 271 (5th Cir).

[111]420 US 469 (1975). Followed in *The Florida Star* v *BJF* 491 US 524 (1989).

[112]However, as Elwood argues, these cases, in effect, concern the extent to which the information has already entered the public domain rather than the 'inherent newsworthiness of individuals' names' (note 100 above), 756. This cannot, however, be said for *Howard* v *Des Moines Register & Tribune Co.* 283 NW 2d 289 (1979), where the Iowa Supreme Court adopted the following reasoning in respect of the naming of a woman who had undergone an involuntary sterilisation: 'Assuming, as the plaintiff agrees, the newspaper had a right to print an article which documented extra-statutory involuntary sterilisations … the editors also had a right to buttress the force of their evidence by naming names…. they had a right to treat the identity of the victims of involuntary sterilisations as matters of legitimate public concern' (*ibid*, 303).

[113]201 Cal Rptr 665 (Cal Ct App 1984).

[114]*Ibid*, 670.

[115]Cf *Sipple*.

[116]188 Cal Rptr 762, 773.

protection was 'to keep the public informed so that they may make intelligent decisions on matters important to self-governing people'.[117] It was further explained that '... the fact that she is a transsexual does not adversely reflect on her honesty or judgment. Nor does the fact that she was the first woman student body president, in itself, warrant that her entire private life be open to public inspection'.[118]

How is this decision to be reconciled with *Sipple*? The answer may lie in the tenor of the *Diaz* article. The newspaper argued that the report was intended to portray the 'changing roles of women in society',[119] but, as Elwood points out,[120] it was clear from the tone of the article that the author's objective stopped at the 'stark revelation'.[121] An important feature of both *Diaz* and *Sipple* is that the articles purported to portray alternative lifestyles. As Joseph Raz has argued:

> An important case for the importance of freedom of expression arises out of the fact that public portrayal and expression of forms of life validate the styles of life portrayed, and that censoring expression normally expresses authoritative condemnation not merely of the views or opinions censored but of the whole style of life of which they are a part.[122]

It is therefore arguable that, if the article about Diaz had seriously intended to portray the changing role of women in society, the court may have resisted calls for its censorship.

In Chapter 2, Schauer's balancing exercise between various sub-classes of society was discussed. Does the status of the subject of the private-facts disclosure affect the application of the newsworthiness defence?[123] Elwood suggests that it does, and further identifies a dichotomy between 'limited-purpose public figures and general-purpose public figures'.[124] The former, those who have voluntarily

---

[117]*Ibid*, 767.
[118]*Ibid*, 773 (footnotes omitted).
[119]*Ibid, loc cit.*
[120]Elwood (note 100 above), 759.
[121]The article ran, 'The students at the College of Alameda will be surprised to learn [that] their student body president, Toni Diaz, is no lady, but is in fact a man whose real name is Antonio. Now I realise, that in these times, such a matter is no big deal, but I suspect his female classmates in PE 97 may wish to make other showering arrangements' (188 Cal Rptr 762, 766).
[122]J Raz, 'Free Expression and Personal Identification' (1991) 11 Oxford J Legal Stud 303, 310.
[123]See Chapter 2.
[124]Elwood (note 100 above), 759.

injected themselves or been drawn into a particular public controversy, lose their right to privacy in respect of the 'events that made them famous'.[125] Diaz, as the first female student body president, became 'a public figure for some purposes'[126] but not in regard to her sexuality, which, accordingly, she was entitled to keep private.

The other category of public figure — general purpose — comprises 'celebrities'.[127] Though the Restatement comments that 'There may be some intimate details of her life, such as sexual relations, which even the actress is entitled to keep to herself',[128] the decision in *Ann-Margret* v *High Society Magazine Inc*[129] illustrates that this delicacy has not yet been embraced by the courts. In that case, an actress was denied relief in respect of the publication of a nude photograph of her, partly because the photograph was of 'a woman who has occupied the fantasies of many movie-goers' and therefore 'of great interest to many people'.[130] The chief ground upon which celebrities are denied protection is that they have consented to publicity and thus, have waived their right to privacy.[131]

Prosser and Keeton enumerate three criteria which must be satisfied to support a finding of implied assumption of risk for *private* figures: the conduct must manifest consent, the risk must be encountered voluntarily, and with full knowledge and appreciation.[132] The case law demonstrates that for private figures, consent must be, at the very least, implied by conduct.[133] Unfortunately, these cases are not followed when the plaintiff is a celebrity. Elwood argues that 'volition' is lacking in many of the cases, e.g., in the *Sidis* case where the plaintiff's entry into the public arena was precipitated by his graduation from college at 16 years of age.[134] He contends that if the courts consider a plaintiff's

---

[125]*Ibid, loc cit.* See Restatement (Second) of the Law of Torts, § 652D, comment f.
[126]*Diaz* 188 Cal Rptr 762, 772–3.
[127]Prosser and Keeton define a public figure as: 'a person who, by his accomplishments, fame, or mode of living, or by adopting a profession or calling which gives the public a legitimate interest in his doings, his affairs, and his character, has become a "public personage".... It includes, in short, anyone who has arrived at a position where public attention is focused upon him as a person' (W Prosser and W P Keeton, *The Law of Torts*, 5th ed (St Paul, Minn: West Publishing Co., 1984), 859–60).
[128]Restatement (Second) of the Law of Torts, § 652D, comment h.
[129]498 F Supp 401 (1980).
[130]*Ibid*, 405.
[131]Elwood (note 100 above), 760.
[132]Prosser and Keeton (note 127 above), 484–92.
[133]E.g., *McCabe* v *Village Voice Inc* 550 F Supp 525 (plaintiff's consent to having his photograph taken for the purposes of the photographer writing a book did not extend to its publication in a weekly newspaper).
[134]Elwood (note 100 above), 761.

privacy in respect of a certain revelation not to have been waived, they take pains to find that the plaintiff was not a celebrity rather than holding that the newsworthiness test has not been satisfied.[135] He points to the need, under general tort law,[136] for the plaintiff to have knowledge not just of the general risk, but of the specific risk that caused his harm for waiver to apply. He submits that, accordingly, waiver should never be implied for sex-related disclosures.[137]

Zimmerman asserts that the courts are most reluctant to examine the boundaries between First Amendment protected and unprotected speech.[138] As Justice Powell commented in *Gertz* v *Robert Welch Inc*, the use of a newsworthiness test:

> ... would occasion the additional difficulty of forcing state and federal judges to decide on an *ad hoc* basis which publications address issues of 'general or public interest' and which do not — to determine, in the words of Marshall J, 'what information is relevant to self-government'.... We doubt the wisdom of committing this task to the conscience of judges.[139]

Zimmerman therefore claims that the courts simply accept the judgment of the press as to what is newsworthy.[140] But her suggestion that 'deference to the judgment of the press may actually be the appropriate and principled response to the newsworthiness enquiry'[141] overlooks the reason why the subject is contentious at all. She observes that 'The economic survival of publishers and broadcasters depends upon their ability to provide a product that the public will buy'[142] and argues that market-place competition breeds into the papers a 'responsiveness to

---

[135]*Ibid, loc cit,* 261 noting T Gerety, 'Redefining Privacy' (1977) 12 Harv CR–CL L Rev 233, 295, n 215 (Wacks, *Privacy I* (Chapter 1 note 1 above)). Gerety concludes that the Supreme Court's reluctance to find the plaintiff a public figure in *Time Inc* v *Firestone* 424 US 448 (1976): 'derives from the legitimate concern that *as to sexual intimacy at least* none of the parties in fact intended to waive their rights to privacy'.

[136]Referring to Prosser and Keeton (note 127 above), 487.

[137]Elwood (note 100 above), 761.

[138]Zimmerman (note 100 above), 343.

[139]418 US 323, 346 (1974), citing the words of Marshall J in *Rosenbloom* v *Metromedia Inc* 403 US 29, 79 (1971).

[140]Zimmerman (note 100 above), 353, citing, e.g., *Jenkins* v *Dell Publishing Co.* 251 F 2d 447 (3d Cir).

[141]Zimmerman, *ibid, loc cit.*

[142]*Ibid, loc cit.*

what substantial segments of the population want (and perhaps even need) to know to cope with the society in which they live'.[143]

The concept of public interest all too easily camouflages the commercial motives of the media. Worse, it masquerades as the 'democratic' exercise of consumer choice: we get the sensationalism we deserve. Both forms of cynical tabloidism neglect the consequences for individuals who happen to be public figures who are unfortunate enough to be catapulted into the public eye.

Proposals for reform in England

The Law Commission

The Commission recommends that '... the courts should have a broad power to decide in an action for breach of confidence whether in the particular case the public interest in protecting the confidentiality of the information outweighs the public interest in its disclosure or use'.[144] Its proposals, discussed above, are embodied in clause 11 of the draft Bill.

As to the substantive requirements of the test,[145] the plaintiff must satisfy the court that the public interest relied upon by the defendant is 'outweighed by the public interest involved in upholding the confidentiality of the information'.[146] This deliberately vague statement may be amplified in two respects. First, the *Lion Laboratories* test has been adopted in that the defence may apply 'notwithstanding that the information does not relate to any crime, fraud or other misconduct'.[147] Secondly, in its balancing function, the court is directed to have regard, in general, to 'all the circumstances of the case' and, in particular, to the 'extent and nature' of the disclosure,[148] the manner in which the

---

[143]*Ibid*, 353–4. Similar arguments inform the writings of the distinguished guru of the economic analysis of law, Richard Posner. See, in particular, R Posner, 'The Right of Privacy' (1978) 12 Ga L Rev 393. Cf C E Baker, 'Posner's Privacy Mystery and the Failure of the Economic Analysis of Law' (1978) 12 Ga L Rev 475; and E J Bloustein, 'Privacy Is Dear at Any Price: A Response to Posner's Economic Theory' (1978) 12 Ga L Rev 429. For further references and a brief discussion of this approach, see Wacks, *Personal Information* (Chapter 1 note 1 above), 28–30.
[144]*Breach of Confidence* (note 1 above), para 6.77.
[145]The Commission was wary of calling it a defence (*ibid*, para 4.53). For a discussion of this point see text after note 14 above.
[146]*Ibid*, app A, clause 11(1)(b).
[147]*Ibid*, clause 11(3) (although, of course, at the time the Commission proposed the Bill, *Lion Laboratories* had yet to be decided).
[148]*Ibid*, clause 11(4)(a).

information was acquired,[149] and the 'time which has elapsed since the information originally became subject to the obligation of confidence'.[150]

The generality of the Commission's proposals is in accordance with the approach of the courts in the cases examined above. However, the Commission differs from the courts in its insistence upon the plaintiff's having to disprove the public interest issue in all cases, and its inclusion of the means of acquisition of the information as a factor to be taken into account in balancing the competing public interests. As to the former, the better approach is that adumbrated by Lord Goff in *Spycatcher (No. 2)*,[151] which distinguishes actions between individuals and those between an individual and the State, placing the burden of disproving the defence on the plaintiff only in the latter situation. This reinforces the view that disclosures of information concerning an individual's private life which bear no relevance to his or her position as a holder of public office or which relate to a public event, have no intrinsic or instrumental value. The self-governance theory, outlined in Chapter 2, is inapplicable to such revelations and hence the principle of freedom of expression forfeits its privileged status.

If a defence is raised by the defendant, he should therefore carry both the evidential and legal burden, as in normal civil practice, because the public interests which the courts must balance, in such a case, are equal.

As to the manner of acquisition of the information, the Bill has introduced an irrelevant factor into the balancing process because, as argued above in relation to motive,[152] this factor ought not to be conceived as an interest to be balanced; it is neither an element of the public interest in freedom of expression nor a component of an individual's interest in privacy.

Finally, it should be noted that the Commission's proposals do not prevent an obligation of confidence from arising or subsisting,[153] and thus, as outlined above in the current treatment of this issue by the courts, an obligation may be *recognised* notwithstanding that it is not granted protection. This enables the court to consider alternative equitable remedies apart from the injunction. The question remains whether a broad test is desirable, leaving the gaps to be filled by a

---

[149]*Ibid*, clause 11(4)(b).
[150]*Ibid*, clause 11(4)(c).
[151]See note 94 above.
[152]See text after note 78 above.
[153]Cripps (note 1 above), 367.

case-by-case analysis. This is discussed below,[154] but it is useful to consider here the other tests which have been proposed.

Other solutions[155]

The National Heritage Select Committee recommends a defence of public interest which, as defined, would include any act done for the purpose of preventing, detecting or exposing the commission of any crime; or informing the public about matters directly affecting the discharge of any public functions of the individual concerned; or preventing the public from being harmfully misled by some public statement or action of the individual concerned; or for the protection of health or safety; or under any lawful authority.[156] This mirrors quite closely the test propounded by the Calcutt Committee except that the Calcutt formulation eschews the emphasis on the 'public interest' and, instead, justifies specific revelations which expose crime or seriously antisocial conduct,[157] or protect the health or safety of the public, or concern the behaviour of an individual in his private life which so adversely affects his public duties or is so hypocritical, that the public is likely to be seriously misled.[158]

The Calcutt *Review* only adds to the Committee's list the defences of lawful authority and where the act is done for the purpose of informing the public about matters directly affecting the discharge of any public function of the individual concerned.[159] The Consultation Paper of the Lord Chancellor's Department embraces the test set down in the Calcutt

[154]See M W Bryan, 'The Law Commission Report on Breach of Confidence: Not in the Public Interest?' [1982] PL 188.
[155]See L Blom-Cooper and L R Pruitt, 'Privacy Jurisprudence of the Press Complaints Commission' (1994) 23 Anglo-Am L Rev 133.
[156]National Heritage Select Committee, *Fourth Report, Privacy and Media Intrusion*, 294–I, 1993, para 55.
[157]Following from the comments of Donaldson MR in *Francome*: 'The "media" ... are an essential foundation of any democracy. In exposing crime, antisocial behaviour and hypocrisy and in campaigning for reform and propagating the views of minorities, they perform an invaluable function' ([1984] 1 WLR 892, 898).
[158]Committee on Privacy and Related Matters, *Report of the Committee on Privacy and Related Matters*, Cm 1102, 1990, paras 3.19–3.27 and 12.20–12.23. The precise formulation of the 'hypocrisy test' is: 'there would, but for the publication, be a real risk that the public, or some section of the public, would be materially misled by a statement previously made public by or on behalf of any individual whose privacy would otherwise be infringed (whether the plaintiff or otherwise)' (*ibid*, para 12.23).
[159]Sir David Calcutt QC, *Review of Press Self-Regulation*, Cm 2135, 1993, para 7.18.

Report and *Review*, but leaves for further consideration how closely the term 'seriously antisocial conduct' ought to be defined.[160]

Conclusion

The question of public interest is, on the whole, satisfactorily analysed in the decisions reviewed above. *Lion Laboratories*, in particular, has helped to illuminate the main grounds upon which the court exercises its exclusive discretion to decide what is in the public interest. This general discretion should, however, be subject to the following principles.

First, the abandonment of the rigid 'misconduct' test is to be welcomed. In the context of personal information, such a test unduly restricts the disclosure of information whose publication is in the public interest. In particular, it might exclude reports of the conduct of holders of public office which have a bearing upon their fitness for that office. Thus should a factual situation such as arose in *British Steel* occur again, the mismanagement of a public undertaking should be considered to be in the public interest.[161] But the defence should not extend to the disclosure of civil wrongs, i.e., the *Weld-Blundell* case should be followed.

Secondly, in respect of the burden of proof, the sensible distinction between private and public law breach of confidence actions should be retained. In the latter, the court will, to use Mason J's expression in *Commonwealth of Australia* v *John Fairfax & Sons Ltd*,[162] 'look at the matter through different spectacles'. If the information is in the private sphere, but has a public relevance (the example given above is the free movement of information concerning advances in medicine) this should not result in the burden of disproving the defence being laid upon the plaintiff. The standard of proving the defence should remain on the defendant but, in such cases, the weight of the evidential burden on the defendant should be decreased (i.e., the plaintiff has to adduce a greater weight of evidence in rebuttal).

---

[160]*Infringement of Privacy*, Lord Chancellor's Department, Scottish Office, 1993, para 5.66.
[161]In that case, Lord Wilberforce, as mentioned in note 54 above, remarked: 'The most that it is said the papers reveal is mismanagement and government intervention'. Such revelations are in the public interest if the Meiklejohnian argument of self-governance is adopted. See A Meiklejohn, 'The First Amendment is an Absolute' (1961) S Ct Rev 245, and Chapter 2.
[162](1980) 147 CLR 39, 51, which was quoted with approval by the House of Lords in *Attorney-General* v *Guardian Newspapers Ltd (No. 2)* [1990] 1 AC 109 (e.g., 283 per Lord Goff).

Thirdly, the American distinction between private and public figures ought to be incorporated into the public interest test but only to the extent that the public status of the individual affects his position as the holder of a public office. Accordingly, the approach of the Calcutt Committee (as closely followed by the Calcutt *Review* and the National Heritage Select Committee) should be adopted. This means that revelations should not be censored where they relate to the behaviour of an individual in his private life which so adversely affects his public duties, or is so hypocritical, that the public is likely to be misled. Nor should the public interest defence be extended to cover the actions of celebrities and, thus, the American approach in this regard should not be adopted. The fact that an individual is in the public eye cannot be a licence to disclose intimate facts about him which he wishes to keep private.

Implicit in this formulation is the exception that if the individual's conduct is such that it may be assumed that he has waived his rights in respect of a particular invasion of his or her privacy, then disclosure *in respect of that particular invasion* may not be prohibited. This is not a question of the scope of the public interest defence but an application of the public domain test. Thus *Woodward*, to the extent that it was decided on the basis that it was in the public interest to disclose the activities of the pop stars by virtue only of the fact that they sought publicity for their own gain, is wrongly decided. The public domain aspect of this case is considered in Chapter 3.

At the interlocutory stage, the references to disclosure of the information to institutions other than the press are sound, but only as a means of reconciling the public interest in *the investigation* of misconduct with the protection of the complainant's rights at the interlocutory stage. At trial it is for the court to determine whether the balancing test comes down in favour of suppression or revelation of the information in question. If disclosure is ordered, then the court should not circumscribe the class of its recipients. Conversely, if the obligation of confidence is enforced by the court, the value of that right should not be attenuated by the sanctioning of limited disclosure to, for example, the Jockey Club. If the court is uncertain as to the light in which the information should be viewed, this is a matter for expert evidence at trial, not for post-trial investigations.

These suggestions are not dissimilar to those propounded by the various committees that have examined the matter over the years. Legislation still remains the preferred option. The prospects of Parliament grasping the nettle seem increasingly slim. Under these circumstances the action for breach of confidence presents an imperfect, but workable substitute.

5

Media Intrusion

The pursuit of information often requires the use of intrusive methods: deception, zoom lenses, hidden devices, the interception of telephone conversations or correspondence, and other forms of spying and surveillance. While the issue of regulating such activities is beyond the scope of this book,[1] the relevance of such methods to the question of the disclosure of personal information, either in breach of confidence (considered in Chapter 3) or generally, is the difficult problem which is the subject of this Chapter.

There is a tendency to conflate the 'intrusion' practised by the prying journalist with the publication of the information thereby acquired. I shall argue that the two be kept separate. First, I briefly examine the law in England and the United States, and proposals for reform in this area,[2] and then suggest how the problem might be resolved.

The United States[3]

William Prosser,[4] in his fourfold classification of the Warren and Brandeis 'right to privacy',[5] included the right to be free from intrusion

---

[1] See, generally, Wacks, *Personal Information* (Chapter 1 note 1 above), ch 7 and bibliography.

[2] Law Commission, *Breach of Confidence*, Cmnd 8388, 1981; Committee on Privacy and Related Matters, *Report of the Committee on Privacy and Related Matters*, Cm 1102, 1990; National Heritage Select Committee, *Fourth Report, Privacy and Media Intrusion*, 294–I, 1993; and Sir David Calcutt QC, *Review of Press Self-Regulation*, Cm 2135, 1993.

[3] A Hill, 'Defamation and Privacy under the First Amendment' (1976) 76 Colum L Rev 1205; and Note, 'The Right of the Press to Gather Information' (1971) 71 Colum L Rev 838.

[4] W Prosser, 'Privacy' (1960) 48 Calif L Review 383 (Wacks, *Privacy II* (Chapter 1 note 1 above), 47).

[5] S D Warren and L D Brandeis, 'The Right to Privacy' (1890) 4 Harv L Rev 193 (Wacks, *Privacy II* (Chapter 1 note 1 above), 3).

upon one's seclusion or solitude or into one's private affairs and the right to prevent the public disclosure of embarrassing private facts about oneself. Accordingly, the common law tort of 'invasion of privacy' is *prima facie* capable of dealing with both the means of obtaining private facts and their eventual disclosure.

In Chapter 4 the dramatic effect of the defence of 'newsworthiness' on the private facts tort was seen.[6] Does this defence also undermine the intrusion tort where newsworthy information is intrusively garnered for publication?

In *Dietemann* v *Time Inc*[7] two reporters of *Life* magazine tricked the plaintiff, a virtually uneducated plumber who purported to diagnose and treat physical ailments, into allowing them access to his home and there set up hidden surveillance devices to monitor his activities. Plainly the resulting article informed the public about a newsworthy topic — the unlicensed practice of medicine — but the court had to consider whether this would grant immunity to the reporters in respect of their surreptitious news-gathering techniques. On appeal, the judgment of $1,000 in the plaintiff's favour for invasion of privacy was upheld. In answer to the defendant's claim that the First Amendment's shield extended not only to publication but to investigation, the court remarked that the Amendment 'has never been construed to accord newsmen immunity from torts or crimes committed during the course of newsgathering'.[8] Significantly, in its assessment of damages, the court took into account not only the nature and extent of the intrusive acts, but also the publication. It noted that '... there is no First Amendment interest in protecting news media from calculated misdeeds [thus] damages for intrusion [may] be enhanced by the fact of later publication'.[9]

In respect of the First Amendment, the 'right to gather information is logically antecedent and practically necessary to any effective exercise of [the right to publish] and ... cannot be given full meaning unless that antecedent right is recognised'.[10] In the United States, no less than in

[6]See J Elwood, 'Outing, Privacy, and the First Amendment' (1992) 102 Yale LJ 747; D L Zimmerman, 'Requiem for a Heavyweight: A Farewell to Warren and Brandeis's Privacy Tort' (1983) 68 Cornell L Rev 291 (Wacks, *Privacy II* (Chapter 1, note 1 above), 433); and generally Restatement (Second) of the Law of Torts, § 652D, comments d, g.
[7]449 F 2d 244 (9th Cir 1971).
[8]*Ibid*, 249.
[9]*Ibid*, 250.
[10]Note (1971) 71 Colum L Rev 838, 843.

England, a general privilege to gather information has been denied to the press.[11]

Accordingly, the court correctly separated the two questions of intrusion and disclosure, assessing the reasonableness of the defendants' newsgathering techniques in the light of the common law principles developed under the former, while reserving any First Amendment argument exclusively for the latter.

The award of enhanced damages illustrates, however, the considerable difficulty of disengaging the two issues at all stages of the inquiry. The answer lies in the formulation of independent criteria by which to assess when an individual's seclusion may justifiably be violated, just as there are standards by which to test when the disclosure of private facts may be justified in the public interest.

Professor Hill usefully divides this problem into two scenarios: the first where there is intrusion without disclosure; the second where disclosure follows intrusion.[12] The former is easily analysed, being free from First Amendment considerations: the invader is liable for his acts of intrusion.[13]

The second scenario may, following Hill, be further subdivided into cases where the discloser is not the intruder but disseminates the information with knowledge of the means of its acquisition, and cases where the discloser has participated in the intrusion.[14]

Discloser not intruder

In *Pearson* v *Dodd*,[15] employees and ex-employees of a US Senator surreptitiously removed papers from his files, copied them and handed the duplicates to two newspaper columnists. The journalists, with full knowledge of the circumstances of its acquisition, included the information in their column. The court held, dealing separately with disclosure and intrusion, that, as to the former, the First Amendment protected the revelation of such information[16] and, as to the latter, the columnists could not be liable for the intrusion merely upon proof of their knowledge of its occurrence.

---

[11]In the United States, the denial was by the Supreme Court in *Houchins* v *KQED Inc* 438 US 1 (1978).
[12]Hill (note 3 above), 1279–85.
[13]E.g., *Hamberger* v *Eastman* 106 NH 107, 206 A 2d 239 (1964).
[14]Hill (note 3 above), 1279–85.
[15]410 F 2d 701 (DC Cir), *cert denied*, 395 US 947 (1969).
[16]The court labelled it information of 'general public interest' (410 F 2d 701, 703). This test has since been superseded by the newsworthiness inquiry.

It does not follow from this decision that damages could not be recovered for the intrusion. The court held merely that Dodd could not recover such damages from the journalists. This, of course, raises the question in what circumstances the media should be compelled to disclose their sources. In effect, source-protection in cases like *Pearson* denies the plaintiff a remedy for his common law right.

Moreover, First Amendment protection extends only to disclosure. Hill points out, in regard to the protection afforded to the media by the newsworthiness defence to otherwise actionable disclosures of private facts, that 'The values of the First Amendment would be seriously subverted if such protection were withdrawn on the ground of knowledge on the part of the media that the truth had come to light through legally reprehensible means employed by others'.[17]

But should similar protection be accorded to intrusion? The answer must be in the negative. The justifications for free speech (canvassed in Chapter 2) which form the rationale of First Amendment protection of disclosure, do not apply to cases of intrusion. Thus, as *Dietemann* correctly held, the media should be liable for intrusive investigative methods. Accordingly, the central question becomes whether mere *knowledge* on the part of the columnists in *Pearson* ought to have been sufficient to hold them liable for the tort of intrusion.

Discloser is intruder

Dietemann protects journalists' disclosure of newsworthy information to the public at large, while reproving their intrusive newsgathering. This sensible approach is buttressed by the remarks of the trial court in *Pearson* which reasoned that where the discloser and intruder are the same person, liability should be imposed for the intrusion even though the disclosure was protected by the First Amendment.[18] Where the trial court differs in *Pearson* from the decision in *Dietemann* is that, in respect of the question of damages, the former supported compensation for the intrusion alone whereas in *Dietemann* the court spoke of 'enhanced' damages.

---

[17]Hill (note 3 above), 1280.
[18]279 F Supp 101, 105–6 (D DC 1968). And see Hill (note 3 above), 1281.

Hill prefers the *Dietemann* view, calling in aid the facts of *Barber v Time Inc*[19] in support.[20] The plaintiff in *Barber*, a woman with a serious eating disorder, was surreptitiously photographed by a newspaper reporter, and the picture was published by the defendant. Hill argues that 'Here it would be unseemly to deny damages caused by the publication'.[21]

Of course, in most mixed intrusion/disclosure cases *but for* the reprehensible news-gathering techniques, the defendants would not have got their story. And equally, *but for* those techniques, not only would the plaintiff not have suffered a violation of his seclusion but he would also have been spared the trauma of being named in the newspaper. However, in *Barber* the Missouri Supreme Court refused to grant protection to the journalist and hence the plaintiff recovered damages for both intrusion and disclosure (though the award for intrusion was almost certainly an integral part of the larger award for disclosure, rather than the court separately quantifying the two).

The conundrum here is that if the photograph attracts First Amendment protection why should the journalist be punished by enhanced damages for his intrusion? The law appears to be giving with one hand constitutional protection to disclosure whilst taking it away with the other when it comes to assess damages for intrusion. And this produces the anomaly that where the discloser publishes newsworthy information which has not been obtained by intrusion, he is not liable to the plaintiff at all, whereas if the information has been so obtained, he is liable, in effect, both for the intrusion and the disclosure; the disclosure being reflected in the form of enhanced damages for intrusion. The fact of intrusion has subverted the protection given to the publication through the public interest test.

A more satisfactory approach may lie in developing separate criteria establishing in what circumstances, and the extent to which, intrusion may be justified. This is considered below.

England

English law protects an individual's solitude by the torts of trespass (to the person and to land) and nuisance. The primary difficulty with these

---

[19]348 Mo 1199, 159 SW 2d 291 (1942).
[20]Hill suggests that the more satisfactory approach 'would be to allow, against any party at fault, damages for the anguish brought about by the intrusion and more particularly by the publication' (note 3 above, 1284).
[21]*Ibid*, 1282.

common law actions is that, traditionally, they may be brought only by an individual with an interest in the land over which the infringement has occurred.[22] As *Kaye v Robertson*[23] amply illustrates, a plaintiff whose 'privacy' is infringed while he occupies property belonging to another is left with little legal redress.[24]

In practice there is only one cause of action[25] in which the question of the relationship between intrusion and disclosure arises, namely the equitable remedy for breach of confidence which now calls for analysis.

Breach of confidence[26]

As discussed in Chapter 3, where the third party is a stranger it is uncertain whether an action lies. And even where confidential information is acquired by the use of 'reprehensible means' (electronic surveillance, spying, and other forms of intrusive conduct), the authorities suggest the third party is not liable when he uses it. The apparent explanation for this 'glaring inadequacy'[27] (which means that if confidential information is obtained by improper means, it receives less protection by the law than if it were confided to a party who was under an obligation not to use or disclose it) is the absence of a relationship of

---

[22]Trespass to land is entering, remaining, or placing or projecting any object, upon land in the possession of the plaintiff. See, e.g., Salmond and Heuston, *The Law of Torts*, 20th ed (London: Sweet & Maxwell, 1992), 44. In *Cunard v Antifyre Ltd* [1933] 1 KB 551, 556–7 per Talbot J, private nuisances were defined as: 'interferences for a substantial length of time ... with the use or enjoyment of neighbouring property'. In the 'privacy' arena, the most common cause of complaint would fall under the category of: 'some interference with the beneficial use of the premises occupied by the plaintiff' (Salmond and Heuston, *ibid*, 61). However, in *Khorasandjian v Bush* [1993] QB 727 the Court of Appeal held that there was a jurisdiction in private nuisance to grant an injunction restraining persistent harassment by unwanted telephone calls notwithstanding that the recipient of the calls had no proprietary interest in the land where the calls were received. See J Bridgeman and M A Jones, 'Harassing Conduct and Outrageous Acts: A Cause of Action for Intentionally Inflicted Mental Distress?' (1994) 14 LS 180, especially 183–192.
[23][1991] FSR 62.
[24]Although, Prescott comments that: 'There is not a hospital in London ... which would not gladly consent to be joined as a co-plaintiff in a situation of the *Kaye v Robertson* type' (P Prescott, '*Kaye v Robertson* — A Reply' (1991) 54 MLR 451, 452). This point is considered in Chapter 6.
[25]Omitting those that may arise in respect of seditious, blasphemous, obscene or racially inflammatory information. Prescott (*ibid*, 452–3) argues that an injunction could be granted by the court in a trespass action under the equitable auxiliary jurisdiction (citing *Crossley v Derby Gas Co.* (1834) 4 LJ Ch 25).
[26]See in particular, M Richardson, 'Breach of Confidence, Surreptitiously or Accidentally Obtained Information and Privacy: Theory Versus Law' (1994) 19 Melb U L Rev 673; and G Wei, 'Surreptitious Takings of Confidential Information' (1992) 12 LS 302.
[27]*Breach of Confidence* (note 1 above), paras 5.5 and 6.28.

confidence between the party who wishes to keep the information confidential, on the one hand, and the 'surreptitious taker', on the other.

But this may be a difficult position to defend. Thus, it has been argued[28] that in these circumstances the taker, since he *knew* that the information was confidential (why else would he be surreptitiously obtaining it?), is under an imputed duty no different from that which applies to the ordinary recipient of confidential information. For Professor Jones:[29]

> It would be rash ... to conclude that the stranger who sells information obtained, for example, from the use of electronic bugs cannot be enjoined and is not liable to make any recompense or account for his profits to the plaintiff. Equity, to borrow a metaphor, should not be past the age of child-bearing. A defendant who has taken good care not to enter any relationship of any sort with the plaintiff and who has obtained confidential information by reprehensible means should be in no better position than a defendant who is given and deliberately breaches the plaintiff's confidence.

There are dicta in two eighteenth-century cases which have been interpreted to suggest that there may be a remedy where the defendant employs improper methods to obtain information. In *Webb* v *Rose*[30] the court awarded an injunction to prevent the printing of conveyancing precedents which had been removed from a conveyancer's offices. *Millar* v *Taylor*[31] involved the reprinting of a book of poems. Yates J held that an injunction would lie to prevent 'surreptitiously or treacherously publishing what the owner had never made public at all, nor consented to the publication of'.

---

[28]G Jones, 'Restitution of Benefits Obtained in Breach of Another's Confidence' (1970) 86 LQR 463; J and R Jacob, 'Confidential Communications' (1969) 119 NLJ 133; Lord Goff of Chieveley and G Jones, *The Law of Restitution*, 4th ed (London: Sweet & Maxwell, 1993), ch 35; Committee on Privacy, *Report of the Committee on Privacy*, Cmnd 5012, 1972, app 1, 287; R P Meagher, W M C Gummow, and J R F Lehane, *Equity: Doctrines and Remedies* (London: Butterworths, 1992), 870–4; and, F Gurry, *Breach of Confidence* (Oxford: Clarendon Press, 1984), 163–5.

[29]Jones, *ibid*, 482. Warren and Brandeis themselves suggest (pointing to the judgment of Lord Eldon in *Yovatt* v *Winyard* (1820) 1 Jac & W 394, 37 ER 425, in which he granted an injunction prohibiting the defendant's making any use of or communicating any recipes contained within, a book he had acquired surreptitiously while in the plaintiff's employ) that 'it would seem to be difficult to draw any sound legal distinction between such a case and one where a mere stranger wrongfully obtained access to the book' (note 5 above, 212).

[30](1732) cited in *Millar* v *Taylor* (1769) 4 Burr 2303, 2330, 98 ER 201, 216.

[31](1769) 4 Burr 2303, 2378, 98 ER 201, 241.

In both decisions, however, the court was concerned with copyright rather than confidence; it was the form in which the ideas were expressed rather than the ideas themselves (the major breach of confidence issue) which formed the basis for the granting of the injunction. Indeed, in *Millar* v *Taylor* Yates J declared 'Ideas are free. But while the author confines them to his study, they are like birds in a cage, which none but he can have a right to let fly: for, till he thinks proper to emancipate them, they are under his own dominion'.[32]

More recent breach of confidence cases lend slightly stronger support to the view that protection is not confined to consensual disclosures of confidential information. In *Lord Ashburton* v *Pape*,[33] a decision which involved a breach of confidence by a solicitor's clerk, the Court of Appeal referred to its power to enjoin the publication of information 'improperly or surreptitiously obtained'. More significantly, in *Franklin* v *Giddins*[34] the Supreme Court of Queensland allowed an action for breach of confidence where the defendant had, in the absence of any confidential relationship, stolen genetic information in the form of cuttings from the plaintiff's unique strain of cross-bred nectarines. Dunn J said:[35]

I find myself quite unable to accept that a thief who steals a trade secret, with the intention of using it in commercial competition with its owner, to the detriment of the latter, and so uses it, is less unconscionable than a traitorous servant.

A persuasive case in support of the contention that the eavesdropper may be held liable for a breach of confidence is, of course, *Francome* v *Mirror Group Newspapers Ltd*[36] where the Court of Appeal granted an injunction to restrain the defendants from using information that had been obtained (by parties unknown) through the use of radio-telephony. But it conflicts with the decision in *Malone* v *Commissioner of Police of the Metropolis (No. 2)*[37] in which Megarry V-C declined to make a declaration that telephone tapping by the police was a breach of the victim's right of confidentiality in the intercepted conversations. In his view, an individual who divulges confidential information cannot

---

[32] 4 Burr 2303, 2378–9, 98 ER 201, 242.
[33] [1913] 2 Ch 469, 475; cited with approval in *Commonwealth of Australia* v *John Fairfax & Sons Ltd* (1980) 147 CLR 39, 50 per Mason J.
[34] [1978] 1 QdR 72.
[35] *Ibid*, 80.
[36] [1984] 1 WLR 892.
[37] [1979] 1 Ch 344.

complain when someone within earshot overhears his conversation. In the case of telephone conversations:

> ... the speaker is taking such risks of being overheard as are inherent in the system.... In addition, so much publicity in recent years has been given to instances (real or fictional) of the deliberate tapping of telephones that it is difficult to envisage telephone users who are genuinely unaware of this possibility. No doubt a person who uses a telephone to give confidential information to another may do so in such a way as to impose an obligation of confidence on that other: but I do not see how it could be said that any such obligation is imposed on those who overhear the conversation, whether by means of tapping or otherwise.[38]

He was in no doubt that 'a person who utters confidential information must accept the risk of any unknown overhearing that is inherent in the circumstances of communication'.[39] Relying on this dictum, the defendants in *Francome* argued that the plaintiffs had no cause of action against them or the eavesdroppers for breach of an obligation of confidence. The Court of Appeal rejected this contention on the ground that in *Malone* the court was expressly concerned only with telephone tapping effected by the police for the prevention, detection and discovery of crime and criminals. Fox LJ distinguished the two forms of intrusion in the following terms:

> Illegal tapping by private persons is quite another matter since it must be questionable whether the user of a telephone can be regarded as accepting the risk of that in the same way as, for example, he accepts the risk that his conversation may be overheard in consequence of the accidents and imperfections of the telephone system itself.[40]

In other words a telephone user's 'reasonable expectation of privacy' may be vindicated when the eavesdropper turns out to be a private individual, but not when it is the police acting under lawful authority. It has been suggested that this judgment suffers from a 'fundamental misconception':

---

[38]*Ibid*, 376.
[39]*Ibid, loc cit.*
[40][1984] 1 WLR 892, 900.

... that because equity acts *in personam* it responds to some personal dealing between the parties so that the eavesdropper is in a quite different case to the confidant. But what the maxim indicates is that equity responds to unconscionable conduct by the defendant; this may but need not flow from any consensual dealing with the plaintiff. Accordingly, it requires no great effort, no straining of principle to restrain the activities of the eavesdropper.[41]

Nevertheless, to catch the eavesdropper, the Younger Committee considered legislation necessary:[42]

> We think that the damaging disclosure or other damaging use of information acquired by means of any unlawful act, with knowledge of how it was acquired, is an objectionable practice against which the law should afford protection. We recommend therefore that it should be a civil wrong, actionable at the suit of any person who has suffered damage thereby, to disclose or otherwise use information which the discloser knows, or in all the circumstances ought to have known, was obtained by illegal means. It would be necessary to provide defences to cover situations where the disclosure of the information was in the public interest or was made in privileged circumstances. We envisage that the kinds of remedy available for this civil wrong would be similar to those appropriate to an action for breach of confidence.

One difficulty with this approach is that the Younger Committee rejected the introduction of an action for unwanted publicity; the only remedies considered necessary in cases of 'public disclosure' were the action for breach of confidence, and the 'illegal means' tort which would assist the plaintiff only where the information was acquired *unlawfully*. This means that where, say, a journalist obtains personal information *lawfully*, the plaintiff may well have no remedy. But should *unlawful* means be employed, an action may lie, subject to the proposed defence of 'public interest'. In other words, in the view of the Younger Committee, the only circumstances in which a civil action should lie where there has been disclosure of personal information are where the means used to obtain the information are unlawful. And this confuses the interests in issue in 'intrusion' with those that arise in 'disclosure'; the availability of remedy for *disclosure* is made dependant on whether

---

[41]Meagher *et al* (note 28 above), 871-2. See my attempt to justify this distinction in Wacks, *Personal Information* (Chapter 1 note 1 above), 256–9.
[42]Committee on Privacy (note 28 above), para 632.

there had been an *intrusion*. This factor ought *not* to be of primary importance in cases of disclosure. Equally, unlawful means ought not to be permitted merely because the eventual disclosure is justified. The two questions should be kept separate.

A further difficulty arises in respect of personal information. If liability for the use or disclosure of information is made to turn on the method of its acquisition it follows that the *nature or quality* of the information ceases to be a qualifying factor. Thus, in recommending the creation of a criminal offence in respect of the improper obtaining of information, the law reformer is explicitly concerned with the *means* employed to obtain the information, rather than the information itself or its use or disclosure. But in its proposal that an obligation of confidence should arise in respect of information acquired in certain improper circumstances, the Law Commission[43] necessarily addresses itself to defining those circumstances. The information in issue would, presumably, need to have the necessary quality of confidence in order to be protected in the first place. The Commission points out[44] that 'information' is used here (as elsewhere in the report) to mean 'information which is not in the public domain'.[45]

The Law Commission recognises that there is an important distinction between the imposition of an obligation of confidence in the normal case, and in the case of improper acquisition, when it states:[46]

> There is undoubtedly a considerable difference in nature between on the one hand the obligation imposed on a person for breaking an undertaking to another to keep information confidential and, on the other, an obligation imposed on a person as a result of his having used improper means to gain information which may, indeed, be so secret that the plaintiff has never entrusted it to anyone, not even in confidence. Nevertheless, we believe that it is possible to encompass both forms of behaviour within the framework of our new statutory tort.

It concludes that the common feature in both cases is that the receiver of information is in a position where it is *reasonable* to impose a duty of

[43]*Breach of Confidence* (note 2 above), paras 6.28–46.
[44]*Ibid*, para 6.46, n 635.
[45]In its report the Scottish Law Commission suggests that in this context the obligation of confidence should not 'depend on a test such as the nature of the information: it should extend to any information so obtained, however trivial it might seem to an outsider' (*Breach of Confidence*, Cmnd 9385, 1984, para 4.38).
[46]*Breach of Confidence* (note 2 above), para 6.30.

confidence upon him. It therefore proposes a number of situations[47] in which the acquirer of information should, by virtue of the manner in which he has acquired it, be treated as being subject to an obligation of confidence:

(a) by unauthorised taking, handling, or interfering with anything containing the information;

(b) by unauthorised taking, handling, or interfering with anything in which the matter containing the information is for the time being kept;

(c) by unauthorised use of or interference with a computer or similar device in which data are stored;

(d) by violence, menace, or deception;

(e) while he is in a place where he has no authority to be;

(f) by a device made or adapted solely or primarily for the purpose of surreptitious surveillance where the user would not without its use have obtained the information;

(g) by any other device (excluding spectacles and hearing-aids) where he would not, without using it, have obtained the information, provided that the person from whom the information is obtained was not or ought not reasonably to have been aware of the use of the device and ought not reasonably to have taken precautions to prevent the information being so acquired.

This approach is potentially restrictive: by prescribing a catalogue of specific forms of conduct there is a danger, especially in an area which is constantly undergoing technological change, of new methods of intrusion developing which call for legislative adaptation. A preferable analysis (suggested by the Scottish Law Commission)[48] is to refer in a general manner to the acquisition by illegal means or by means which would be regarded as improper by a reasonable person. This has the advantage of anticipating advances in electronic surveillance technology. The English Law Commission would impose automatic liability 'without qualification'[49] for the use of confidential information upon a person who obtains such information with the assistance of a device which is 'clearly designed or adapted solely or primarily for the

---

[47]*Ibid*, para 6.46.
[48]Scottish Law Commission (note 45 above), paras 4.36–41.
[49]*Breach of Confidence* (note 2 above), para 6.35.

surreptitious surveillance of persons, their activities, communications or property'.[50]

The Law Commission draws a distinction between such devices and those, such as binoculars or tape recorders, which are not in themselves designed primarily for that purpose, although they are capable of being so used. In the case of the latter, liability for the subsequent use or disclosure of the information should arise only if the subject was not or ought not reasonably to have been aware of the use of the device and failed to take precautions to prevent its acquisition.[51] This would seem to be a sensible distinction, though it is unclear what is to be understood by the Law Commission's following observation:

> It might be argued that the use of any form of surveillance device, whether or not designed primarily for that purpose, should be wrongful. However, to give a remedy merely because information is acquired by one of these means would amount to the creation of a right of privacy — a right, for example, not to be photographed even if the photographs were later never published.[52]

But, since the Law Commission is here concerned only with the *use or disclosure* of confidential information acquired by improper means, this would not be the case. And even the point that to allow a remedy where, say, an ostensibly innocuous device were used for spying, e.g., binoculars, would be tantamount to recognition of a 'right of privacy', seems to be misconceived for that would be true (in this context) whatever device, even if none at all, were used.

The Scottish Law Commission would impose an automatic obligation on a person not to use or disclose *any* information acquired by improper means 'however trivial it might seem to an outsider'.[53] The obligation is therefore not dependent on the nature of the information acquired; it is not restricted (though, in practice, will normally relate) to confidential information. While consistent with the general concern to prevent intrusive activities (and not merely their consequences), this proposal again demonstrates the different objectives of the control of *intrusion*, on the one hand, and the protection against the *misuse* of personal information, on the other. The former extends beyond (but may accommodate) the present concern with confidential information and,

---

[50]*Ibid, loc cit.*
[51]*Ibid*, para 6.38.
[52]*Ibid*, para 6.36.
[53]Scottish Law Commission (note 45 above), para 4.38.

a fortiori, personal information, and is, of course, in any event, more satisfactorily dealt with by the criminal law or by administrative control. The present statutory controls[54] are extremely limited in scope and there have been several attempts to introduce more explicit legislation.[55]

Thus, several decisions discussed in Chapter 3, involve not information being imparted in confidence by A to B, but B's 'surreptitiously taking' the information without A's knowledge.[56] I argued there that no obligation of confidence should be imposed upon a 'surreptitious taker' by virtue only that he used illicit means to obtain the information. Liability should always rest upon general principles of unconscionability; the fact that improper means were necessary to acquire the information is a persuasive factor in determining whether the defendant had constructive knowledge, but is not an inexorable rule of law.

To what extent, if at all, is the fact of intrusion punished by the action for breach of confidence? As in the American jurisprudence, the English case law manifests a tendency to confuse intrusion and disclosure. In *Malone*, the plaintiff's telephone had been tapped by the Post Office under a warrant signed by the Secretary of State; Malone being under suspicion of handling stolen goods. In the course of his judgment, Megarry V-C, having adverted to Lord Denning's 'just cause or excuse' formulation for the public interest defence,[57] remarked that 'The question is ... whether there is just cause or excuse for the tapping and

---

[54]In particular, the Wireless Telegraphy Act 1949. Section 1(1) prohibits the unlicensed installation or use of any apparatus for wireless telegraphy, defined in s. 19(1) as 'the emitting or receiving, over paths which are not provided by any material substance constructed or arranged for that purpose, of electromagnetic energy'. It was argued in *Francome v Mirror Group Newspapers Ltd* [1984] 1 WLR 892, that the Act does not give rise to a right enforceable by a private individual, an argument which Donaldson MR was not called upon at the interlocutory stage to decide, though he did comment: 'Suffice it to say that I am far from sure that the plaintiffs do not have rights under the Act of 1949, if they have suffered damage by breach of the Act which is special to them: see *Gouriet v Union of Post Office Workers* [1978] AC 435' (*ibid*, 897). Cf *McCall v Abelesz* [1976] 1 QB 585. Under s. 7 of the Wireless Telegraphy Act 1967 the Secretary of State is vested with power to make orders forbidding the manufacture and importation of wireless telegraphy apparatus in order to prevent or reduce the risk of interference with wireless telegraphy. However, the purpose of orders under this section is to stop the manufacture of radio-telephonic equipment which uses those frequencies employed by many VHF receivers.
[55]In particular, the Unauthorised Telephone Monitoring Bill, 741 *Hansard*, HC, cols 1051–5 (20 Feb 1967); the Industrial Information Bill, 775 *Hansard*, HC, cols 802–28 (13 Dec 1968); the Private Investigators Bill, 782 *Hansard*, HC, cols 1443–6 (30 Apr 1969); and the Control of Interception Bill, 1161 *Hansard*, HC, cols 474–9 (20 Feb 1980).
[56]Namely, *Franklin v Giddins* [1978] 1 QdR 72; *Malone v Commissioner of Police for the Metropolis (No. 2)* [1979] 1 Ch 344; and, *Francome v Mirror Group Newspapers Ltd* [1984] 1 WLR 892.
[57]See *Fraser v Evans* [1969] 1 QB 349, 362.

for the use made of the material obtained by the tapping'.[58] This is to confuse the two issues.

Consider A who, acting upon the suspicion that B has been doing something that the public would like to know about, taps B's telephone and, after having collected the information, threatens to disclose it to the press. The proper enquiry should be: Was A justified in tapping B's telephone? This depends *inter alia* upon who A is, what B is suspected of doing, and what methods A used to acquire the information. The courts should not look to the eventual outcome of the tapping, nor should they apply the 'just cause or excuse' test, to resolve the issue of intrusion. The 'just cause or excuse' formulation ought to be reserved for the second element of the enquiry which considers what *use* may be made of the acquired information.

Hill[59] suggests that the criminality of the plaintiff's behaviour may be an important consideration in assessing the reasonableness of the intrusive activity, but it is difficult to follow the logic of this reasoning unless one accepts that it is right to create a civilian police force with the power to search, snoop and seize in the hope of discovering information which would, if published, be protected in the 'public interest'.

Megarry V-C's question (when may a person's telephone be tapped by the police acting in the course of their duty to prevent crime?) should therefore be asked separately of intrusion and disclosure. Where he holds that '. . . there should be grounds for suspecting that the tapping of the particular telephone will be of material assistance in detecting or preventing crime',[60] he should be understood as referring to *intrusion*. His statements that '. . . no use should be made of any material obtained except for [the purposes of crime prevention or detection]' and '. . . any knowledge or information which is not relevant to those purposes should be confined to the minimum number of persons reasonably required to carry out the process of tapping'[61] should be applied exclusively to *disclosure*.

As will be recalled, in *Francome* the Court of Appeal upheld the granting of an interlocutory injunction to prevent the defendants from disclosing information concerning the jockey Peter Francome which had been obtained by telephone tapping. An important distinction

---

[58][1979] 1 Ch 344, 377.
[59]Hill (note 3 above), 1283. On a more general level, Hill remarks that 'in the light of the public interest, it may be determined that the investigatory activity of reporters and photographers was not tortiously intrusive in the first instance' (*ibid*, 1284).
[60][1979] 1 Ch 344, 377.
[61]*Ibid, loc cit.*

between this decision and *Malone* is that in the latter the defendant was both the intruder and the potential discloser, whilst in *Francome* the intruders were not party to the proceedings. Thus, maintaining the rigid and logical distinction suggested above, the only pertinent question here is whether the *Daily Mirror* received the information subject to an obligation not to disclose it to others. Again, the fact of the tapping does figure in this assessment, but only in so far as it might determine what reasonably constitutes unconscionable behaviour.

The analysis of Donaldson MR is in this respect correct. That he realised that intrusion was not in issue is clear from his comment that the question at trial 'is likely to be whether the defendants can make any, and if so what, use of the fruits of [the illegal tapping]'.[62]

Whether the English courts would compensate a plaintiff for intrusive news-gathering, over and above the compensation for breach of confidence in disclosing the information without just cause or excuse, is hard to say. No decided case has involved such facts. What do the law reformers propose?

Reforming the law

As mentioned in Chapter 3, in its report, the Law Commission advocates the creation of a statutory tort of breach of confidence. Having concluded that, under the existing principles of the equitable action for breach of confidence,[63] a plaintiff has no protection where information is surreptitiously taken from him (as opposed to his having imparted it to another in circumstances imposing an obligation of confidentiality[64]), the Commission proposed that if information were so acquired, the 'surreptitious taker' and any person obtaining the information from him, with knowledge, would be under an obligation of confidence by virtue solely of that surreptitious taking.[65]

This approach conflates disclosure and intrusion; the fact of intrusion is the basis upon which disclosure is to be prevented or compensated. And the Law Commission proposes no separate sanctions against

---

[62][1984] 1 WLR 892, 895.
[63]See *Saltman Engineering Co. Ltd* v *Campbell Engineering Co. Ltd* (1948) 65 RPC 203.
[64]In *Breach of Confidence* (note 2 above), para 5.5, the Commission states: 'It is a glaring inadequacy of the present law that ... the confidentiality of information improperly obtained, rather than confidentially entrusted by one person to another, may be unprotected'. The reasoning by which the Commission reaches this conclusion is set out in paras 4.7–4.10.
[65]This proposal is embodied in clause 5 of the draft Bill (*ibid*, app A).

intrusion itself.[66] In clause 14(1)(b) of its draft Bill, the Commission defines recoverable damages to include those in respect of 'any mental distress, and any mental or physical harm resulting from such distress' in consequence of the defendant's breach of confidence. This explicit restriction of those damages to distress suffered in consequence of the breach[67] suggests that, along with the narrowness of the Commission's terms of reference mentioned above, it is highly unlikely that the Commission contemplated an enhancement of these damages by virtue of additional distress caused by the intrusion.[68]

What of the situation in which A discovers certain information about B by intrusion, and then passes it to C, who takes it with knowledge of that intrusion? Is C liable for the intrusion as well as for any subsequent publication? In clause 5(5) of the draft Bill the Commission directly addresses the *Pearson* scenario; that the discloser is not the intruder but has knowledge of the intrusion. In such circumstances, the clause would impose an obligation of confidence upon the (potential) discloser. But what is not clear is whether the discloser is liable for the *intrusion*.

It must be recalled that the Commission was discussing the circumstances in which an obligation of confidence would be imposed. Clause 5 is necessary to perform the 'constructive knowledge' function which, in the common law, is effected by reference to what is reasonable. It is not directed to the third party recipient's responsibility for the intrusion through which, indirectly, he acquired the information.

The Law Commission proposed no sanctions for the act of intrusion *per se*, preferring, as is logically consistent with its terms of reference, to use the intrusion as a springboard from which to attach an obligation of confidence to prevent or compensate disclosure.

In its report, the Calcutt Committee[69] recommended that three forms of physical intrusion should be criminal offences, namely:

(a) Entering private property, without the consent of the lawful occupant, with intent to obtain personal information with a view to its publication.

---

[66]Though this may be readily explained having regard to the terms of reference of the Commission's enquiry. The relevant term asks the Commission to: 'consider and advise what remedies, if any, should be provided ... for persons who have suffered loss or damage *in consequence of the disclosure or use of information unlawfully obtained* and in what circumstances such remedies should be available' (*ibid*, para 1.1, emphasis added).
[67]Clause 14 of the draft Bill (*ibid*, app A).
[68]This view is supported by para 6.106, *ibid*, where the Commission confines its analysis to 'mental distress ... suffered as a result of the *disclosure*' (emphasis added).
[69]Committee on Privacy and Related Matters (note 2 above).

(b)   Placing a surveillance device on private property, without the consent of the lawful occupant, with intent to obtain personal information with a view to its publication.

(c)   Taking a photograph, or recording the voice, of an individual who is on private property, without his consent, with a view to its publication with intent that the individual shall be identifiable.[70]

It proposed a public interest type defence to these offences.[71]

Just as the Law Commission concentrates exclusively on disclosure, so the Calcutt Committee directs its legislative recommendations at intrusion, leaving disclosure to the regulation of a newly formed Press Complaints Commission.[72] The prospect of confusion between the two issues is thus obviated.

But is a public interest type defence appropriate to intrusion? What of the question of the reasonableness of the intrusion?

In the one instance where the Calcutt Committee does make a recommendation pertaining to disclosure, it addresses directly the subject of what use may be made of information acquired by intrusion. This, like the approach of the Law Commission, represents a confusion between the two acts: the fact of intrusion leads to a remedy to prevent disclosure. A statutory right of action is granted to 'anyone having a sufficient interest' to prevent disclosure, by way of injunction, or to be compensated for its occurrence, by way of damages or an account of profits.[73] What is not made clear is whether the right of action applies when A obtains the information and passes it to B for publication; A not being an employee of the disclosing newspaper. It ought to apply, though, once more, in this *Pearson* scenario, the Committee is silent as to whether the damages would be enhanced by the fact of intrusion. Again, intrusion is being conflated with disclosure.

The National Heritage Select Committee[74] recommends the introduction of a Protection of Privacy Bill, one part of which concerns what the

---

[70]*Ibid*, para 6.33.

[71]*Ibid*, para 6.35. The defences are: '(a) for the purpose of preventing, detecting or exposing the commission of any crime, or other seriously antisocial conduct; or (b) for the protection of public health or safety; or (c) under any lawful authority'. This approach was again proposed (with minor alterations) by Calcutt in his *Review* (note 2 above), paras 7.1–7.26.

[72]Committee on Privacy and Related Matters (note 2 above), paras 15.1–15.31. This is subject to one exception, which is discussed below.

[73]*Ibid*, para 6.38. In the preceding paragraph, the Committee rejected a criminal offence for publication of personal information obtained through intrusion. It was 'wary of creating an offence of publishing material in a newspaper where the point at issue would be how it was obtained rather than the content'.

[74]National Heritage Select Committee (note 2 above).

Committee calls 'the main civil offence', namely infringement of privacy[75] and it is clear from the definition of that offence that liability attaches to both 'obtaining and/or publishing' personal information.[76] Here, intrusion and disclosure are entirely separate, each, independently, giving rise to a cause of action.

But, again, it is to be regretted that a public interest defence is proposed to apply both to acts of publication and to the *obtaining* of the personal information.[77] The Bill includes provisions along the lines of the Calcutt *Report* for the introduction of criminal sanctions against certain intrusive techniques.[78]

Conclusion

The law should provide separate and distinct causes of action for both intrusion and disclosure. That is to say, even if both are subsumed within an actionable right to privacy, the intrusive activity by which the information is obtained must be treated distinctly from its subsequent disclosure and independent relief should be provided for both, or either, as the case may be.

Against intruder who is not discloser; information not in public interest

The question here is should the plaintiff be compensated for the intrusion *simpliciter* or for the intrusion and the subsequent publication of the personal information obtained thereby, by way of *Dietemann* 'enhanced damages'? The National Heritage Select Committee's Bill makes the intruder liable for infringement of the plaintiff's 'privacy' right, but the report omits to mention whether the damages should be increased if publication does ensue. The better view is not to award enhanced damages against the intruder, because in such cases the plaintiff will invariably be able to proceed against the publisher in what should be a combined action against both intruder and discloser. Accordingly, the plaintiff will recover for both the intrusion and the publication.

---

[75] *Ibid*, para 48.
[76] *Ibid, loc cit*.
[77] *Ibid, loc cit*, and see para 55.
[78] *Ibid*, para 52. See the discussion of these sanctions above.

Against intruder who is not discloser; information in public interest

The public interest test should not apply to acts of intrusion. The theoretical underpinnings of the principle of freedom of expression which justify the defence in respect of disclosure, do not apply with equal force to intrusion. Instead the test should be one of reasonableness. Thus, the intruder's liability for the intrusion would be unrelated to the nature of the information. If the intrusive activities were in themselves unreasonable, the intruder would be liable to compensate the plaintiff but only for the damage caused directly by the intrusion, physical and emotional. As in the first situation above, the intruder should not be required to compensate the plaintiff for the subsequent act of publication.

Against intruder who is discloser; information not in public interest

The defendant is liable for his acts of intrusion and disclosure. The law should be careful not to fuse the issues in respect of damages. The plaintiff should not recover less than he would have done in an action against an intruder and a separate discloser (as in the first situation above).

Against intruder who is discloser; information in public interest

The defendant remains liable for his acts of intrusion notwithstanding the protection afforded to the publication by the public interest test, unless those acts are reasonable in themselves (that is, without reference to the nature of the information thereby obtained).

6

Remedies

This Chapter considers the principal common law remedies available to a plaintiff who complains that personal information has been obtained by intrusive means or that such information (whether obtained by intrusion or otherwise) has been published without his consent.

Trespass and nuisance

Damages

The tort of trespass to land normally compensates the plaintiff for a 'temporary loss of use of his land'.[1] Where, in pursuit of personal information, an intrusive journalist or photographer trespasses on my land, however, it is hard to establish such loss. An alternative basis of relief is thus required. One possibility is 'loss of reputation'. In *McCarey* v *Associated Newspapers Ltd (No. 2)*,[2] Diplock LJ held that 'loss of reputation' comprised not only the non-pecuniary loss itself, but also the pecuniary loss flowing therefrom.[3] But the act of trespass is unlikely

---

[1] A S Burrows, *Remedies for Torts and Breach of Contract*, 2nd ed (London: Butterworths, 1994), 169. An indication of the limitations of both trespass and nuisance as remedies for an alleged 'invasion of privacy' may be found in *Bernstein of Leigh (Baron)* v *Skyviews & General Ltd* [1978] QB 479. See R Wacks, 'No Castles in the Air' (1977) 93 LQR 491.
[2] [1965] 2 QB 86.
[3] *Ibid*, 108. This was a libel action, but damages for loss of reputation have also been recovered for false imprisonment (*Childs* v *Lewis* (1924) 40 TLR 870), malicious prosecution (*Savile* v *Roberts* (1699) 1 Ld Raym 374, 91 ER 1147), and where goods infringing the plaintiff's intellectual property rights are so inferior to the plaintiff's product that they devalue his reputation (*A G Spalding & Bros* v *A W Gamage Ltd* (1918) 35 RPC 101). However, it is necessary to distinguish between recovery for pecuniary loss consequent upon loss of reputation and recovery for the loss of reputation itself; the latter is, for certain torts, irrecoverable. See, Burrows (note 1 above), 226.

to be the cause of loss of the plaintiff's reputation. It is the act of publication of the information which has the potential to lower his standing in the eyes of the public. Moreover, the complaint is likely to be that the facts disclosed (which are probably true) offend 'privacy' rather than reputation, though the two are, as has been seen, sometimes closely related. Hence Gorden Kaye was unable to show that he had suffered such loss by virtue merely of the public seeing pictures of him convalescing in hospital after a serious operation.[4]

A more effective tortious remedy to compensate a plaintiff for intrusion is damages for mental distress, 'for example, disappointment, worry, anxiety, fear, upset, grief and annoyance'.[5] Such damages have been awarded for distress caused by false imprisonment,[6] nuisance,[7] and also for trespass to goods.[8] And there seems to be no reason why damages under this head may not also be recovered for trespass to land. However, once more, it is important to separate the mental distress caused by the intrusion from that caused by the publication of the personal information so gathered. A trespasser will be liable only for distress caused by the former because, to put it crudely, there is no tort of publication of true facts.

Moreover, it is also questionable whether the plaintiff's fear of subsequent publication of the information obtained by the intrusion may be taken into account in the assessment of damages for mental distress. Where the plaintiff seeks compensation for trespass, he faces the obstacle that the tort is not directly referable to the acquisition of personal information. His only complaint in law is that 'somebody was on my land', restricting the award to his anxieties and fears *directly* stemming therefrom. Damages in tort will do little to assuage his real grievance: the unsolicited publicity accorded to his private life.

Injunction

A plaintiff may, under s. 49 of the Supreme Court Act 1981, combine a claim for common law damages with a prayer to the court for the

[4]*Kaye v Robertson* [1991] FSR 62. See Chapter 1. Though it is interesting to note that both Glidewell (*ibid*, 66–7) and Bingham LJJ (*ibid*, 70) considered that Mr Kaye had a strong *prima facie* case in defamation on the authority of *Tolley v J S Fry and Sons Ltd* [1931] AC 333. This could not afford the plaintiff interlocutory relief on the basis of the principle that injunctions are to be used sparingly in libel actions.
[5]Burrows (note 1 above), 231.
[6]*Walter v Alltools Ltd* (1944) 61 TLR 39.
[7]*Bone v Seale* [1975] 1 WLR 797.
[8]*Owen and Smith v Reo Motors (Britain) Ltd* (1934) 151 LT 274.

exercise of its equitable discretion to award an injunction. Can the plaintiff, who complains that journalists have acquired personal information by intrusive means with intent to publish it, obtain an injunction in such terms as to prevent, in effect, the information being disclosed?

Once reporters have acquired information, retaining it, be it a photograph or a tape recording of a conversation, is not a tort.[9] Prescott argues that the court has an inherent jurisdiction 'to prevent wrongdoers retaining the fruits of their wrongdoing, even though the act of retention as such gives rise to no cause of action and the plaintiff has no right to the thing retained'.[10] He regards such an action to be an implicit part of the court's duty to 'give the plaintiff adequate relief in respect of a cause of action otherwise arising'.[11] Thus he suggests the court could, in respect of reporters who possess personal information about the plaintiff obtained by trespassing upon his property, order the delivery up of the information for destruction or enjoin them from publishing it by permanent injunction.[12]

But can the court restrain journalists from publishing the information (or passing it on to others for them to publish)? Section 37(1) of the Supreme Court Act 1981 empowers the granting of an injunction 'in all cases in which it appears to the court to be just and convenient to do so'. Despite the sweeping ambit of this provision, it is clear that a plaintiff cannot invoke the section without a cause of action.[13] In other words, an injunction may only issue to protect a right that is known to law or equity.[14] Prescott refers to *Chappell & Co. Ltd* v *Columbia Graphophone Co.*[15] in which the plaintiff's sheet music was copied by the defendant in breach of copyright and used by studio musicians to recreate the pieces which were recorded on graphophone discs. Even though the second phase of the defendant's activities — recording the studio musicians — infringed none of the plaintiff's rights, the Court of Appeal

---

[9]P Prescott, '*Kaye* v *Robertson* — A Reply' (1991) 54 MLR 451, 452. Moreover, as noted above, the acquisition of the information is not a tort save to the extent that the reporters trespass upon the plaintiff's land.

[10]*Ibid, loc cit.*

[11]*Ibid,* 453.

[12]*Ibid, loc cit.*

[13]*Ainsbury* v *Millington* [1986] 1 All ER 73. See, generally, H Hanbury and J E Martin, *Modern Equity,* 14th ed (London: Sweet & Maxwell, 1993), ch 24; Burrows (note 1 above), ch 9; and I C F Spry, *The Principles of Equitable Remedies,* 4th ed (London: Sweet & Maxwell, 1990), ch 4.

[14]*Siskina (Cargo Owners)* v *Distos Compañía Naviera SA* [1979] AC 210, 254 per Lord Diplock. And note the recent acceptance of this position, despite the wording of s. 37(1) of the Supreme Court Act 1981, in *Khorasandjian* v *Bush* [1993] QB 727, 732 per Dillon LJ.

[15][1914] 2 Ch 745.

ordered the delivery up of the graphophone records for destruction. Prescott[16] cites Swinfen Eady LJ who said:

> The order for delivery up for destruction is not based upon any notion that the property has passed to the plaintiffs. Whether the property has passed to the plaintiffs or not, the articles may be ordered to be delivered up for destruction, because they are articles manufactured in violation of the plaintiffs' rights, and there is general jurisdiction in the court to order such articles to be destroyed.[17]

Prescott refers also to *Crossley* v *Derby Gas Co.*,[18] where it was held that the Court of Chancery had the power to restrain the selling of articles infringing an expired patent if they were produced during the currency of the patent.

These decisions, however, are not authority for the proposition that the court can restrain an intruder from using the fruits of his intrusion and/or order the delivery up of any materials which embody the personal information obtained during the trespass. They involve intellectual property rights in respect of which the court, in the exercise of its equitable discretion, may well enjoin a defendant from 'profiting from the fruits of his wrongdoing' because those profits are a *natural and logical consequence* of the original infringement. In *Chappell* no other conclusion could have been reached than that for every sale of the graphophone records, which could not have been manufactured but for the copyright infringement, the defendant reaped a reward directly flowing from the abuse of the plaintiff's proprietary rights. In the case of trespass to land, therefore, the court may protect only the plaintiff's *rights over his land*. Otherwise the court would be bestowing on the plaintiff property in the personal information acquired by the intruder.

In respect of an order for delivery up, the court may grant such relief under the provisions of the Torts (Interference with Goods) Act 1977 or by virtue of its equitable jurisdiction. The Act does not apply where there has been a trespass to land because the plaintiff has no proprietary rights over any photographs or notes taken by the intruder.[19] As to the

---

[16]Prescott (note 9 above), 452.
[17][1914] 2 Ch 745, 756.
[18](1834) 4 LJ Ch 25.
[19]Torts (Interference with Goods) Act 1977, s. 3(2)(a) and (b). In the words of the Law Commission, 'the latter is concerned with "goods", defined as including "all chattels personal other than things in action and money"', in which, broadly speaking, the plaintiff had an interest prior to the "wrongful interference" of which he complains' (Law Commission, *Breach of Confidence*, Cmnd 8388, 1981, para 4.103).

latter equitable jurisdiction, it would appear to be restricted to the infringement of intellectual property rights including, *inter alia*, a breach of the equitable obligation of confidence.[20]

The whole basis of the exercise of the court's discretion is that it is a further remedy to protect the plaintiff from a feared future breach of his rights.[21] This explains the cases cited by Prescott. The respective remedies were granted to address the likelihood of prospective loss to be suffered by the plaintiff resulting from the original infringement. They do not extend to an independent, extra-legal right. This interpretation of cases such as *Chappell* emerges from the following dictum of Lord Cozens-Hardy MR in that decision:

> As to the form of the judgment, I think the authorities which have been cited justify us in saying that this is a case in which things have been produced *by the use of the infringing copy*, and it is a case in which it is right to hand over those, including the matrix and the records which have been made, for destruction.[22]

Breach of confidence

Damages[23]

The scope of Lord Cairns's Act,[24] as re-enacted by s. 50 of the Supreme Court Act 1981,[25] must be assessed against the background of the Supreme Court of Judicature Acts 1873 and 1875, which did not fuse the substantive rules of law and equity[26] but removed the barriers in the

---

[20]See Burrows (note 1 above), 458.

[21]See *Breach of Confidence* (note 19 above), para 4.102.

[22][1914] 2 Ch 745, 752 (emphasis added).

[23]See D Capper, 'Damages for Breach of the Equitable Duty of Confidence' (1994) 14 LS 313. And, generally, Burrows (note 1 above), 242–7; Spry (note 13 above), ch 7; and F Gurry, *Breach of Confidence* (Oxford: Clarendon Press, 1984), ch 23.

[24]Chancery Amendment Act 1858, s. 2.

[25]This section provides, 'Where the Court of Appeal or the High Court has jurisdiction to entertain an application for an injunction or specific performance, it may award damages in addition to, or in substitution for, an injunction or specific performance'.

[26]Note Lord Diplock's dictum in *United Scientific Holdings Ltd* v *Burnley Borough Council* [1978] AC 904, where he remarked: 'to perpetuate a dichotomy between rules of equity and rules of common law which it was a major purpose of the Supreme Court of Judicature Act 1873 to do away with, is, in my view, conducive to erroneous conclusions as to the ways in which the law of England has developed in the last hundred years' (*ibid*, 924). This has been characterised as 'a fundamental error as to the purpose of the Judicature Acts' (Capper (note 23 above), 316).

administration of those rules.[27] Accordingly, to ascertain the existence, or otherwise, of a jurisdiction of the court to award damages in equity, it is necessary to determine whether the old Court of Chancery enjoyed these powers prior to the Judicature Acts.

It is unlikely that the Court of Chancery has an inherent jurisdiction to award damages for the infringement of a purely equitable right.[28] Lord Cairns's Act provides therefore the only possible source of a jurisdiction to award damages in these circumstances. The Act almost certainly conferred jurisdiction upon the Court of Chancery to award damages in addition to, or in substitution for, the granting of other equitable relief (such as an injunction).[29] Consequently, after the Judicature Acts directed that the rules of equity could be administered in a court of law, where an action for breach of confidence is before a court, damages may be awarded if the court could, in the exercise of its equitable discretion, grant some other relief.

What is to be understood by the words 'where [the court] has jurisdiction to entertain an application for an injunction'?[30] The answer is crucial in determining the efficacy or otherwise of the action for breach of confidence in certain circumstances.[31] One view is that damages may be awarded only in circumstances where the court could grant an injunction *de facto*, i.e., the procedural rules which have been developed to control the use of the injunction have been satisfied. The alternative position is that Lord Cairns's Act applies whenever the court may issue an injunction *de iure*. According to Spry, '... the statutory power of awarding damages subsists whenever at the material time ... the right in question is susceptible of protection by injunction, *whether or not relief might be refused on a discretionary ground*'.[32] Thus, it is essential to differentiate between matters that go to the court's jurisdiction to award equitable relief and those which merely influence its discretion.

In an action for breach of confidence the significance of this distinction is most evident where the defendant has derived little profit from the dissemination of the information obtained from the plaintiff

---

[27] See Capper, *ibid*, 316.

[28] P M McDermott, 'Jurisdiction of the Court of Chancery to Award Damages' (1992) 108 LQR 652. Capper agrees with this conclusion (*ibid*, 318). The theory that damages could be awarded by the Court of Chancery was effectively exploded by Lord Eldon in *Todd* v *Gee* (1810) 17 Ves Jun 273, 279, 34 ER 106, 108, when he remarked: 'The plaintiff must take that remedy, if he chooses it, at law: generally, I do not say universally, he cannot have it in equity'. Cf Spry (note 13 above), 607–10.

[29] See Gurry (note 23 above), 429.

[30] Supreme Court Act 1981, s. 50.

[31] See Capper (note 23 above), 314.

[32] Spry (note 13 above), 611 (emphasis added).

and there is no likelihood of further breaches by the defendant. In this scenario, the remedy of an account of profits is unhelpful because it yields little profit. Moreover, if the view is adopted that the court is deprived of its jurisdiction to grant damages in lieu of an injunction because there is 'nothing to injunct the defendant against', then the plaintiff is left without a remedy.[33] The remarks of Megarry V-C in *Malone* v *Commissioner of Police for the Metropolis (No. 2)*[34] may be taken as support for this view:

> [The right of confidentiality] is an equitable right which is still in course of development, and is usually protected by the grant of an injunction to prevent disclosure of the confidence. Under Lord Cairns's Act 1858 damages may be granted in substitution for an injunction; yet if there is no case for the grant of an injunction, as when the disclosure has already been made, the unsatisfactory result seems to be that no damages can be awarded under this head. . . . In such a case, where there is no breach of contract or other orthodox foundation for damages at common law, it seems doubtful whether there is any right to damages, as distinct from an account of profits.[35]

The better view is that Lord Cairns's Act *would* apply in such circumstances. First, the plaintiff is rarely unlikely to convince the court that there is *some* likelihood of a repetition of the breach by the defendant. This ought to suffice to bring the matter within the ambit of the Act. In *Hooper* v *Rogers*,[36] Russell LJ noted that to award damages in lieu of an injunction it was enough that equitable relief could be granted, 'however unwisely'.[37] Again, recourse should be had to s. 37(1) of the Supreme Court Act 1981[38] and the court's wide discretion to grant an injunction when it is 'just and convenient' to do so. In addition, as Capper argues, decisions like *Malone* may not represent the modern judicial approach.[39] A more flexible attitude is illustrated by *Race Relations Board* v *Applin*[40] where the court awarded a declaration instead of an injunction because almost two years had passed since the

---

[33]Capper (note 23 above), 314. See *Proctor* v *Bayley* (1889) 42 ChD 390.
[34][1979] 1 Ch 344.
[35]*Ibid*, 360. See Capper (note 23 above), 314.
[36][1975] 1 Ch 43.
[37]*Ibid*, 48.
[38]See note 13 above.
[39]Capper (note 23 above), 320–21. He points out that the remarks in *Malone* concerning the jurisdiction of the court to award damages in lieu of an injunction were *obiter*.
[40][1973] 1 QB 815.

defendant's last infringement of the plaintiff's rights. However, as Capper notes,[41] Lord Denning MR, in a majority judgment of the Court of Appeal, seemed to consider that jurisdiction to grant an injunction still existed.[42] Gurry claims that '... the court has a power of choice between the grant of an injunction and the award of damages *whenever the plaintiff has established the breach of an equitable obligation of confidence'.*[43]

To summarise:

(a) The weight of academic opinion denies the existence of an inherent jurisdiction to grant damages for the infringement of a purely equitable right.[44] Accordingly, any damages awarded must be by virtue of Lord Cairns's Act.

(b) Damages may be awarded under this provision in any situation where the court has jurisdiction to grant, *inter alia,* an injunction irrespective of whether it would decline to do so in the exercise of its discretion. Damages have been awarded under this head in breach of confidence actions.[45]

(c) Under Lord Cairns's Act, the plaintiff may recover damages both in substitution for, *and* in addition to, injunctive relief.[46]

A further difficulty concerns whether equitable damages may be awarded to compensate the plaintiff for both prospective *and* retrospective loss. Gurry thinks they may.[47] He refers to *Saltman Engineering Co. Ltd v Campbell Engineering Co. Ltd*[48] where the Court of Appeal

[41]Capper (note 23 above), 321.
[42][1973] 1 QB 815, 829.
[43]Gurry (note 23 above), 437 (emphasis added). See too J A Jolowicz, 'Damages in Equity — A Study of Lord Cairns's Act' [1975] CLJ 224.
[44]Cf Spry (note 13 above), 608–10 (citing *Phelps v Protheroe* (1855) 7 De G M & G 722, 44 ER 280).
[45]*Saltman Engineering Co. Ltd v Campbell Engineering Co. Ltd* (1948) 65 RPC 203. The case of *Seager v Copydex Ltd* [1967] RPC 349, requires a little care; the Court of Appeal did not mention the jurisdictional basis upon which it was ordering an inquiry as to damages for the breach of confidence. Gurry correctly opines that the court was proceeding under Lord Cairns's Act (note 23 above, 428–9). In *Nichrotherm Electrical Co. Ltd v J R Percy* [1956] RPC 272, Harman J suggested that damages could be awarded in the absence of a prayer for equitable relief (*ibid*, 279–81). This 'mildly revolutionary' view, implying the fusion of law and equity, was left open by Lord Evershed MR in the Court of Appeal ([1957] RPC 207, 213–14).
[46]As to the awarding of damages in addition to an injunction, see *London & Provincial Sporting News Agency Ltd v Levy* (1928) MacG Cop Cas (1923–8) 340; *Cranleigh Precision Engineering Ltd v Bryant* [1966] RPC 81; *Peter Pan Manufacturing Corporation v Corsets Silhouette Ltd* [1963] RPC 45. See, generally, Gurry (note 23 above), 437–40.
[47]Gurry, *ibid*, 434.
[48](1948) 65 RPC 203.

'expressed reluctance to make any order which would involve the destruction or sterilisation of tools which might serve a useful purpose, since under Lord Cairns's Act the court could award damages, to cover both past and future acts, in lieu of an injunction'.[49]

The Law Commission, on the other hand, refers to *Seager v Copydex Ltd*,[50] and concludes:

> It is a reasonable inference from the decision ... that damages are awardable for a past breach of confidence. On the other hand it can be argued that it is not clear from that case whether the damages which were ordered to be assessed were intended to include loss suffered in respect of the past breach of confidence or only to provide compensation in lieu of an injunction.[51]

It also cites the remarks of Megarry V-C in *Malone*[52] (set out above).[53] But the Vice-Chancellor's statement relates to the precise nature of the jurisdiction to award damages in lieu of an injunction under Lord Cairns's Act, rather than to the *assessment* of those damages once jurisdiction is found to exist. It is the latter which is my present concern, and Gurry's view is the better one: damages may address past wrongs because the court has jurisdiction to restrain the commission of *continuing* wrongs.[54]

Finally, what heads of damages may be recovered in a breach of confidence action? In particular, can a plaintiff in a 'privacy' context obtain damages under Lord Cairns's Act for mental distress? As Gurry points out, 'A claim for damages for breach of a personal confidence may in essence be a claim for injury to feelings'.[55] But the Law Commission holds the opinion that 'So far as non-contractual breach of confidence is concerned, there is no authority to support an award of damages for mental distress'.[56] No award of such damages in a breach of confidence case has been made, although in *Woodward v Hutchins*[57] the majority of the Court of Appeal were content, in an interlocutory application to enjoin the publicity agent of a group of pop stars from

---

[49]*Ibid*, 219.
[50][1967] RPC 349.
[51]*Breach of Confidence* (note 19 above), para 4.76. And see, generally, paras 4.75–4.77.
[52]*Malone* v *Commissioner of Police for the Metropolis (No. 2)* [1979] 1 Ch 344, 360.
[53]See note 35 above.
[54]Gurry (note 23 above), 434.
[55]*Ibid*, 442.
[56]*Breach of Confidence* (note 19 above), para 4.82.
[57][1977] 1 WLR 760.

revealing details of their private lives, to allow the agent to disclose the information leaving the plaintiffs to seek damages at trial.[58]

Limited recognition of damages for injury to feelings has been given in a contractual setting. In *Jarvis v Swans Tours Ltd*[59] damages in respect of a disappointing holiday were awarded to take into account 'the disappointment, the distress, the upset and frustration' caused by the defendant's breach of contract.[60] However, as the Law Commission notes,[61] this consequence of the breach must be foreseen by both parties to the contract.[62] A court would thus be unlikely to extend this principle to purely equitable breaches of confidence.[63]

Certain statutory provisions exist which are roughly analogous to breach of confidence. So in *Williams v Settle*,[64] in the context of a claim for 'such additional damages . . . as the court may consider appropriate in the circumstances' under s. 17(3) of the Copyright Act 1956, Sellers LJ had regard to the 'scandalous conduct' of the defendant, and the fact that it was 'in total disregard not only of the legal rights of the plaintiff regarding copyright but of his feelings and his sense of family dignity and pride'.[65] The Law Commission adds that '. . . there is no statutory basis for awarding damages in respect of mental distress caused by a breach of confidence'.[66]

In *Francome v Mirror Group Newspapers Ltd*[67] Donaldson MR listed the plaintiff's claims for relief, one of which was exemplary damages for breach of confidence.[68] *Rookes v Barnard*[69] establishes that, for a claim for exemplary or punitive damages, the conduct by the defendant must be calculated to give him a profit likely to exceed the compensation payable to the plaintiff.[70] The problem is that where the defendant's profit from the breach of confidence is large, the plaintiff is adequately compensated by the remedy of an account of profits. Damages are, in

---

[58]Lord Denning MR remarked: 'Any remedy for [the plaintiffs] should be in damages and damages only' (*ibid*, 764). See Wacks, *Personal Information* (Chapter 1 note 1 above), 121–3.
[59][1973] 1 QB 233.
[60]*Ibid*, 238 per Lord Denning MR.
[61]*Breach of Confidence* (note 19 above), para 4.80.
[62]*Heywood v Wellers* [1976] 1 QB 446, 461 per James LJ.
[63]See *Breach of Confidence* (note 19 above), para 4.80.
[64][1960] 1 WLR 1072.
[65]*Ibid*, 1082.
[66]*Breach of Confidence* (note 19 above), para 4.82.
[67][1984] 1 WLR 892.
[68]*Ibid*, 894.
[69][1964] AC 1129.
[70]*Ibid*, 1226–7 per Lord Devlin.

the present context, sought where the defendant's gain is small but the emotional cost to the plaintiff is high.

In the archetypal 'privacy' case, where, for instance, the plaintiff is betrayed by a confidant who sells the information, imparted in confidence, to a newspaper for a large fee,[71] the most appropriate and efficacious remedy is an account of profits.

Account of profits

In its Working Paper on *Breach of Confidence*,[72] the Law Commission stated:

> In contrast to damages, which seek to compensate the defendant for the loss he has suffered, an account of profits seeks to recover from the defendant the profit he has made. Where both remedies are available, they are always alternative, since if both were granted the plaintiff would receive a double benefit for the same wrong; but as one remedy may be more beneficial to the plaintiff than the other, it is at the plaintiff's option (subject to the discretion of the court in granting the equitable remedy of an account) which remedy he will take.[73]

In relation to the combination of the equitable remedies possible in a breach of confidence action, Gurry explains that damages and an account of profits are mutually exclusive, but that 'each is available in addition to an injunction and an order for the delivery up or destruction of material made or acquired in breach of confidence'.[74] As is generally accepted,[75] quantification of the amount due by way of account of profits is frequently 'a difficult, laborious and expensive operation'.[76] However, in the 'privacy' sphere, at least in the context of a defendant accepting money from a newspaper to reveal information in breach of

---

[71]E.g., *Stephens* v *Avery* [1988] 1 Ch 449.

[72]Law Commission, *Breach of Confidence* (Working Paper No. 58), Cmnd 5012, 1972.

[73]*Ibid*, para 123 (set out in its report (note 19 above), para 4.86).

[74]Gurry (note 23 above), 417–18 (footnotes omitted). See *Peter Pan Manufacturing Corporation* v *Corsets Silhouette Ltd* [1963] RPC 45 (injunction, order for delivery up, and enquiry as to damages).

[75]See *Breach of Confidence* (note 19 above), para 4.86 (setting out the Commission's comments in its Working Paper); Gurry (note 23 above), 418–9.

[76]G Jones and Lord Goff of Chieveley, *The Law of Restitution*, 4th ed (London: Sweet & Maxwell, 1993), 690.

confidence, it accords the plaintiff simple and effective relief. The more intricate situation is the quantification of the account to be made by a newspaper said to have profited from publishing information knowingly in breach of confidence.

The only issue concerns the circumstances in which the court will exercise its discretion to order this remedy. Gurry concludes from *Seager v Copydex Ltd*[77] that the court may not order an account when the defendant has acted innocently, leaving the plaintiff to his remedy in damages.[78] As *Seager* itself demonstrates, the concept of innocent breach of confidence is recognised by the law but it has little application to the communication of personal information. The approach of Pennycuick J in the *Peter Pan* case[79] is therefore to be preferred: that the plaintiff should be given the choice between damages and an account, and the court should, save in exceptional circumstances, give effect to that election.

In conclusion, it should be noted that the profits accounted for must only be those which are 'attributable to the misuse of confidential information'.[80]

Injunction[81]

Equitable damages under Lord Cairns's Act may, as described above, be awarded in lieu of the granting of an injunction. Unlike the remedy of account of profits (and any common law measure of damages for breach of a contractual obligation of confidence), the injunction is primarily directed towards any future loss that may be caused to the plaintiff by the continuing effect of an existing breach of confidence or through further breaches feared by the defendant. The latter purpose of this discretionary remedy has two vital ingredients. First, the plaintiff may gain injunctive relief for an apprehended infringement of his equitable rights notwithstanding that no breach has yet occurred. This is the so-called '*quia timet*' injunction to restrain the defendant from committing an apprehended wrong to the plaintiff. In these circumstances the court, in exercising its discretion, embarks upon

---

[77][1967] RPC 349.
[78]Gurry (note 23 above), 420–1.
[79][1963] RPC 45, 58.
[80]Gurry (note 23 above), 423 and especially 424–7.
[81]See Burrows (note 1 above), ch 9; Spry (note 13 above), ch 4; Gurry (note 23 above), ch 19 and ch 20.

'balancing the magnitude of the evil against the chances of its occurrence'.[82]

Secondly, the most appropriate remedy available where the plaintiff has not yet had his rights infringed, is the interlocutory injunction. This is a crucial weapon by which to prevent the plaintiff's rights from being eroded before he can proceed to substantive trial. In many cases, in exercising its discretion not to grant the plaintiff interim relief, the court is effectively deciding the substantive issue. This is particularly so in personal information actions where, with regard to the inadequacy of the measure of damages discussed above and because the plaintiff's only concern is usually to prevent the information from being disclosed at all, the plaintiff will rarely proceed to trial after failing to gain interlocutory relief.

Interlocutory injunction

This is 'a remedy that is both temporary and discretionary'.[83] It is temporary in that it seeks to prevent the impairment of the plaintiff's rights during the time between issue and resolution of proceedings. The well-established principles adopted by a unanimous House of Lords in *American Cyanamid Co.* v *Ethicon Ltd*[84] altered the standard of proof which the plaintiff had to satisfy. Before *American Cyanamid*, the plaintiff had to establish what was commonly termed 'a *prima facie* case'.[85] Lord Diplock pointed out that the effect of that test was:

> ... that the court is not entitled to take any account of the balance of convenience unless it has first been satisfied that if the case went to trial upon no other evidence than is before the court at the hearing of the application the plaintiff would be entitled to judgment for a permanent injunction in the same terms as the interlocutory injunction sought.[86]

The court rejected this approach in favour of a less stringent, more flexible test. Lord Diplock remarked that 'The court no doubt must be satisfied that the claim is not frivolous or vexatious; in other words, that

---

[82]*Earl of Ripon* v *Hobart* (1834) 3 My & K 169, 176, 40 ER 65, 68. See Spry (note 13 above), 369–73.
[83]*American Cyanamid Co.* v *Ethicon Ltd* [1975] AC 396, 405 per Lord Diplock.
[84]*Ibid, loc cit.*
[85]E.g., *Norman* v *Mitchell* (1845) 5 De G M & G 648, 675, 43 ER 1022, 1033 per Turner LJ. See also *J T Stratford & Son Ltd* v *Lindley* [1965] AC 269 (HL).
[86][1975] AC 396, 407.

there is a serious question to be tried'.[87] The next step is to consider the 'balance of convenience'. If the injunction were *issued*, could the defendant be adequately compensated in damages if he were to resist the plaintiff's action at the substantive trial? If, on the other hand, the court *refused* to enjoin the defendant, would the plaintiff be adequately recompensed in damages if 'the uncertainty were resolved in his favour at the trial?'[88] Should this balancing of the parties' competing interests not point clearly to whether the injunction should be granted, Gurry, while stressing that the test is to remain flexible and unfettered by strict rules, suggests three further considerations:[89]

(a) All things being equal, the court ought to preserve the *status quo*.[90]

(b) The general terms of the injunction must be sufficiently precise to leave the defendant in little doubt about what he may or may not do. Accordingly, an all-embracing draft order may militate against the grant of interim relief. In *Potters-Ballotini Ltd* v *Weston-Baker*,[91] Scarman LJ said that he 'would not suggest that this factor can itself be decisive, but it is a factor to be brought into account when striking the balance'.[92]

(c) Where the defendant raises a defence it may affect the court's willingness to grant an injunction. It is not clear from the case law whether the existence of a defence ought to be taken into account under the heading 'a serious issue to be tried' or as a factor in the balance of convenience.[93] I return to this question below.

Finally, Lord Diplock commented that '... it may not be improper to take into account in tipping the balance the relative strength of each party's case as revealed by the affidavit evidence adduced on the hearing of the application' if the assessment of whether either side could not be compensated in damages at trial proves inconclusive.[94] He

---

[87] *Ibid, loc cit.*
[88] *Ibid,* 406.
[89] Gurry (note 23 above), 392–5. Lord Diplock remarks that 'there may be many other special factors to be taken into consideration in the particular circumstances of individual cases' (*American Cyanamid* [1975] AC 396, 409).
[90] E.g., *Standex International Ltd* v *C B Blades* [1976] FSR 114. In *Dunford & Elliott Ltd* v *Johnson & Firth Brown Ltd* [1978] FSR 143, an injunction would have upset the *status quo*, and was thus not granted.
[91] [1977] RPC 202.
[92] *Ibid,* 209. See the comments of Lord Denning MR in *Woodward* v *Hutchins* [1977] 1 WLR 760, 764.
[93] Gurry (note 23 above), 392–5.
[94] [1975] AC 396, 409.

warned, however, that this 'should be done only where it is apparent upon the facts disclosed by evidence as to which there is no credible dispute that the strength of one party's case is disproportionate to that of the other party'.[95]

An analysis of the balancing test employed by the courts in determining whether to grant an injunction in personal information breach of confidence cases is complicated by the fact that the invariable defence is that the breach was in the public interest. This defence is itself subject to a balancing test and thus it is often very difficult to distinguish the one test from the other; the court frequently deals with the two together.[96]

In *Woodward* v *Hutchins*[97] the plaintiffs were three pop stars who sought to restrain their publicity agent from disclosing information regarding their private lives to a newspaper. Lord Denning MR looked no further than the public interest defence. He concluded that such an interest existed and, drawing an analogy with libel cases where the courts are most reluctant to enjoin the defendant from disclosing the contested information, he said, 'If there is a legitimate ground for supposing that it is in the public interest for [the information] to be disclosed, the court should not restrain it by an interlocutory injunction, but should leave the complainant to his remedy in damages'.[98]

This approach is exemplified by Lord Denning MR's dissenting judgment in *Schering Chemicals Ltd* v *Falkman Ltd*.[99] It will be recalled that this case concerned the intended broadcasting of a television programme which highlighted potential side-effects of the plaintiff's pregnancy testing drug Primodos. The Master of the Rolls dispensed at once with the orthodox *American Cyanamid* approach. In respect of the plaintiff's application for an injunction to restrain the broadcast, he reasoned that 'Such an injunction falls into a special category because it encroaches upon one of our most fundamental freedoms — the freedom of the press. So I put on one side [the *American Cyanamid* case].'[100] He then identified the doctrine of prior restraint, which generally precludes the court from enjoining the disclosure of information to the public, although he recognised that the action for breach of confidence

---

[95]*Ibid, loc cit.*
[96]In *Breach of Confidence* (note 19 above), para 4.49, the Law Commission, in reference to *Schering Chemicals Ltd* v *Falkman Ltd* [1982] 1 QB 1, advert to this difficulty.
[97][1977] 1 WLR 760.
[98]*Ibid*, 764. See R Wacks, 'Pop Goes Privacy' (1978) 31 MLR 67.
[99][1982] 1 QB 1.
[100]*Ibid*, 16.

represents an exception to this rule.[101] Throughout his judgment, Lord Denning was concerned only with the balancing test to resolve in whose favour the public interest should fall, and he was not referring to the narrower competing interests of the parties to the action. He was:

> ... clearly of opinion that no injunction ought to be granted to prevent the publication of this information, even though it did originate in confidence. It dealt with a matter of great public interest. It contained information of which the public had a right to know. It should not be made the subject of an injunction.[102]

Shaw LJ adopted a different approach which seems to use the defence as a filter. If the public interest balancing process favoured the disclosure of the information then the obligation of confidence could be 'overborne'.[103] However, if the balance favoured the plaintiff then the more orthodox *American Cyanamid* balancing would have to be undertaken. After performing the public interest balancing (and concluding, unlike the Master of the Rolls, that it favoured Schering) Shaw LJ observed that 'There remains the question whether Schering's remedy should sound only in damages. This is a case in which the injury to Schering's interests might well be irreparable.'[104] Templeman LJ adopted yet a more traditional standpoint. He considered the public interest test to be a *factor* in the *American Cyanamid* balance of convenience test.[105] What is not clear is whether the defence has primacy over the other factors to be weighed up in deciding whether to grant injunctive relief. Somewhat cryptically, he observed:

> It has been suggested that an injunction restraining breach of confidentiality should only be granted in circumstances in which the right to preserve confidentiality is so important that it takes priority over the freedom of the press. If this means that the court should consider the consequences to the public of withholding or granting an injunction, then I fully agree.... These consequences must be weighed against the argument that, if an injunction is granted, the public will be deprived of information.[106]

---

[101] *Ibid*, 21.
[102] *Ibid*, 22.
[103] *Ibid*, 27.
[104] *Ibid*, 29.
[105] This can be deduced from the fact that the judge discussed the public interest defence directly *after* the *American Cynamid* 'balance of convenience' test (*ibid*, 38).
[106] *Ibid*, 39–40.

As discussed in Chapter 4, there is no analogy to be drawn between defamation and breach of confidence actions.[107] Apart from this crystallisation of the guiding principles for the granting of an injunction, the precise approach of the courts remains uncertain. In *Francome* the plaintiff, a champion horse jockey, sought an interlocutory injunction to restrain the defendant from publishing the details of telephone calls between himself and his wife which had been unlawfully tapped and which allegedly revealed 'breaches of the rules of racing'. Donaldson MR clarified the position:

> I stress, once again, that we are not at this stage concerned to determine the final rights of the parties. Our duty is to make such orders, if any, as are appropriate pending the trial of the action. It is sometimes said that this involves a weighing of the balance of convenience. This is an unfortunate expression. Our business is justice, not convenience. We can and must disregard fanciful claims by either party. Subject to that, we must contemplate the possibility that either party may succeed and must do our best to ensure that nothing occurs pending the trial which will prejudice his rights.[108]

The Master of the Rolls exercised this balancing of 'justice' in a manner that is both simple and logical. He largely ignored the public interest question, stating that this was an issue which would have to be resolved at trial.[109] Instead he examined the respective positions of the parties and concluded that it would be far more unjust to allow publication upon the questionable premise that the recordings revealed iniquitous conduct on the part of the plaintiff than it would be to preserve the plaintiff's rights until trial, after which the defendant, if successful, could proceed with publication.[110] Fox LJ underscored this approach when he remarked:

> The *Daily Mirror* states that it will rely on iniquity and public interest as a defence to any claim of confidentiality. The claim of confidentiality and the claim of iniquity raise questions of law and fact which cannot be determined on an interlocutory application. They require a

---

[107]Lord Denning MR's remarks in *Woodward* were not followed in *Francome v Mirror Group Newspapers Ltd* [1984] 1 WLR 892, 899 per Fox LJ nor in *Lion Laboratories Ltd v Evans* [1985] 1 QB 526, 538 per Stephenson LJ.

[108]*Francome* [1984] 1 WLR 892, 898.

[109]*Ibid*, 896.

[110]He also gave the defendant the opportunity to apply to the court to sanction limited disclosure of the information to the police or the Jockey Club (*ibid*, 898 and 899).

full trial. If the *Daily Mirror* is permitted to publish the tapes now, the consequent harm to Mr Francome might be such that he could not be adequately compensated in damages for any wrong thereby done to him whatever the result of subsequent proceedings.[111]

It is hard to see why similar reasoning was not adopted in *Woodward*. In effect, Lord Denning MR determined the substantive issue *at the interlocutory stage*. In consequence, the plaintiffs were left with a worthless, potential right to damages.

The final case to be considered is *Lion Laboratories Ltd v Evans*.[112] The plaintiff company was the sole manufacturer of a device used to test for drink-driving by measuring the percentage of alcohol in the breath exhaled by the driver. The defendants were ex-employees of the plaintiff who wished to expose alleged serious inadequacies in the Intoximeter's calibration. The Court of Appeal refused to enjoin publication. From the outset, Stephenson LJ spelt out that, at the interlocutory stage, it was for the defendant to show 'a legitimate ground for supposing it is in the public interest for [the confidential information] to be disclosed'.[113] He added that '... to see if there is a serious defence of public interest which may succeed at the trial, we have to look at the evidence and if we decide that there is such a defence, to perform a balancing exercise'.[114] This balancing exercise constitutes the substantive test for resolving on which side the public interest falls. If this issue were resolved in favour of disclosure, Stephenson LJ thought that an injunction should not be granted but only after 'considering and weighing in the balance all relevant matters such as whether damages would be an adequate remedy to compensate the plaintiffs if they succeeded at the trial'.[115]

The first feature of this reasoning is that it is nearer the *American Cyanamid* test than Lord Denning MR's judgment in *Woodward*. Stephenson LJ specifically notes that the resolution of the public interest balancing test is not to be the sole factor in deciding whether to grant interim relief. But the *American Cyanamid* principles appear to have been inverted. The narrow balance of convenience/'justice' between the parties is merely a *factor* to be taken into account when assessing the competing public interests of confidentiality and disclosure (and not

---

[111]*Ibid*, 900.
[112][1985] 1 QB 526.
[113]*Ibid*, 538 (citing the remarks of Sir David Cairns in *Khashoggi v Smith* (1980) 130 NLJ 168).
[114][1985] 1 QB 526, 538–9.
[115]*Ibid*, 538.

vice versa as envisaged in *American Cyanamid*). The difficulty with this approach is that it imports the characteristics of a substantive trial into the interlocutory hearing.

This may occasionally be justified. In *Lion Laboratories*, as Stephenson LJ was careful to emphasise, the public interest issue was 'a serious question concerning a matter which affects the life, and even the liberty, of an unascertainable number of Her Majesty's subjects'.[116] It would be a perverse logic that favoured preserving the plaintiff's potential rights when the effect of that preservation was to subject civilians to criminal sanctions. In the personal information context, however, the *American Cyanamid* test should not be relegated to the status of a component of the public interest test. A balancing test which has as its primary concern the *public* interest should not override one which is designed to resolve the short-term individual anxieties of the parties to the action.

Perpetual and quia timet *injunctions*

Quia timet injunctions are available both in the form of interlocutory and perpetual injunctions.[117] In the personal information context, it is, of course, the *quia timet* interlocutory injunction that is likely to be of the greatest utility to the plaintiff. A 'privacy' plaintiff will frequently seek to restrain continuing acts of disclosure by the defendant, though in a paradigmatic 'privacy' case the plaintiff seeks to enjoin the defendant from making any disclosure at all. As already mentioned, if the plaintiff is unsuccessful in this attempt, he is left with a hollow right, especially in the light of the uncertainty surrounding awards of damages in equity.

The principles by which the court is governed in the granting of *quia timet* injunctions are relatively settled. According to Spry:

> It may properly be said that wherever a court with equitable jurisdiction might enjoin an act if that act had been commenced, it may, in the exercise of its discretion, enjoin the act although it has not yet commenced, provided that its imminence is sufficiently clearly established in order to justify intervention in all the circumstances.[118]

He criticises those cases which hold that the degree of risk of a breach of his rights that the plaintiff must prove for the court to exercise its discretion is fixed and independent of the other circumstances of the

---

[116]*Ibid*, 546.
[117]E.g., Spry (note 13 above), 369–73, 459–61.
[118]*Ibid*, 369–370.

extant case.[119] He prefers the view espoused by Russell LJ that '... the degree of probability of future injury is not an absolute standard: what is to be aimed at is justice between the parties, having regard to all the relevant circumstances'.[120] If the defendant has already committed breaches, this is an evidentiary matter which the court will take into account, but in all cases the issue is whether it has been sufficiently clearly shown that the defendant intends to repeat those infringements.[121]

The matter of a perpetual injunction (both *quia timet* and to restrain a continuing wrong) lies, once more, within the discretion of the court.[122] In *Shelfer* v *City of London Electric Lighting Co.*,[123] A L Smith LJ stated 'as a good working rule' that damages in substitution for an injunction may be given:

(1)   if the injury to the plaintiff's legal rights is small,

(2)   and is one which is capable of being estimated in money,

(3)   and is one which can be adequately compensated by a small money payment,

(4)   and the case is one in which it would be oppressive to the defendant to grant an injunction.[124]

But the factors which the court takes into account when exercising its discretion are more numerous, and their interrelation more complicated, than this dictum would suggest. It is plain that the court will not readily sanction the infringement of a plaintiff's rights by awarding damages in lieu of an injunction.[125] This principle is especially appropriate to personal information cases where the aim of the plaintiff is to *prevent* publication rather than to obtain fair compensation for its *use*.[126] The court will also qualitatively assess the nature of the information. (See Chapter 3 where this question is considered at some length.) Suffice

---

[119]*Ibid*, 371.
[120]*Hooper* v *Rogers* [1975] 1 Ch 43, 50.
[121]*Kernot* v *Potter* (1862) 3 De G F & J 447, 45 ER 951. See, Spry (note 13 above), 372.
[122]See, generally, Spry (note 13 above), 373–435; Gurry (note 23 above), ch 20; *Breach of Confidence* (note 19 above), para 4.99; Burrows (note 1 above), 387–423.
[123][1895] 1 Ch 287.
[124]*Ibid*, 322–3.
[125]*Ibid*, 322.
[126]This approach is borne out by the case law. See, e.g., *Pollard* v *Photographic Co.* (1889) 40 ChD 345; *Duchess of Argyll* v *Duke of Argyll* [1967] 1 Ch 302. But in *Attorney-General* v *Hallett* (1847) 16 M & W 569, 581, 153 ER 1316, 1321, Parke B remarked that equity would only intervene to prevent irreparable injury: 'such an injury as could not be compensated in damages'.

it to say here that the court will not restrain the publication of mere 'trivial tittle-tattle'.[127] Indeed, this factor is best regarded as a substantive requirement of the obligation of confidence, i.e., one that precludes the court from granting *any* equitable remedy.[128]

It should also be noted (and this is also a matter examined in detail in Chapter 3) that the court will not restrain the disclosure of information which has entered the 'public domain' or is about to do so since, as Lord Eldon LC remarked in *Williams* v *Williams*, '... the injunction can be of no use'.[129] This requirement is also best categorised as a component of the obligation of confidence, going to the question whether the information is capable of being confidential. Thus, as Gurry points out,[130] as long as the courts are willing to consider the information confidential, the defendant may be restrained from publication notwithstanding that wide disclosure has already occurred. In *Gilbert* v *The Star Newspaper Co. Ltd*[131] Chitty J enjoined the defendant from publishing further extracts from the plaintiff's forthcoming comic opera after having already done so in one edition of the newspaper. He is reported to have commented that:

> No doubt the injury which the plaintiff complained of would to a large extent already have been done, but that was no ground why the court should decline to stop, although only for a few hours, that which, speaking on the evidence before it, appeared to be unjustifiable.[132]

As to the requirement that some detriment be shown, this should not prevent the granting of an injunction, especially in personal information cases, as Gurry rightly argues.[133] In *Prince Albert* v *Strange*, Knight Bruce V-C thought that an individual was entitled to relief whenever 'the produce of his private hours'[134] was used, irrespective of his being shown in a good or bad light thereby.

---

[127]*Coco* v *A N Clark (Engineers) Ltd* [1969] RPC 41, 48 per Megarry J.
[128]See the principles expounded by Lord Greene MR in *Saltman Engineering Co. Ltd* v *Campbell Engineering Co. Ltd* (1948) 65 RPC 203, 215.
[129](1817) 3 Mer 157, 160, 36 ER 61, 62.
[130]Gurry (note 23 above), 399–400.
[131](1894) 11 TLR 4.
[132]*Ibid*, 5. And see *Pollard* v *Photographic Co.* (1889) 40 ChD 345.
[133]Gurry (note 23 above), 407–8.
[134](1849) 2 De G & Sm 652, 697, 64 ER 293, 312.

Finally, as with all equitable remedies, the court will not grant an injunction where the plaintiff has been guilty of fraud,[135] or does not come to court with 'clean hands'.[136]

Delivery up[137]

A further equitable, discretionary remedy which the courts may grant in addition to an injunction is the order for the defendant to deliver up or to destroy on oath any material in his possession which is the result of, or contains information in, breach of confidence.[138] There are two situations in which the court will consider granting this remedy. First, if the confidential information is contained in physical material which belongs to the plaintiff and which the defendant has taken, the usual order will be for him to deliver up that object and to deliver up for destruction, any copies or extracts made therefrom (which the plaintiff cannot retain because he has no proprietary right in them).[139] Also, and this is particularly pertinent in the 'privacy' context, the court will order the defendant to deliver up for destruction any records of, or 'products embodying',[140] the confidential information where he took no permanent physical material from the plaintiff.[141]

Such orders will not be sanctioned as of right. Their purpose is well described by Russell J in *Mergenthaler Linotype Co. v Intertype Ltd*,[142]

[The plaintiff] is protected as to further manufacture of infringing articles by the injunction which he obtains, but there remains this, that, so long as there is still what I might call infringing stock in the possession of the infringer, he may be subject to too serious and grave a temptation and may thereby be tempted to commit a breach of the injunction which he would not otherwise commit. Accordingly, in order to assist the plaintiff and as a relief ancillary to the injunction he

---

[135]E.g., *Pride of Derby and Derbyshire Angling Association Ltd v British Celanese Ltd* [1953] 1 Ch 149, 181.
[136]E.g., *Litvinoff v Kent* (1918) 34 TLR 298.
[137]Gurry (note 23 above), ch 21; Burrows (note 1 above), 458–61.
[138]*Mergenthaler Linotype Co. v Intertype Ltd* (1926) 43 RPC 381, 382 per Russell J.
[139]See *Alperton Rubber Co. v Manning* (1917) 86 LJ Ch 377; and *Prince Albert v Strange* (1849) 2 De G & Sm 652, 64 ER 293.
[140]Gurry (note 23 above), 413.
[141]See, *Prince Albert v Strange* (1849) 2 De G & Sm 652, 64 ER 293.
[142](1926) 43 RPC 381.

has obtained, the court may in its discretion make an order for the destruction or delivery up of infringing articles.[143]

One consequence of this approach is that the reliability of the defendant in honouring the injunction is, in effect, assessed by the court. Thus in *Industrial Furnaces Ltd v Reaves*[144] Graham J stressed that he was making the order because '... the defendant was not reliable. In those circumstances, even if I would otherwise not make an order for delivery up, it seems to me that the court is in the position of not necessarily being able to rely on the oath of the defendant [to destroy the infringing articles]'.[145]

The final question is whether the extent to which the personal information is used in the infringing publication affect the court's willingness to order delivery up. In simple cases, such as the defendant having a photograph of the plaintiff, obtained in confidence, the likelihood of his having to deliver up the negative and any existing copies may depend upon the court's assessment of the defendant's probity. Where the defendant is a third-party newspaper, straining to print the next edition, the matter of confiscation may be more complicated. If free speech is to be protected, it is hard to see how destruction of an entire publication can be justified. Since the offending article is unlikely to occupy more than one page, and given the facility with which computerised copy may be edited, the embarrassing personal information may easily be 'severed' from the whole; the newspaper having to deliver up any notes including the personal information in question.[146]

Other Remedies

Equitable compensation[147]

Following a breach of the equitable obligation of confidence, a court may order a defendant 'who has not benefited from a breach of duty to compensate the plaintiff for any loss the latter has sustained'.[148] There

---

[143]*Ibid*, 382.
[144][1970] RPC 605.
[145]*Ibid*, 627.
[146]E.g., *Warne & Co.* v *Seebohm* (1888) 39 ChD 73; *Boosey & Co.* v *Whight & Co. (No. 2)* (1899) 81 LT 265.
[147]See Capper (note 23 above), 321–8.
[148]*Ibid*, 321.

is, as Capper shows, a paucity of English authority on this point; it is settled law, however, that such compensation is available against trustees[149] and other fiduciaries.[150] In a non-fiduciary context, in *Parker-Tweedale* v *Dunbar Bank plc (No. 1)*,[151] Nourse LJ was of the opinion that a mortgagee's duty to the mortgagor to secure the best price reasonably obtainable for the property in the exercise of his power of sale arose in equity[152] and not, as had been formerly suggested,[153] in tort. However, in *Banque Financière de la Cité SA* v *Westgate Insurance Co. Ltd*[154] the Court of Appeal refused to award damages for breach of an insurer's duty of good faith because it took the view that it entitled the plaintiff only to rescind the contract.[155]

If such compensation is available, it acts in a manner indistinguishable from the operation of common law damages, making good the plaintiff's loss.[156] In the New Zealand decision of *Mouat* v *Clark Boyce*[157] the plaintiff was awarded NZ$25,000 for, *inter alia*, mental distress. With respect to the recoverability of damages for mental distress in contract and tort, Cooke P maintained:

There appears to be no solid ground for denying that equitable compensation can likewise extend so far. It would be anachronistic to draw distinctions in this respect between the various sources of liability, dictated as they are by the same considerations of policy.[158]

However, as Capper points out, it is too early for definite conclusions to be drawn concerning the applicability of this remedy in an English court.[159] It would certainly assist a 'privacy' plaintiff who could otherwise not obtain relief because the defendant has not profited from the breach of confidence and is unlikely to repeat the infringement, thus precluding an award of damages in lieu of an injunction under Lord Cairns's Act. It is to be hoped that the courts would not allow this

[149]E.g., *Re Bell's Indenture; Bell* v *Hickley* [1980] 1 WLR 1217.
[150]*Nocton* v *Lord Ashburton* [1914] AC 932.
[151][1991] Ch 12.
[152]*Ibid*, 18–19.
[153]*Standard Chartered Bank Ltd* v *Walker* [1982] 1 WLR 1410, 1415 per Lord Denning MR.
[154][1990] 1 QB 665.
[155]*Ibid*, 782–9. The House of Lords dismissed the appeal on other grounds, but Lords Templeman and Jauncey were in agreement with the Court of Appeal on the issue of the damages for breach of the duty (*Banque Financière* [1991] 2 AC 249, 280–1).
[156]Capper (note 23 above), 323.
[157][1992] 2 NZLR 559.
[158]*Ibid*, 569.
[159]Capper (note 23 above), 326–8.

technicality to thwart compensation of a meritorious plaintiff who has suffered as a consequence of sensationalist or intrusive journalism.

In its report on breach of confidence, the Law Commission recommended the enactment of a new statutory tort of breach of confidence.[160] This tort would extend the right to damages both to past and prospective wrongs[161] and in respect of mental distress.[162] The remedy of an account of profits would remain,[163] but would not be additional to damages.[164] Damages in lieu of an injunction could still be awarded as 'adjustment orders': the award should be discretionary and the basis of assessment flexible and tailored to the circumstances of each case.[165]

Intentional infliction of emotional distress

The possibility of the principle in *Wilkinson v Downton*[166] supplying a means by which to prevent unwanted disclosures of personal information was canvassed in Chapter 3. It was suggested that, especially since its recent application in *Bradley v Wingnut Films Ltd*[167] and *Khorasandjian v Bush*,[168] a plaintiff might be able to recover for the 'nervous shock'[169] (today generally called 'recognisable psychiatric illness')[170] threatened or caused by the intrusion.

Indeed, it may be that the court is able to protect the plaintiff where there is only a *risk* of nervous shock later resulting from the cumulative effect of the defendant's conduct.[171] The Court of Appeal's decision in *Khorasandjian* appears to stretch *Wilkinson* to cover purely emotional distress where an injunction is being sought,[172] though the major obstacle remains the need to prove that the act was calculated to cause

---

[160]*Breach of Confidence* (note 19 above), para 6.2.
[161]*Ibid*, para 6.105.
[162]*Ibid*, para 6.106.
[163]*Ibid*, para 6.107.
[164]*Ibid*, loc cit.
[165]*Ibid*, para 6.110. See clauses 13–16 of the draft Bill for the implementation of these proposals (*ibid*, app A).
[166][1897] 2 QB 57. See too *Janvier v Sweeney* [1919] 2 KB 316.
[167][1993] 1 NZLR 415.
[168][1993] QB 727.
[169]See *Janvier v Sweeney* [1919] 2 KB 316; *Burnett v George* [1992] 1 FLR 525; and *Khorasandjian v Bush* [1993] QB 727.
[170]*Hinz v Berry* [1970] 2 QB 40, 42 per Lord Denning MR.
[171]See J Bridgeman and M A Jones, 'Harassing Conduct and Outrageous Acts: A Cause of Action for Intentionally Inflicted Mental Distress?' (1994) 14 LS 180, 192–201; F A Trindade, 'The Intentional Infliction of Purely Mental Distress' (1986) 6 Oxford J Legal Stud 219.
[172]Cf *Burnett v George* [1992] 1 FLR 525.

physical harm. There is also the possibility that for the intentional tort under *Wilkinson*, the court will award damages for purely emotional distress. These issues are briefly explored in Chapter 3.

7

The Future

There is no golden fleece. Enactment tomorrow of a 'privacy' statute would generate new problems for the judicial construction of victims' rights against unsolicited intrusions into private lives. Nor would these difficulties be diminished if, as suggested in this book, the judges pursue a common law route toward protection.

The press would continue to be tested daily (with minds more concentrated) as to whether stories are in the 'public interest':

How far is the sexual deviancy of a family doctor of legitimate interest to his patients? How far is a schoolteacher's adherence to Satanism of legitimate interest to parents? Is there a public interest in revealing the true behaviour of pop stars or sportsmen, who may serve as role models to thousands of adolescents? If a member of Parliament has an affair and is deceiving either his family or his mistress, is the public interest served by allowing voters to know, so that they may form a view about his stewardship of office?[1]

Nothing will make these questions go way. The real issue is whether the interests of the individual are invariably to be sacrificed at the altar of a contrived 'public interest'?

A killjoy's charter?

Opponents of legal, or even non-legal, checks on unwanted public disclosure like to depict concern for the victim as quaint, even prudish.

---

[1] C Munro, 'Press Freedom — How the Beast Was Tamed' (1991) 54 MLR 104, 107. Professor Munro describes these as 'formidable difficulties' and is generally sceptical of the Calcutt Committee's arguments and recommendations (*ibid*).

This is contrasted with the aggressively robust pursuit of the truth by the press. In many cases, of course, newspapers, like all commercial institutions, are moved by the interests of their shareholders who may evince less interest in what appears in the paper than what appears in its balance sheet. Moreover, since the press, in its code of conduct, has itself recognised that it should not publish hurtful disclosures of private facts, it is hardly in a position to characterise such apprehensions as pious or censorious.

Advocates for 'privacy' may well include enemies of free speech, but that is no more a legitimate argument against them than that advocates of free speech include avaricious newspaper proprietors.

A good deal may transpire in the time between the processing of these words and their appearance on this page, yet the likelihood of MPs (some of whom must dream of little else) passing legislation on this explosive subject remains negligible.

The power of the press lobby can never be underestimated. How many politicians, whose careers often hang by a slender thread, wish to invite the animosity of the tabloids by championing curbs on reporting of what has come to be called 'bonk journalism'?

The press, while quick to condemn the exposure of private lives in the name of the 'public interest', inevitably close ranks against legislation. The following argument, expressed by a former editor of The Times, and member of the Calcutt Committee, is typical:

> My objection is not to the gun but to its aim, the archaic obsession of the tabloids with sex. All but two of the 17 scalps that Fleet Street claims to have cut from the heads of senior Tories of late are for sexual 'misbehaviour'. The misbehaviour is usually of a sort that none of the journalists would recognise as such in themselves or their colleagues. No politician is hounded from office for incompetence or wasting public money. It simply does not happen. The thinnest of justifications for sexual intrusion is that the victims are 'hypocrites', that those who preach family values and back-to-basics lay themselves open to intrusion, even if they are doing nothing that impinges on their public duties. That is garbage.[2]

The truth is, as Jenkins points out, that while most tabloids preach family values, they show little concern or respect for the families of their victims. Nor does the cry of 'investigative journalism' wash:

[2]Simon Jenkins, The Spectator, 15 April 1995.

The revelation of the contents of private phone calls or of the personal misfortunes of relatives of the royal family are ethically indefensible. They are rarely 'investigative' and merely involve paying money to a snooping intermediary. They are also breaches of the code drawn up by all newspapers back in 1990.[3]

Yet despite this scathing indictment of press conduct, he rejects a 'privacy law': 'I cannot imagine anything more ludicrous or cumbersome or ineffective. I appreciate the tabloids and the irresponsibility and tastelessness they bring to Britain's otherwise dour public life.'

The logic of this line of reasoning is obscure. The charges against the tabloids include humbug (for its disingenuous use of 'public interest'), hypocrisy (for exposing intimate information about all except journalists), duplicity and chicanery (for tricking victims or others into disclosing sensitive facts), dishonesty (for defending virtually any disclosure of private lives as being connected to public office), and insensitivity (for intruding on private grief). The indictment nevertheless fails to disclose a case for legislative protection which is summarily dismissed as 'ludicrous', 'cumbersome', and 'ineffective'. The charges are then dropped for the evidence reveals no case to answer!

It hardly requires stating that these three colourful epithets might themselves apply to the press's own attempts at self-regulation. More importantly, however, any serious argument against the statutory protection of 'privacy' surely rests on none of these grounds, but on the possible 'chilling effect' such legislation might have. While it would be foolish to predict the fallout (though the evidence from other jurisdictions gives little cause for pessimism) it is hoped that this book has sketched an adequate case in support of the proposition that legislation which protects only publications that are not in the public interest (carefully defined) poses no threat to free speech and the good government it engenders.

The suggestion by a respected journalist that to value 'privacy' is somehow wimpish ('irresponsibility' becomes a virtue) or puritan ('tastelessness' is laudable) is curious enough. But the rationale for this exercise of free speech is grotesque: to enliven Britain's allegedly dull

---

[3]*Ibid, loc cit.* The code defines 'public interest' to include detecting or exposing crime, serious misdemeanours, or seriously antisocial conduct, protecting public health, and preventing the public from being misled. 'The public interest does not include whatever the public is interested in, and it was crucial to maintain the distinction — especially for those in public life. This is a distinction which will cause considerable problems for many tabloid editors in future' (R Snoddy, *The Good, the Bad and the Unacceptable* (London: Faber, 1992), 112).

public life. This end could, of course, be achieved by any number of artless endeavours. Are those who suffer genuine emotional distress or embarrassment at the hands of the press to be told that they ought not to complain, for their humiliation has invigorated our political life?

Privacy preserved?

A statutory cause of action for the public disclosure of private facts (subject, of course, to the accepted defences) remains the best way forward. But if Parliament is unwilling to grasp the nettle, the courts must. The combined force of three recent developments provides ample support for initiative in an appropriate case properly pleaded: the expanding equitable remedy for breach of confidence, the revived tort of inflicting emotional distress, and the growing influence of the international recognition of 'privacy', especially the jurisprudence of the European Convention on Human Rights. With these weapons to hand, the campaign demands only modest judicial heroism.

Index

Index

Index